SOMETHING IN THE WIND

Something in the Wind

Spirits, Spooks & Sprites
of the San Juan

MaryJoy Martin

PRUETT PUBLISHING COMPANY
BOULDER, COLORADO

Printed in the United States of America

10 09 08 07 06 05 04 03 02 01   5 4 3 2 1

Library of Congress Cataloging-in-Publication Data
Martin, MaryJoy, 1955–
     Something in the wind : spirits, spooks & sprites of the
San Juan / MaryJoy Martin.
          p. cm.
     Includes bibliographical references.
     ISBN 0-87108-913-0 (alk. paper)
     1. Ghosts—San Juan Mountains (Colo. and N.M.). I. Title:
Spirits, spooks & sprites of the San Juan. II. Title: Spirits,
spooks, and sprites of the San Juan. III. Title.

BF1472.U6 M36 2001
133.1'09788'3—dc21   00-062785

Cover and book design by Julie Noyes Long
Book composition by Lyn Chaffee

To my sister Jeanne
who walked across my grave,
To my brother Pete P.
who came back from the dead,
To sweet Rebecca
who is with me forever,
And to her sister Lisa and all my nieces and nephews
who love it when I scare them to death:
This book is yours, with love.

S.D.G

Contents

ℐLLUSTRATIONS

ACKNOWLEDGMENTS

Many thanks to all the people who have shared their ghost stories and history with me since 1976, those who have sent me clippings and letters and led me into the delightful world of spirit-tracking, those who have since died, and those who have shared their parents' and grandparents' tales of hauntings and strange spirit encounters, and to all of you who have contributed to this book in some way, including my proofreader, Joyce, and my ghost-hunting partners, Jeanne and Pete. I could never have written it without you. My gratitude is forever. A very special thanks to the following:

Allen Nossaman, who deserves a medal for being one of the greatest archivists and researchers in the San Juan region.

Alta Cassietto, long-time postmaster of Telluride, whose love for her hometown spans nine decades.

Ernie Kuhlman and the lads of the Old Hundred Mine who love Tommyknockers enough to share their Twinkies with them. The boarding-house at Seven Level has been repaired (the boulder removed and the roof fixed) and the Old Hundred itself is now the best educational mine tour in the San Juans, recommended by *National Geographic* and other publications.

Dorothy Patton, unflagging interlibrary loan specialist of the Montrose Library District who hunted down every obscure book I asked for.

Rich Fike, BLM archaeologist and character extraordinaire, who has been instrumental in the stabilization and restoration of many beloved buildings from the San Juan mining era.

Bruce Hanson, Denver Public Library, Western History Department. Adam Chosovi, Alan Reed, Albert Fuentes, Ann Hoffman, Bob Curvey, Charles Hosner, Chay Rees, Clyde Benally, Davine Pera, Dawna and Jerry O'Rourke, Doris H. Gregory, Dr. Jim Parker, Ernest Beyale, Frank Massard, Gene Amole, George and Gay Cappis, Ginni Bosse, Grant Houston, Harry B. Wright, Jacob Ferrari (Strater Hotel), Joel Swank, John Motter, John Walter "Shorty" Larson, Kimberley Sheek, Lillie Padilla, Oran David "Shorty" Campbell, Peggy Jacobson, Perk Vickers, Robert W. Wilson, Rosie Hall, the Anderson Family, Verena Jacobson, Stan Zuege.

And to the wonderful people of: Adams State College, Center of Southwest Studies, Fort Lewis College, Chicago Historical Society, Colorado State Archives, Colorado State Historical Society Library, Denver Public

Library, Western History Department, Hall Realty, Library of Congress, New York Historical Society, Ouray County Historical Society, Philadelphia Historical Society, San Juan County Historical Society, San Miguel County Historical Society, the Slideprinter (Suzy and the great crew), University of Colorado Archives, Western State College, Wilkinson Library, Telluride.
GOD BLESS THEM, EVERY ONE!

$\mathscr{P}$REFACE

Ghost stories are born from our ancient tribal origins, from that time when we knew how to gather our ancestors from the realm of the dead, knew how to bring them from the darkness to stand in strength beside us. In the dim, unwritten past we believed in spirit, the power of spirit, the insatiable appetite of the universal spirit, and thus we entombed our daughters on the frozen heights of the Andes and enshrined our Qin emperors with life-sized, imperial armies of terra-cotta to guard their decaying bones. Every tribal child knew there was a place—whether it was called Valhalla (the Norse hall of the dead) or Maski (the Hopi house of the dead) or countless other names—there was a place where the dead awaited us . . . a place from whence their souls occasionally slipped out and came back.

They came in our dreams. They spoke to us. They gave us their secret knowledge.

They came in our waking. They took the shape of other creatures. They helped us fight battles. They protected us against sorcerers who could speak to the bones of the dead, who could use dark knowledge to cripple our own souls.

Suddenly steel, steam power, and rocket fuel stripped us of our connection to the spirit world. Our ancient tribal stories, diluted and corked, were placed on the shelf merely for entertainment. Those who still had the power to reach through the mist were labeled and boxed and sent to psychiatric wards, or scoffed at, jeered, called liars and eccentrics.

The relentless explosion of technology is eroding our beliefs, replacing our storytelling, gradually sucking away our power to touch unseen, living energy. Although enthralled by fiber optics and silicon chips, something deep in our bones clamors for spirit. Gone is our ability to gather our ancestors, yet the vestiges of our longing manifest in the increasing popularity of genealogical research, of our fascination with movies like *Ghost, The Sixth Sense,* of programs such as *Unexplained Mysteries* and *Sightings.*

Science cannot explain spirit. Nor can it show us the realms of the heart. Storytelling can. The folk stories of our grandparents and theirs before them, that vast spirit-filled oral tradition, is in danger of being lost, even among modern tribal peoples. In the region of southwestern Colorado known as the San Juan, oral tradition comes through a marvelous mix of cultures, from the ancient Puebloans to the modern Utes, from the migratory gold seekers to the hungry immigrants straight off the boat. Woof and warp, these tales weave a unique tapestry that matches the mystery and majesty of the mountains.

My aim is not to convert the skeptics. I was born a skeptic. My personal approach to unexplained phenomena is scientific: no conclusion is formulated until data is collected through observation, physical evidence, etc. Yet it is science that maintains matter is energy and a scientist, Sir George Wade of England, who explained his belief that phenomena classified as "ghosts" are not the disembodied spirits of the dead, but the energy diffused by death, an energy as real as electricity or nuclear fusion.

What is this universal thing we call spirit? World-renowned Swiss psychologist Carl G. Jung believed in its myriad forms and relationships, relating his own psychic experiences in *Memories, Dreams, Reflections.* "There are indications that at least a part of the psyche is not subject to space and time," he wrote. Like him, I have not been satisfied with the singular explanations of "spirit" phenomena as "hallucinations," or "psychic compensation," or "imagination twisting ordinary sounds or shadows into extraordinary things." Psychic energy, emotional energy is little understood. Too often, exploration of it is left in the hands of quacks or pseudoscientists; consequently, legitimate paranormal phenomena are condemned as inane, and those who experience it, categorized as "loony tunes."

Yet psychologists are finding that many people who sever the spiritual aspect of their lives are unable to reach their full potential. If we tap into the psychic energy or soul energy we all possess, energy present in our dreams, our visions, our intuitive communications, the possibilities of life, of healing, of creating become tremendous. Is this the ancient "magic" of our ancestors? They could communicate beyond space and time, connect through the pathways of the universal collective psyche. We've all had the occasional experiences of absolutely knowing a loved one many miles away is in trouble, injured, or ill. Some of us have met a stranger and suddenly know private details of his or her life without the subject saying one word.

One terrible and baffling experience, enough to convince my skeptic's mind (although my jury of wee scientists continues debating it), occurred late Sunday night, January 15, 1984. Just writing the date still makes my heart race. At the time, I was living in the Denver metro area and had gone to bed late that Sunday night without a care. Before I was asleep, horrible images came out of the darkness. I was a small blonde girl being viciously attacked in my bed by a man with a claw hammer. The terror, the pain was real.

I sat up to escape the "dream," but the blows of the hammer, the dark form of the man came at me again. I was an older little girl now, and I was terrified for my sister. Where was my sister? My mother—? I *was* my mother—I too was struck and beaten, the crashing blows sounded unbearably loud in my head. Suddenly I was a man, and I could feel the cold sweat running into my mustache and brushed it away, my heart racing. I started down the stairs, a long kitchen knife in my hand. Two men wearing navy ski masks were coming at me, one with a bloody hammer. The scent of them, death in their eyes, the hardness of their bodies, the blows, the knife wrenched out of my hand, the strange sensation of the blade across my neck, the stairway flying up to meet me, desperation to save my family . . . and abruptly the "dream" or "vision" ended.

I was sick the rest of the night, unable to shake the nightmare, unable to understand it, the suddenness of it, the utter chaos and confusion, the actual feeling of pain, the clarity of "being" someone else. In the morning I rang up my mother to tell her about it and to clear the horrible cobwebs and blood spatter from my mind before I returned to the writing project I was working on. That evening, as I sat down to supper, I tuned to KVOD radio to listen to my favorite classical music. Instead, the news was on. The first report stopped my heart cold. A man, his wife, and their two little girls had been found murdered in the exact way as I had experienced and at the same hour. They lived twenty miles across the metro area in Aurora. I did not know the Bennett family, had never even heard of them.

What terrible rift in time and space, in the fabric of the collective psyche was this? What purpose was there in my experiencing it? I had no intention of taking the story to the police. What good would it do? Certainly they would write me off as a total nutcase. Thus, the experience went no further than family and close friends. (Not until ten years later did I find out the youngest Bennett child had actually survived her attackers.)

This made me less skeptical and more open to the possibility that psychic phenomena don't merely reside in the imagination. Whether the manifestations are something "felt" or seen, whether they are disembodied spirits, nature spirits, psychic energy, emotional energy, or some unlabeled nuclear impulses, they need to be explored. And that is the aim of this book.

Whenever possible, I have given the precise location of these haunted places. Many of the buildings are still standing or have enough visible fragments to find them. Old jack trails and four-wheel drive roads lead to secluded basins and forgotten mine complexes where spirits wander.

As in *Twilight Dwellers: Ghosts, Ghouls, and Goblins of Colorado,* this book does not include the countless haunted houses of the region, simply because there are too many, the sites are private, and the ghosts are personal.

The majority of this volume's tales originated before the 1920s, most going back to the gold rush days and beyond. They have come from many sources and each was researched to its roots if possible, whether it was a family tale or a popular community story. All conversational quotes derive from original documents, newspapers, or eyewitness accounts, including private journals and letters. I was allowed to use some of the family stories only if I agreed to protect the identity and maintain the privacy of the informants. Many people are reluctant to shoulder the notoriety, ridicule, or inquiries ghost stories generate.

A number of stories were told to me or sent to me as long ago as 1978, and unfortunately, some newspaper clippings or photocopies had no dates or even the name of the paper they came from. Colorado ghost stories surprisingly appeared in the news as far away as the San Francisco *Chronicle* and the Philadelphia *Ledger.*

I present each spook as through the eyes of the witnesses, painting a portrait in words as the police artist sketches the face of a suspect, not to convince the reader of its reality, but to show the ghost as the witnesses experienced it, for they were convinced of its reality. Their beliefs, their fears, their awe may be more tangible with such a presentation. Our ancient tribal storytellers, the bard, the shaman, the *seanachaidh,* told tales in this fashion to give heart to the telling.

It is the heart of some of these ghosts that spoke to me, beckoning me to search through the past and uncover their truths. Thus the mysterious tale of William J. Barney (Chapter 9: The Bowels of the Earth) is presented but briefly here, reserved for the full telling in another book I am writing on him and the Telluride labor wars. I hope to do the same for Richard Krueger's witch.

Folklore has historical validity, giving life to many stories that are merely a collection of dry facts. Author Alfred Metraux wrote in the *Journal of American Folklore* (Vol. 59): "Folklore, if properly handled, constitutes the most valuable document not only to understand the nuances of the culture, but to grasp the general psychological pattern of those who share it." Storytelling was the path to the heart, from the heart, and this collection of tales demonstrates the beliefs of the times, the heart stories, the hopes and dreams and fears of the men and women who called the San Juan home. I not only desire to preserve their heart stories, that oral tradition that is nearly lost, but also hope readers will use this book to explore the haunted sites and to court the possibility of brushing up against the realm of spirit.

Soirbheas math leat!
MaryJoy Martin
Animas Forks, June 21, 2000

$\mathcal{I}$NTRODUCTION

S pirits, spooks, and sprites have shadowed the San Juan since the first nomadic shaman danced them from the flames of a midnight fire. They spoke from the sky. They drummed beneath the earth. They showed themselves like mist over the boiling spring waters.

As Puebloan stone-builders migrated north, their great Maasaw, god of fire, god of death, followed them through the *sipapu*. Their priests summoned kachinam from the belly of the kiva and *soyoko* ogres from canyon and cave. Wandering Utes sang Sinapi out of the sky, fled the *si-a-ci's* grisly appetite for human flesh and cowered before the *nusak-wu-ci*, the spirit of the dead. Ghost fires terrified the Dineh in the darkest San Juan nights and the *chindi* was avoided at all costs.

Spanish explorers dragged their *brujas* and *santos* and *demonios* into the heart of the Shining Mountains. Sidling in after them, French trappers released the wraith of the Countess of Artois from their knapsacks.

Loups-garous, the she-wolf of Auvergne, and the dark spirit Astramon curled out of the smoke of their pipes.

In only the flap of a demon's wing, gold seekers, dream chasers, merchants, preachers, and prostitutes deluged the San Juan with their own denizens of the dark. From Saguache to Paradox, Montrose to Durango, a virtual host of ethereal beings cluttered the wind and water and burrowed deep in the earth. Tommyknockers sprang from Cornish gripsacks. Banshees and leprechauns slipped out of Irish satchels. Poltergeists and kobolds escaped German trunks and *domoviks* squeezed out of Russian apron pockets. English children imported bundles of fairies while Scots trundled in cartloads of imps, hags, selkies, and enough ghosts to hang a mist over the mountains. The Chinese ferried in their ancestors, and the Italians lugged in their pepperoni. Nothing more terrifying than the ghost of a pepperoni.

Supernatural creatures crossed cultural lines, perhaps even interbred, creating tales to match the mountains: mysterious, spectacular, magical. Once conglomerated, the spirits failed to limit themselves to their own particular origins. A nonsuperstitious white Philadelphian named J. S. Gallagher encountered an ancient Puebloan *soyoko* or the Maasaw along the Rio Mancos. Greedy cowboys were slain by a Dineh *chindi* while engaged in the sport of grave robbing. La Llorona descended on an Anglo boy at Pagosa Springs. The editor of the Rico newspaper interviewed a witch imported by a young German. Tommyknockers went bad in the Virginius Mine when non-Cornish miners insulted the wee men. Although the Swedes and Italians refused to believe in them, the knockers sent a number of them to the doctor and the undertaker.

Whether sweet or sour, Tommyknockers and their Teutonic cousins, the kobolds, were clearly sprites, diminutive supernatural creatures like leprechauns. Elusive and mischievous, sprites usually were helpful to humans, performing odd chores or protecting us from danger. If insulted or neglected, sprites exacted their revenge in dreadful ways, like the knockers of the Virginius and other mines. Historically, tales of sprites in the San Juan were probably confined to children's bedtime stories, but a few were scattered among the Cornish, Irish, Scottish, and German miners. English children near Ophir cultivated the friendship of a band of displaced fairies in the hills above town. The Utes consulted a diminutive man called *pituku-pi*, a supernatural creature that lived underground and had healing powers. More modern tales of the *pituku-pi* have him dressed in green and looking suspiciously like a suntanned leprechaun.

Trunk loads of sprite tales have disappeared from the San Juan region, siphoned off by the advance of technology faster than any other folklore. Belief in them was less widespread than belief in spirits and ghosts and thus their demise went unnoticed. Tommyknockers and kobolds are all that remain and they, too, are vanishing as mines continue to close down. Not far behind them are the nature spirits, elementals, or spirits of the earth, still abundant among the Puebloans, but nearly gone from pioneer settlements. Belief in them is again on the rise, with ordinary farmers leaving them offerings in the fields and Hollywood divas calling on them for consultation. Many, such as Spider Woman, Raven Mother, the Elegant Lady of Animas Forks, and perhaps the stray witch of Richard Krueger, might still be glimpsed in the San Juan.

Most abundant in the region are the ghosts. Whether they are astral bodies of the deceased or some sort of psychic energy left over from life, tales of them survive from more than a century ago. Accidental or pre-meditated violent death produced the majority of them. Since death was constantly on the prowl, sometimes scooping armfuls of helpless humans to her bosom at once, ghost stories proliferated. Murder and lynching victims were the quickest to come screaming back. Strangely, they often failed to haunt their dispatchers and turned up to terrify innocent children or their own families. (They would have rendered good service had they popped up in front of Ouray's self-righteous editor, David F. Day, and scared him out of his knickers.) Suicide and avalanches invariably resulted in hauntings, the latter creating so large a spook population that old-timers dubbed their collective moaning "the Voice of the Winter Wind."

During the 1880s and 1890s, spiritualists and their followers rapped and tapped these ghosts out of the woodwork, their favorite place for a séance being the cemetery. More ghosts were reported during those decades than any other time. Ghosts attached to houses and hotels were called forth, interviewed, offered holy water and bratwurst, and sent on their way. "Lay-ing a ghost" or putting it "to rest" was quite a common practice and totally ineffective. Only those ghosts that were "thought-forms"—an astral body produced from the thoughts of mediums or sorcerers—were successfully exterminated. The others went on clanging and banging and knocking up the walls. Many can still be encountered in the deserted mining camp boneyards, abandoned buildings, and deadly mines. The energy of things not human, such as dogs, frogs, stagecoaches, and trains, also has manifested in the San Juan, with spiritualists responsible for inadvertently releasing at least some of this rambunctious energy into the hills. S. S. Merry, the bighorn ram, would have stayed in his grave if a medium had not disturbed his decaying hide.

Often San Juan ghosts manifested in a material, physical form, which witnesses mistook for a living person. In the mines they appeared covered with gore. In houses, hotels, and other buildings, they were less visible, frequently no more than a shadow or a cold spot. Sometimes only a scent announced their presence. A few spooks never showed themselves at all, simply content to drive humans to distraction with scratching and rapping on walls or flinging items around the room.

One of the most delightful manifestations of San Juan ghosts is music, from haunting pipe tunes to lyrical vocals, from violin solos to piano concertos. Many a man, woman, and child who died in this region left the music of their lives echoing throughout the mountains. No other place claims as many musical ghost stories. There is no explanation for it, except in the landscape itself. This glorious, vertical masterpiece called the San Juan, scarred by wind and water, painted in hues of red, green, blue, and dazzling white, gouged with deep passions and gut-wrenching tragedy, this masterpiece of living rock *is* music, rhapsody, opus, sonata, cantata. Perhaps this is why the music of those who lived here remains forever a part of the peaks and valleys, each person adding a note to the symphony.

From the highest mountain to the deepest canyon, no place in the San Juan lacks for a spirit, spook, or sprite. Some places, however, have more than a decent share. A "ghost belt" runs directly through the heart of the range, in a jagged line from Creede to Lake City to Silverton to Telluride to Rico, the terminus of that line virtually bloated with supernatural gasses. Humble, dog-eared Rico, a town with more guts than glory, has from the earliest days courted spooks. Many a Rico editor gave space to ghosts, even advertised for them to collect their bones at the news office. The town's appetite for violence was no greater than other raw Western camps in those early years, having assorted shootings, lynchings, and suicides to keep up with her neighbors, yet she collected far more ghosts. One per dead citizen was hardly enough. Spare ones drifted in on the wind, were draggled in by dogs with a fondness for thighbones, thundered in on the rails, and cackled in on broomsticks. At present there is far less town than in her boom days, and far more ghosts. Everyone who ever died here seems to be still hanging around and has invited kith and kin, for each house and building boasts not just one or two ghosts, but half a dozen . . . or more. One witness claims to have even seen the "ghost" of the old Foote Saloon on Glasgow Avenue one rainy evening. Rico has a passionate love for her spooks, willingly introducing those dark, obnoxiously scented "things" procreating in the jail cells at the courthouse as "friends."

Lake City also embraces her spook population with gusto. Under the guidance of the inimitable Grant E. Houston, editor of *Silver World*, ghost tales are served on a walking tour.

Ghosts are an integral part of this region. Despite the "ghost busters" and the spiritualists who blow through now and again, attempting to "release" the spirits from their perceived agonies or to "lay them to rest," the spirits, spooks, and sprites of the San Juan will continue with their moaning and rattling, their chanting, and their magic until no one is left to listen to them. They are the mist on the mountains. They are the music at twilight. They are the soul of the San Juan, that mysterious something in the wind.

And they are forever.

1

THE $\mathcal{G}$APING $\mathcal{G}$RAVE

N o breeze stirs. No bird calls. Twilight spreads a mantle of eerie silence beneath a silver-blue sky. Fading light glints off polished metal fleurs-de-lis and dresses whitewashed picket fences in an otherworldly gleam. Long-neglected grave monuments tilt against tree trunks or hide in the overgrown snarl of a rambling rose. The pines embrace tombstones and iron fences like great dark-robed angels gathering the dead in their arms.

Off in the gloom something glows with a white luminescence, beckoning, as a soft misty rain begins to fall. The pines give perfect shelter until the rain ceases to whisper in their boughs and low clouds leave a trailing mist along the hem of City Cemetery. Now the sky is darker, the trees are blacker, and the sweet-scented stillness heavier, pressing in from all sides. Even the highway offers no sound and seems to have vanished from the cemetery's fence line.

Something moves. A whir, a twitter, and sharp wings brush the edge of the sky . . . only a night bird. Ahead, in the heart of the graveyard, the white, luminous form still beckons: come closer . . . closer. It is only a thin marble tombstone, a cold, arched slab standing in a neglected enclosure of rusty rails and stocky posts. The afterlight plays on it, that mysterious silver light left by the dying sun, drawing a glow out of white marble. And yet, no other stones are so easy to read in the growing darkness.

"Patrick Smith. . . ." Whisper the name or the dead will awaken. "Native of the County West Meath, Ireland . . . died October 30, 1883 . . . age 45." Forgotten now, this son of Eire, but for the twilight's luminous caress, for no one comes to shed tears on his grave.

"Patrick . . ." a sudden breeze seems to whisper. "Patrick. . . ." The word falls soft through the sway of the pines, bringing another sweep of light rain with it. Something moves in the enclosure of Pat Smith's grave. A shadow, a light . . . a haze of shawl fringe, a mist of white lace . . . there is someone reaching out toward the tombstone, a longing in her action as if she is afraid to come too near, afraid to disturb his peace, yet wanting him, wanting him in her arms. What gulf yawns between them? What dream did they share?

For over a century she has been coming here, seen faintly in the shadows of twilight, her faded dress, feathered hat, and tattered black shawl suggestive of a dance-hall girl or a woman of poverty who bought one fine dress and kept it long after the fashion had gone. In the 1880s and 1890s those who saw her believed she was a dead "girl of the row," since Pat Smith's life had ended in acute syphilis with softening of the brain. Some identified her as Maggie Hartman, a Lake City prostitute who died in 1880. Later legends claimed Maggie was the woman who nursed a sick miner named Crowley back to health at Sherman and then succumbed to the disease herself, Crowley being Pat Smith. Other tales wove the ghost as Lizzie West (a.k.a. Lizzie DePendergast), an Irish prostitute from Ouray who killed herself in Denver in the spring of 1884. As the story went, Lizzie and Pat had fallen in love and he promised to marry her when he struck it rich. Some years passed and finally he was on the edge of a good deal, about to sell his share of the Carbonate Queen Mine, claim his girl, and retire. But his "old illness" struck again, "taking away his reason," snuffing out his life.

This tale matched many of the facts, yet in the early 1900s the *Rocky*

Mountain News published an altogether more curious tale, casting greater mystery over the ghost at Pat Smith's grave.

Patrick Smith was born in County Westmeath in the shadow of Athlone Castle on the banks of the River Shannon. He left his widowed mother in the care of his brothers and eventually arrived in the San Juans when he was thirty-seven years old. He worked hard prospecting and mining, finally becoming a partner in the rich Carbonate King Mine in Corkscrew Gulch above Ouray. He had bouts of illness that laid him low, but for the most part he appeared hale and hearty. Then in September of 1883 his illness ripped through him again, torturing him with debilitating headaches and nausea, racking him with hallucinations. His friends brought him to Lake City. Doctors could do nothing. With his friends at his side, though he was unable to recognize them, Patrick Smith died at the American House that October.

Not his ghost, but the ghost of a mysterious golden-haired woman soon appeared at Pat's grave. Schoolboys dared each other to stay in the cemetery after dark; stay and wait . . . see what comes. With shrieks, they threw stones at the foggy form and fled. She never seemed to notice.

Somewhere around this time a Pinkerton detective sidled into Lake City. After similar inquiries at Guston, Ouray, and Silverton, he asked after the whereabouts of one Patrick Smith. His wife, Mrs. Patrick McAbley of Athlone, County Westmeath, Ireland, was desperately seeking him. Patrick Smith was Patrick McAbley, by the detective's account, and his wife wanted to see him one last time before she died. The Pinkerton discovered Pat Smith had died and shortly learned Mrs. McAbley had also died, her heart broken, far from the only man she ever loved. She had spent her last farthing, had scraped and sacrificed in order to find Pat, her beauty fading, her blonde tresses streaked with silver.

The ghost at Pat's grave was his faithful wife, still longing to touch his face, still separated by the strange weave of time and an impossible gulf.

Other lovers in City Cemetery at least had each other, their shadowy forms seen only at twilight or midnight. These were said to be Jessie Landers and Louis Estep, united at last in death.

Jessie was a dance-hall girl working for Clara Ogden in Lake City's tenderloin. A few minutes before midnight on June 10, 1896, Jessie boiled out of her room, shooting at Frank McDonald, a man she accused of badly mistreating her. Instead of killing McDonald, the bullet missed its mark, striking Louis Estep. He died instantly. Louis and Jessie were engaged, their wedding date already set. The horror of her action drove her outside where she turned the gun on herself.

Jessie recovered from the wound but not her broken heart. Judge Gabbert sentenced her to the state prison for voluntary manslaughter. She served only part of her term, returning ill to Lake City in 1900 where she died in May.

Shunned, broken by life, tormented with guilt, Jessie found peace at last, her frail ghost running into the arms of her young lover. Their tragic spirits were united in an embrace "beneath the tall pine tree just above the river."

Cemeteries are the first place one expects to see ghosts, a place where centuries of tradition throughout the world had the dead come creeping out of their graves. "Rest in Peace" was no idle or sentimental phrase. It was a command. Ancient tombs were feared. Walking at night through cemeteries, or even near them, was dreaded. Horror stories of being bitten by the hungry dead abounded. Walking skeletons, bloodthirsty phantoms, and evil spirits stalked the graveyards of Europe, giving rise to spells, potions, and special behaviors to protect against them. Many American tribal peoples stayed away from the dead and from burial grounds, believing contact with ghosts caused illness and death.

None of this terrifying tradition seeped into the village cemeteries of the San Juan mining towns. The most frightening ghosts seemed to be kept in the mines, while the cemeteries hosted unaggressive wraiths that hovered near their graves, undisturbed by onlookers, never inclined to wander past the iron gates. Seeing them may have unnerved the living, but no San Juan cemetery spook was ever said to have snared a schoolboy and pulled him down among the worms as ghosts did in Scotland. Schoolboys were the first to spread graveyard tales and bet against each other's bravery, yet none ever lost to a hell-bent specter that ripped off boys' heads and fled with the prize as the dead did in Hungary.

Most San Juan cemetery spooks were described as "melancholy," "lonely," or even "beautiful," never terrifying. Rarely were they drenched in gore, as were the phantoms in the mines. Many were lovers, like Jessie and Louis, seen as a pair. Among these were John B. Frasher and his wife, whose shades hovered near their graves in Lone Tree Cemetery at Telluride.

Frasher tumbled into a bottomless melancholy when his wife died in 1896. He had been Telluride's postmaster in the 1880s and served as county clerk from 1894 to 1900, having gained numerous friends. But friends failed to fill his emptiness or quiet his fears, and on July 20, 1903, Frasher walked into the cemetery, despondent, lost. That afternoon he was found lying across his wife's grave, a bullet hole through him, a revolver in his hand. In his pocket was a letter he had written two days earlier to his grown children, asking their forgiveness, telling them to "be good to each other," and ending with "Good bye Millie, Elsie, Georgie, and Johnny. Your loving father."

The cemetery sexton was the first to see John and his wife arm in arm at her grave. Initially he mistook them for a living couple, recognizing them only as he drew nearer, startled to see the smiling face of the man he had buried only months before.

Like the Frashers, a couple who appeared at Silverton's Hillside Cemetery walked arm in arm in the alpenglow, their spirits eternally united. They were believed to be Anna Pearce and her English husband Jack, who died within days of one another in 1894.

Other ghostly lovers were lost in eternal longing and despair as they waited alone for the objects of their hearts to return to them, as was the case of Red McCann, a gambler shot to death by a deputy sheriff in Dave Long's saloon at Creede. Red loved a spicy woman named Devita Fleur, who visited his grave on the hill each day during the summer of 1892. She left the territory sometime that fall, and Red's ghost became lonely. At the sound of footsteps, particularly ladies' footsteps, the lonely shadow of the gambler rose from his grave, looking for Devita.

Similarly, the ghost of Elmer E. Kerr was aroused by the presence of ladies in the Lone Tree Cemetery, as if he were looking for his sweetheart. His sweetheart stopped going to Elmer's grave for fear of the tormented phantom, who was rumored to have frightened her by wrapping his arms around her. She never actually saw him, just felt him or heard his voice "fraught with despair." Twenty-seven-year-old Elmer had died unexpectedly

September 17, 1888, from "compression of the brain," as the doctor termed it, just three days before he was to be married.

In 1888 this cemetery had a rash of ghosts churning the air, and reporters surmised it was due to the weedy, haphazard condition of the place. "There is no system at all in regard to the laying out of graves," said one. The grounds were disorderly, unkempt, with some graves oriented east-west and some north-south and no aisles between. No wonder the dead were restless, what with someone else's toes in their ears and another's teeth on their kneecaps.

Victims of unsolved murders also found no peace. One of them, who was buried at the roadhouse in Stage Station Flat above Sawmill Canyon, Hinsdale County, manifested at the sound of horses' hooves. No one knew who the man was. They had discovered his corpse in the shrubbery in spring 1884, perforated by four bullets, ripe with maggots, and chewed by coyotes. As a spirit his countenance was pleasant, his eyes full of fear. Like the others, he did little more than hover at his grave.

Secluded, remote graves produced the loneliest of wraiths. Stories of mysterious figures seen by a grave on a hillside or near an old homestead or at the side of a forest road abound throughout the San Juan, with spooks equal to the number of graves. Typical of their mention were these enigmatic lines in the *Rocky Mountain News*: "While looking over the Paradox country last month, Mr. G. W. Kramer, stopping to water his horse by a spring a few miles this side of Bedrock, was surprised to encounter a pretty young lady smiling upon him from the hill. He exchanged a few words with her and started up the hill, never taking away his gaze. She was nowhere to be found upon his gaining the hilltop. The grave at his feet explained the vaporous departure." This was probably the ghost of Susie E. Lonsway, buried two miles east of Bedrock in 1896 in a spot as lonely as the far side of the moon. Herbert Daniels, a Paradox man, had also encountered Susie.

These ghosts came at the approach of the living, for in these remote places it was generally believed the spirits felt left behind, waiting for their loved ones to come back for them. Many were young children, and the loneliness on their sad-eyed faces was enough to tear one's heart, although these wee ghosts were often described as "beautiful" or "luminous." Sometimes the presence of women near a grave in Calamity Draw west of Nucla brings a soft voice on the breeze, begging, "Please, stay." At this point a faint

SOMETHING IN THE WIND

apparition of light appears on a rock, arms outstretched, "a beautiful little boy" reaching from beyond time.

Another lonely little boy has been seen in the Howardsville cemetery, lost among the tombstones, waiting for someone who will never come. Silvertonians suggested this is the ghost of Jimmie Miller, who died at the age of nine in 1880.

At Rico's IOOF cemetery, little Georgie Edwards's ghost stood forlorn beneath the trees, calling for his mama. Unknowing visitors at the cemetery were drawn to the sobbing child in the shadows of the towering spruces. Upon inquiry, they found he wished to be taken home. He offered his little hand and was led toward the gate, abruptly vanishing as the compassionate and now confused person stepped through. For Georgie, killed in 1897 when a horse dragged him through rocks and stumps, it was impossible to get beyond the gate, impossible to go home.

Rico also claimed a pair of little spooks in the burial grounds on the opposite side of the highway. These neither spoke nor sobbed. They simply appeared together as luminous forms, beautiful, serene, the bigger boy holding the baby. Some thought the Wakeman boys were trying to convey the message to their grief-stricken mother that they had found one another. Baby Russell Wakeman, an infant of one year, died in 1882 when Fenno Wakeman brought his family from Colorado Springs. Only a week in their new town, the Wakemans were devastated by the boy's death. Jennie Wakeman returned to her parents' home in Watkins, New York, but eventually rejoined her husband, and soon daughters cheered the household. By 1889 she gave Fenno the "apple of his eye," little Ralph, having given birth to the boy in Watkins. Fenno prospered on his leases of the Dayton and Hope-Cross Mines and his wagon business, but suddenly in 1902 his joyous, sprightly, beloved twelve-year-old Ralphie was snatched by diphtheria. No amount of tender words were able to fill his parents' aching hearts, until the luminous apparitions in the graveyard were reported by two of the women from the Ladies Aid Society. Ralphie had found baby Russell and brought him from beyond the bonds of the tomb.

In Cedar Hill Cemetery north of Ouray, it was the ghost of a young mother who carried a babe in her arms. Emma Vorse and the infant daughter named in her honor were glimpsed as "softly translucent figures emanating a warm light." Emma had died in 1890, two weeks after the birth of her baby. Baby Emma died eight months later. The crushed father, John Vorse, turned to a spiritualist for comfort. In the light of a crescent moon, the spiritualist, a woman calling herself Perdita LeBlanc from Montreal, gathered a small group at Cedar Hill and called their beloved dead to "come forth." She must have been paid well, for some of the spirits who came forth never went back from whence they came.

Spiritualists infested Ouray from 1889 for a decade or more. Dave Day scoffed at them, poked fun at them, and gave them a good bit of space in his *Solid Muldoon.* Yet even his ardent skepticism bent a little with esteemed citizens whispering of the spirits these mysterious mediums brought through the veil.

In August 1890 Day wrote, "There are a number of Spiritualists in Ouray, working on the quiet, who have spoken to the *Muldoon* people as to the advisability of holding a séance and admitting the believers and unbelievers alike to the ceremonies. In this age of progression everything goes, and if anyone thinks he can convert the *Muldoon* to this . . . cut loose and give us a chance. We will talk to the spirits and report their conversation as received honestly and without criticism."

Unfortunately, a large majority of spooks remained taciturn when approached by mediums and their breath-holding disciples. A mysterious little girl in the Wilson Mesa cemetery, located up the Big Bear Creek road, was repeatedly interrogated by a candle-toting, chanting pack of spook chasers who simply desired to know who she was. No amount of essence of mandrake or powdered yew berry induced her to speak. Ignoring the lot, she went on hovering beside the grave of a man long after the mob had given up.

Some boneyard bogies do speak, but refuse to show themselves. This was the case of a crusty, London-born Rico gambler known only as "Poker Joe," who died in 1880. Joe was cantankerous, sullen, and rude in life and downright vile in death. His epitaph read, "Hell hath called him." But even hell spit him back out. He not only stunk up the Rico cemetery, his grave sprouted noxious weeds. From his grave, he spewed out unexpected, obscene orders, the mildest of which was "Get on with you, you swine-arsed son of a cheating fishwife!" The shaken victim whirled round to see who spoke and Joe cut loose with a string of scorching insults and curses. Whether the town fathers rooted him up and hurled his remains into the river, after this suggestion was printed in Ouray, remains unknown.

At Guston was a ghost with the temperament of Poker Joe and a tongue nearly as scorching, cooled only by his Irish brogue. Unlike Joe, Tom Barrens was a congenial lad in life, busting up the Red Mountain district saloons with his "sharp wit and convivial disposition." He and his cohorts, Jack Jenkins, Tommie Quail, Evan Lloyd, John Kenaugh, and a few unnamed others, were called a "rascally pack of Hibernians, the lot of them," when it was learned they had been highgrading ore from the Guston and Yankee Girl Mines for months. Highgrading was theft of the best ore. They were arrested in August 1891, all but Tom Barrens. Tom had vanished.

The mill returns, found in Evan Lloyd's trunk, showed they had netted at least $674 in silver and gold from their sneaky operation. They were suspected of having caches of ore "secreted in the region," although searches failed to turn up any. Some fellow countrymen admired them for their cleverness. Kirby and Owen, Red Mountain saloonkeepers, posted their bail, inviting them in for a round. After all, the miners toiled for a measly three dollars a day while the managers and owners, like Captain Harvey of the Guston, lived like lords. Around this time the "laddies," as newsmen referred to them, placed a carved wooden grave marker over the remains of Tom Barrens somewhere up Champion Gulch.

The gavel banged, time passed, and life went on in the Red Mountain district without the "rascally Hibernians," their crimes and misdemeanors forgotten. Almost. Leftover Hibernians at the Guston (the mine was liberally festooned with the sons of Eire) revisited the tale in their free hours at the boardinghouse and saloons, whispering of "a large cache of highgrade ore" waiting for some lucky blighter to discover where Lloyd and Quail had stashed it.

Come summertime 1898, Guston lads Mickey Lonegan, Tom Tierney, Martin Ryan, and Angus McDonald (the Scot was chucked in for good luck) decided Tom Barrens's grave was no grave at all. The highgraders had marked it as a grave to deter the curious from digging up their cache before they came back for it, for who could recall Tom actually dying? And hadn't his friends chosen a curious time to give him a grave marker? Find the grave, find the gold.

The four men searched Champion Gulch from toenail to bald spot, finally locating the weathered board on a shelf high above the Genessee Mine. Tom had worked there once; perhaps highgrade from that mine was in the "grave" as well. "Tom Barrens, Died 1891" was tossed aside and the men began removing rocks with glee. A loud crack hurled Ryan backward into the gulch. Some unseen thing struck Lonegan about his head. With ears ringing, they replaced the marker in terror, scrambling down the side of Red Mountain as if they were hornet-stung.

They had stirred up the ghost of Tom Barrens. Or had they? Someone suggested to them the cracking, buzzing ghost was actually lightning . . . and the lads plucked up their nerve and tried it again.

This time Tom Barrens himself was standing over the grave. And he was rat-spitting mad. Hurling stones, firing a volley of Irish curses, spewing sand, he ended the excursion before it began. Well, said a saloonkeeper, old Tom must be guarding more than his bones to be that riled. Most likely they buried him *and* the ore in that hole.

The story was flying about far too freely at this point and one of the men decided to protect his interest from the rest of the planet by taking the grave marker. Simple to remember where the spot was, he reasoned.

Red Mountain has always been a copper-colored mass of slide rock, thus scree quickly covered all trace of Tom Barrens's grave. No one could find it again, not even Tom. He apparently was out of the grave at the time his marker was pinched, probably pursuing the thief down the gulch, dooming himself to moan and curse and hurl thunderbolts across Champion Gulch until green Eire sinks beneath the sea. Old rumors claim that if anyone ever risks Tom's high voltage and finds the grave, Tom will be grateful indeed, rewarding the finder with whatever is in it.

Cemetery ghosts rarely had the use of lightning, as Tom did. Many were no more than faint light or shadow, unidentifiable manifestations reported throughout the region during the 1880s and 1890s. Spiritualists, who found cemeteries irresistible, were responsible for the majority of the reports, frequently conducting séances on moonless nights, much to the annoyance of the dead and the press.

Outside of the usual tales of "swinging lights as if a specter had a lantern in hand," or of faint flashing lights bouncing from tombstone to tombstone, the most interesting of these was the light at the bone plot in Bachelor, a mining camp above Creede. A "soft beam of green light illuminated" a tombstone while a hazy "finger traced out the name" on the marker . . . and the name was *"NOT* the same as that carved thereon." Someone else was buried in the hole? It wouldn't be the first time.

Lone Tree Cemetery caretakers are the only ones who admit these old graveyards had many a mix-up in the boom days. Totally blootered undertakers and even drunker sextons or grave diggers buried bodies on top of others, misplaced markers, and forgot who was buried where when the tombstone arrived. So many graves went unmarked at Telluride that bones are still being unearthed when new graves are dug . . . and no one knows whose bones they are. Nor is Telluride likely to be the only place in the San Juan where Joe was mixed in with Rita or hauled off by Spot.

Rest in peace?

$\mathcal{M}$USIC IN THE $\mathcal{M}$OUNTAINS

S unlight silvered the wind-polished snow cornices of Mendota Peak as Willie and his burro picked their way down the trail from Governor Basin to Marshall Basin, high above Telluride. Shrouded in a dark mood, Willie paid little attention to the deadly ice underfoot. The snow-packed, crusted trail zigzagged over a thirteen-thousand-foot saddle dividing Ouray County from San Miguel County. Willie wanted to leave his heartache on the north side of that jagged ridge.

He thought he would be celebrating his thirty-fifth birthday in April 1888 with his Highland bride. Instead, he was alone with his burro, staring into the white maw of Marshall Basin.

William R. McKenzie left Scotland only a few years before to seek a better life in the booming mining camps of Colorado. His plan was to find steady work that would support two, then send for his sweetheart. They had promised to marry in April of 1888. From Denver to Leadville and finally to Ouray, Willie labored until he found back-breaking long hours and steady pay at the Virginius in Governor Basin. He sent for his lassie with a joyful heart.

Word came back from across the sea: in his absence she had married another.

William McKenzie's proud Highland heart was broken. He packed his burro and left the Virginius without collecting his pay. The darkness inside him snarled dead loveless words into his injured mind . . . what would it matter if the trail's rotting snow gave way . . . what difference would it make if a spring blizzard howled over and buried him in these snag-toothed mountains? . . .

His "burro disliked the wretched ideas" and sat down in the middle of the trail. Willie refused to argue. He sat beside the beast. Man and burro stared in silence at the white basin below, a rocky bowl garnished with mine tunnels, shaft houses, cabins, and a web of trails. The brilliant blue sky held no sound of wind. An eerie hush hung over the peaks.

Out of this silence slipped the distant, almost inaudible voice of Highland pipes, a sound that brought tears to Willie's eyes. Had he died and Highland seraphim were coming to take him home?

The piping grew more distinct, echoing from the unnamed peaks. Willie stood, astounded, looking all around him. His burro brayed once. A sweet, lilting tune bounded in echoes from Mendota Peak, across the rocky ridges, teasing in its direction.

Willie scanned the cornices and rocky outcrops for sign of the piper. He thought he heard boisterous laughter in the lull of the skirl. He called out, "Piper, show yourself!" No one appeared and the piping fell silent.

In his distraction Willie failed to notice his burro had strayed down the trail. He stumbled over the ice after the animal, stopping abruptly when the piping again wailed out of the rocks above, "like laughter out of the Highlands." This time stubborn Gaelic determination sent Willie chasing the music, up to the very ice cornices, across exposed rock, and back to the trail, taunted by the "ancient and wild tunes of his boyhood," teased by a "hearty rollicking" crow of a laugh.

Scrambling around this inhospitable place on the edge of the sky, his burro braying in amusement, his heart pounding in the excitement and thin air, sparked new life in Willie's bones. He decided this would be his world, his heart, his love. No woman would ever have his heart again. He would give it to these mountains where the piper cheered him.

Still unable to locate the energetic piper, Willie finally turned his burro toward the large mine complex below, for the sun was dipping low in the west and the chill breath of rotting snowfields crept round him. The piper once again had fallen silent. Perhaps the miners knew who he was and where he stayed.

Willie plodded down the trail, reveling in the memory of the music, in the glow of the dying sun that set white peaks ablaze. The soft kiss of an evening song touched the air. Willie turned. Several hundred yards above him "was a Highland piper, wrapped in tattered tartan," his pipes jutting past his broad shoulders. Willie stared in amazement, in awe. The piper grinned. Willie waved and hollered his gratitude. The piper waved back.

At the Mendota Mine Willie told his tale to the miners, who seemed to fall into "uneasy silence." They were reluctant to answer his inquiries about this man with whom he felt a deep bond, a bond beyond blood and bone, a bond as timeless and inexplicable as soul.

Willie pressed them. A few mumbled about hearing the piper over the past five years. No one had seen him. The blacksmith over at the Sheridan might tell Willie the story.

The Sheridan Mine's blacksmith, forty-year-old Frederic Surprise, was built like a gnarled tree trunk and seemed to have a few squirrels loose in his topmost branches. He claimed he gave himself his surname, never knowing his mother or father or place of birth, although some believed he was the brother of an equally peculiar Frenchman who called himself Peter Surprise (a.k.a. Pierre Surprenaut). Freddie never confessed to another name. "Surprise" was the root of many a joke and always an itchy sore on the nose of census takers (one threatening to have him arrested in 1900, so the story goes).

With the gravity of an undertaker, Freddie took Willie aside and told him the Highland piper was a dead man, "dead as spent shot, dead as a coffin nail, dead as a rat in a bucket of pitch," dead, dead, dead. Fred had dug the corpse out of the snow himself some five years ago.

The dead man was Fionnlaigh T. Farquharson, known as "Scotty," not merely because he was a Scot, but because intimidated tongues shied from his Gaelic name. One or two people called him "Fred" or "Frank" or "Fark." Most called him Scotty. He was straight from the heart of Scotland, a native of Glen Garry and the Grampian Mountains. He had a burr as melodious as a rippling brook and a laugh as boisterous as a Highland cataract. Scotty was described as "true-hearted, hard working, manly and handsome of features . . . generous of soul." Tall, broad-shouldered, strong as an ox, with "blue eyes full of the devil," Scotty worked with James and John Burns and Jim Walsh on the Gold Bug claim not far from the Mendota. He was "fiercely proud" of his Highland heritage and bellowed his love of this adopted high country to the surrounding peaks. On bright summer evenings or when he was melancholy, he played his pipes to the wildflowers carpeting the emerald alpine. In the winter his kindly nature dictated he play only the reed chanter or a flageolet or "penny whistle" indoors by the fire . . . the cabin wasn't exactly high enough to accommodate the drones, anyway.

At impromptu gatherings, typical of the era when womenless men danced together for the sheer joy of it, someone produced a fiddle, someone else a tambourine or harmonica, and Scotty joined with his flageolet. Boardinghouse or alpine meadow then filled with merry foot-stomping, toe-tapping, laughing, clapping, hollering miners.

After one long, hard winter day underground, while snow came in wet and heavy over the divide, James Burns and Scotty bedded down in their rough bunks in the low-slung cabin. Late Friday night, December 21, 1883, the snow-loaded ridge above the Gold Bug broke beneath its own weight, a deep rumble, a terrifying boom, a snap of logs all in an instant, then utter silence. The white fury had folded the cabin's walls and roof, dragging bunks and men beneath its deadly shroud.

On Saturday morning, John Burns, the brother of James, along with a crew that included the blacksmith Fred Surprise, dug into the snowpack. They prodded with poles, but their hope faded with each uncovered cabin fragment.

The grim work continued as grey skies boiled overhead. A few yards below the cabin's wreckage, deep in a snowy embrace, James and Scotty were discovered still in their bunks. Crushed instantly in their sleep, the two men appeared to be sleeping yet, never aware of the White Death that claimed them. The *Solid Muldoon* reported: "Burns was lying on his back, his features regular and bearing no evidence of struggle, while 'Scotty' lay on his right side with arms folded." James Burns, a well-known San Juan prospector, had $2,500 tucked into his clothes when his body was found. His San Juan properties totaled about $80,000 according to the *Telluride Journal*.

Both corpses were taken to Telluride and interred in unmarked graves in the cemetery below town (the first cemetery). Scotty was buried in the plaid he loved so well, his family unaware in far-off Scotland.

Avalanches continued to drag men to their deaths that weekend before Christmas 1883, killing nine at the Mendota, destroying buildings, machinery, supplies, and livestock here and at the Sheridan, Union, and Smuggler, all in Marshall Basin. Gloom descended on Telluride as the dead and injured were brought down. The only bright spot was the heroic care of Mary Hinds, a woman who stayed with the victims in town, nursing them without sleeping, lullabying them with Christmas hymns, an "angel at their bedsides." The Mendota boys told the *Journal* "her kindness will never be forgotten."

Due to heavy snowfall assaulting the mountains that winter, Marshall Basin mines were virtually deserted. Howling winds or white silence reigned until spring thaw brought miners, mules, and music back to the alpine bowls. The soft hint of Scotty's pipes or flageolet tunes tripped on the breezes. Miners joked about "Scotty's ghost up in the rocks blowing his penny whistle," but tossed it off by calling the sound a "trick of the wind."

In late summer of 1886, Sheridan trammer and fiddle player, Keenan Riley, was in an impromptu quartet, stirring up dancing feet at the boardinghouse when he suddenly realized the man playing a "flute" beside him was Scotty. No one else saw the fifth man, yet a few "thought" they "may have" heard his music. Riley's disturbed Irish mind (Gaels take their ghosts to heart) and subsequent ridicule sent him to seek other employment in Savage Basin.

Over the years Scotty became just a late night tale more often than not, or the bedevilment of inebriated miners staggering back to Marshall Basin boardinghouses in the wee hours of Sunday mornings. William McKenzie adopted the shade of his fellow countryman, in lieu of losing his heart to a woman, and was the only person who confessed to conversations with Scotty. Willie spent many hours wandering the alpine ridges, listening to the piper's tunes.

A lucrative position was offered him through friends at Aspen, pulling him away from the Marshall Basin mines for nearly a decade. But the piper remained in his heart. In 1898 Willie unhesitatingly took the offer to be night shift boss at the Bullion Tunnel of the Smuggler-Union Company near Marshall Basin. As soon as he returned to San Miguel County, Willie went tramping across the hills in search of the piper.

At this point McKenzie was closer to Savage Basin, with only a zig and zag of trail between the Bullion and the Tomboy, thus it was no surprise for Scotty's piping to be heard there as well, especially since Savage Basin was toe-to-toe with Marshall. As a shift boss at the Smuggler-Union during the tragic fire of November 1901 that killed twenty-four men, Willie, with miners' union president Vincent St. John, was credited for his heroic efforts in trying to save lives. In 1903, during a lull in the bloody and brutal labor wars, he was promoted to night foreman of the Smuggler-Union. Some said the piper played for McKenzie at the Smuggler boardinghouse even in this last year of Willie's life, and the faint sound of the pipes seemed to mourn in the walls of the building the night Willie breathed his last.

William R. McKenzie died suddenly June 11, 1903, at the age of forty-seven. He was working on Level Nine just two hours before and was oddly "pleased to hear his piper" in the belly of the mine. He went to his modest room in the Smuggler boardinghouse, feeling pain in his stomach. He died peacefully in his own bed from what the coroner termed "stomach cancer." Scotty had called Willie home.

In 1907 a small Scottish entertainment company, headed by Peter Menzies, was touring the San Juans. Whether Menzies had heard of Scotty through McKenzie's letters home or McKenzie's half-sister in Ontario is unknown. However, he had heard about the mysterious piping in the basins above Telluride and during his stay, made a few excursions with his wife in hope of hearing it for himself. A few local cards suggested Menzies sign the piper on with the company as an attraction to crown their exhibition of tinted moving pictures.

Back home in Scotland, the Menzies told the tale of Scotty Farquharson, of William McKenzie's attachment to him, of the beautiful, unearthly piping that echoed from the alpine ridges and slipped away on passing winds. A reporter for the Glasgow *Herald* greedily reaped every word. Scots always had a passionate love affair with spirits; their tragic history has wed shadowy wraiths to castle and cairn, ruin and Highland pass alike. The dead cannot be unraveled from the living. Nor are the Gaels far removed from the ancient magic of their ancestors, the days when bog witches called dead heroes from their tombs. Only a veil as fragile as the mists across the green glens separates this world from the rest, and Scotty's breaking through the veil was perfectly acceptable.

The Caledonian Club of Lake City, under the leadership of Kenneth McDonald, learned of Scotty's music and made a few excursions to Marshall Basin in search of it. One time they brought along a spiritualist and quoted Bobby Burns's poetry to the marmots and ptarmigans as a means to entice the piper out of the rocks.

The music of these Shining Mountains can never be beckoned, only discovered. Like the springtime, it is suddenly there, a long-lived San Juan tradition of harmonic spontaneous combustion. Pure delight. Heart-lifting. Melodies spilling out of stone and timber. Even now, in the swift days of cyberspace, the sound of a brass band toe-taps out of nowhere in Silverton, its members, clad in the dress of the Gay Nineties, materializing on Greene Street. This is flesh-and-blood serendipity, and everyone in town gathers along the street, smiling into the past.

From the time of unwritten legend, the men and women who peopled this region had a need to bring music with them, for it more than "soothed the savage soul." Music is the language of the soul.

The Weeminuche, Tabeguache, Capote, Dineh, and Puebloan soul-talked through sacred rattles, drums, and flutes, scattering their magic into the heart of the San Juan. Unable to live without that same soul-talk, Anglo, Finn, Italian, Greek, Prussian, and Mexican strapped fiddles to knapsacks, accordions to mules' backs, and pianos to wagons, and they, too, dragged their music into the heart of these mountains. Somehow the mountains made the music immortal.

Can any other region boast as many spectral symphonies infused into the landscape? Can science explain the proliferation of melodious ghost stories in one place? Perhaps stories are just stories, born from the age-old competition between men and the torment of snowdrift-induced cabin fever: "They have a phantom fiddler at the Forks, so let's have a fiddler and a piper. . . ." And perhaps not.

Distant legends whisper of several places in the San Juan where the haunting notes of a Weeminuche or Dineh courtship flute echo in the trees or drift on the wings of sacred hawks. Had some proud, dark-eyed man, who lost his love to death, poured out his grief to the wind?

As enchanting and mysterious as it is in life, flute music from the misty veil chills the heart. In August of 1878 at sundown, three prospectors making camp at the edge of silver-eyed Ice Lake froze in terror. They peered awestruck into the twilight. Flute music rippled across the smooth surface of the lake, wrapping itself around them, leaving them sleepless and on guard with rifles the rest of the night. In the morning they set out boldly in the sunlight, but again they were struck speechless upon discovering A. Southwell Howe's flute, provisions, and other personal effects rotting in a bank of thawing snow. They concluded an avalanche the previous spring had snuffed out Howe's life, although they found no body. His spirit was bound to this place in haunting melodies.

Less than a mile to the south in the same 12,400-foot basin is another silver-eyed lake with a resident musician-vocalist. In the fall of 1928, an experienced Dutch miner, Peter Izaak Spigt, working for Fredrick Schmelzer of Silverton, set out for the Ice Lake Basin claims. He left word he would return by Thanksgiving. He never returned.

Search parties in December of 1928 failed to find any trace of the Dutchman. Rumors of sightings came from Ophir, Rico, and Durango, yet if anyone actually had seen Spigt, they had seen a ghost.

Each summer Mrs. A. A. Schmelzer sent out search parties. They returned without results, until late August 1932, when Raymond Sutton found coyote-strewn human bones near Fuller Lake in the upper part of the basin. Rubber boots were still on the feet. A belt buckle with the initials "P.I.S." was nearby, according to a *Silverton Standard* report.

The gentle-hearted Dutchman, a man in his late fifties who played violin, cello, and other instruments and who could sing the entire Catholic Latin mass from memory, was buried at the side of the lake where he was found. For Spigt, this was hallowed ground, a fitting place. In a letter written to Schmelzer in September 1928 and discovered in the mine cabin, Spigt had declared, "High up in the Rocky Mountains, in a spot, a wonderful spot, in fact the most beautiful spot on earth—viz., Ice Lake Basin . . . there is, Thank God, where I find peace and happiness and hope to be allowed to spend a long time. . . ."

Peter Spigt has all eternity at the edge of Fuller Lake where clear water reflects majestic Vermilion Peak and the Golden Horn. Like a standing trumpet, the Golden Horn adds to the symphony of this place. As recently as 1998 hikers have been awed by violin music at Fuller Lake, music described as "somehow all around, not coming from one direction," music that took them "out of" themselves.

This is the banner quality that distinguishes spectral music: it takes one out of one's self. Or it drives one out of one's mind. For Julia White, the faint fiddle tunes of very much dead Frank Cooney drove her entirely out of the county.

Frank, described as "one of the nicest young men in San Miguel County," was the carpenter foreman at the Tomboy mill in Savage Basin. He had fallen in love with sweet Miss Julia White in Telluride. Her interest in him was less enthusiastic, although she accepted formal visits. He was said to have wooed her outside her window, playing fairy tunes on his fiddle.

Perhaps due to his state of mind or simply an unfortunate misstep, Frank lost his footing one terrible day on September 30, 1895, pitching into one of the large balance wheels on the crusher shaft at the mill. He was killed instantly. His crushed, mutilated body was packed and painted by the skilled hands of undertaker Isaac Glenn so as to make him appear merely bruised and sleeping. With necessary haste, his fellow lodge members had the corpse shipped back to his adoptive parents in Galena, Illinois. Julia White would never see him again.

Despite the temporal distance between Galena and Telluride, Julia began hearing those old fairy fiddle tunes outside her window. Her family and friends never found any explanation for this, except perhaps Julia was "more sensitive" to such tunes, now that Frank Cooney had died, and she was probably hearing the music of fiddlers about town wafting on the evening air. Whether Frank's spirit played up at the Tomboy is unknown.

For several years he played for Julia, until the disturbances became unbearable for her. In May 1899 she moved to Grand Junction and said she would not be coming back.

The ghost of a mandolin player, sometimes identified as Edward Donnaly, also was said to serenade a few select locations in Telluride, one of which was the old Cosmopolitan, another the vacant and dilapidated rooming house at South Fir and West Pacific Avenue.

At Dublin Dan's saloon in Ophir, a spectral cornet player tipped a few miners toward sobriety when he appeared behind them at the bar and tooted a tune in their ears. This teasing spook was said to be Mark Moyle, who had died as the result of a gunshot received at that saloon.

The most frequently mentioned spectral music in the San Juan came from pianos. The piano was a symbol of culture, of civilization. Men and women were hauling these bulky instruments into the mining camps before the burro trails were wide enough to accommodate wagons. Advent of a piano always warranted mention in the local newspaper. Citizens fondled and gawked at the new arrival as joyfully as if it were a baby. Pianos were sensitive creatures, and on occasion a self-proclaimed piano doctor ran the circuit lecturing on the care and feeding of pianos at high altitudes. In Colorado's dry climate, cheap pianos shrank and popped and lost their hammers.

The earliest keyboard ghost tale was of a piano hauled into the rough and raw tent camp of Howard Fork (Ophir) in the 1870s. After days of packing the instrument over rocky narrow trails, it reached the camp and was set up in a sagging tent, but no one there knew how to play it. Their initial gaiety dampened, the prospectors grumbled back to the mud and muck. One by one they stopped grumbling—someone was tickling the ivories with tunes from "back home." The stranger played all evening, every song requested, reels and Mendelssohn, marches and ballads, bringing tears of joy to the homesick men, until the hour of midnight, when he abruptly vanished before their dumbstruck eyes.

This is so close to the story told by William Devere in his poem, "Jim Marshall's New Pianner," that it is likely inspired by that work. On the other hand, the "stranger" in Devere's poem might have been a ghost. Devere ends the poem:

> *He thundered o'er the treble with a rattle*
> *and a roar,*
> *We heard a crash, and like a flash, he vanished*
> *out the door.*
> *We made a rush to stop him, but he vamoosed*
> *in a wink,*
> *We stood a moment dumbfounded, and then we*
> *took a drink.*

In his introduction, Devere pointed out that "the incidents are all true."

A similar phantom pianist played at the Inter Ocean Hotel on First Street in Durango in the 1880s, vanishing before the eyes of startled onlookers.

Across the San Juan region, otherworldly piano music without the presence of pianist or instrument reportedly has been heard from the 1890s to the present. Sisters Nettie and Maude Heinz were haunted by piano sonatas near the cemetery above Creede in the late 1890s. The girls made it their mission to discover the "tragic and romantic" pianist with whom Nettie had fallen in love. He was never unearthed.

Other ghostly piano concertos have been heard at Animas Forks, Cunningham Gulch, hotels in Durango and Rico, and buildings in Lake City, Telluride, and Ophir.

Animas Forks above Silverton did have a piano once at the Kalamazoo House. The hotel burned down in 1891, and perhaps it was the ghost of the piano itself that was heard in later years.

The piano music in Cunningham Gulch is attributed to Reinhard Niegold, one of the German Niegold brothers who established Niegoldstown at the foot of Stony Pass. Castellated dreams, schemes, and boundless energy led these eccentric brothers into deep, gold-flecked debt. In a short time, even the fine piano Reinhard loved so well had to be sold. He never let go of his collapsed visions and ardent love for Cunningham Gulch, laboring on the toothed flanks of Galena Mountain for years. After his death in 1906, his ashes were scattered to the mountains that were too big for him, and his ghost lingered among the fragmented hopes, playing like wind upon the beloved lost piano.

As if Cunningham Gulch had too few spectral occurrences, what with the spirits in the bowels of the Highland Mary Mine, the supernatural lights across the lakes above, and the assorted ghosts of the Old Hundred and Stony Pass, an archaeologist has lodged yet another piano sprite high on the slope above the mouth of the gulch. As the story goes (and from whence it came the archaeologist has no recollection), the Hawkeye cabin cabled to the twelve-thousand-foot sharp-edged shoulder of Galena Mountain was occupied at one time by a miner who had married a dance-hall girl. Without her adoring fans, the woman grew lonesome. To ease her heartache, the miner dragged a piano up the cliff and it became a better soul mate than the man himself. Eventually, the miner and his wife departed for more reasonable elevations, leaving the piano behind . . . and it began to play by itself, even long after a pack of roguish lads shoved it to its death off the cliff. Since the Hawkeye was once one of the Niegold claims, and since Reinhard's ashes had been scattered over the nearby Veta Madre claim, perhaps Reinhard himself had popped in to play the deserted piano or lugged his own with him . . . at this point it should be very lightweight.

In Lake City mysterious piano music in the Colonel Burgess house initially came from the brass lungs of the corporeal instrument. This piano was a Christmas gift to Bertina, the seventeen-year-old daughter of Dean and Mary Burgess. Bertina was home for the holidays in December 1920. Her father bought her the piano, knowing how much she loved playing, believing the instrument, the music might somehow restore the young woman's failing health. The gift was treasured above all others, and Bertina played the piano each evening as if she knew she had little time with it. Heart disease and its complications were sucking out her fragile life. She slipped away New Year's Day and was solemnly buried from the church of St. Rose of Lima, the bell commemorating each year of her brief life.

Bertina had played the piano just before she died, and now in the silence of the evenings after her burial, her father heard the gentle music in the sitting room once again. The Colonel rushed into the room, calling his beloved only child. Did she want to assure him she was forever at his side?

Colonel Burgess and his wife moved away from the shadows of heartache, and Dean died in California only a few years later. Their house in Lake City still cradled the mysterious music, a faint sound heard on the twilight air, although the piano no longer occupied the sitting room. The house eventually fell into disrepair and was torn down, and Hall Realty was built on the lot. Soft sounds, eerie music, a book inexplicably falling off the shelf, a giggle that makes one turn with a start and hope it was imagined . . . is gentle Mary Bertina Burgess still present, her fingers on the ivories?

Not so gentle was the tortured wraith of Lyle T. Lazelle, alias Lyle T. Stuart, a saloon pianist in Rico who fell in love with a servant girl at the Hotel Enterprise. Lyle had been in Rico for four years, earning his living as a professional piano player at the Rico Beer Hall, the saloon in the St. James Hotel, the Hotel Enterprise, and the Odd Fellows hall. For the most part he used the surname Stuart, afraid his French parentage would prejudice his audience. Furtive and secretive, he had confessed to Fred Archambault, the owner of the St. James Hotel, that he was born aboard a ship off the coast of France to the deflowered daughter of a merchant gentleman. Lyle and his wife, Sadie, lived quietly in a small house on Rico's River Street.

Lyle spent many long hours playing the piano at the Hotel Enterprise on Glasgow Street, hours too long away from his wife. One of the girls employed at the hotel, Alice Downs (a.k.a. Alice Watt), stole away from her duties whenever her employer's eyes were elsewhere and listened to Lyle from a nearby doorway. Listening blossomed into flirtation and before he knew what to do with the consequences, Lyle's hands were exploring the possibilities of Alice's curves in the dim hallway.

This tantalizing backdoor love became a nightmare for Lyle. Already given to the torment of paranoia and a hypochondriac's need for pills and powders, the eccentric thirty-four-year-old Frenchman was unable to stomach guilt. His wife loved him. His mother, God bless her, prayed for his soul in far-off New York. His young daughter, also in New York, loved him. Only death could hold back his sins.

Thursday evening, April 8, 1897, Lyle left the Hotel Enterprise earlier than usual and went home. He asked his Chinese cook to bring him a cup of tea. The cook watched him empty a small packet of powder into his hand—something Lyle did habitually—swallow it, and wash it down with the tea. A short time later Lyle staggered to his bed. His wife, assuming he was under the influence of alcohol, thought he was off to bed early to sleep off his "drunk."

At eleven o'clock that night Sadie became alarmed by her husband's labored breathing. She sent the cook for Dr. Landon, but Landon's antidotes brought Lyle only partway out of the dark portal of death. Before dawn his laboring heart stopped.

Sadie found two cryptic notes on the chest of drawers. One simply said, "Forgive me, Sadie"; the other, "Better this than be untrue to you."

Tormented Lyle Lazelle went to his grave mourned by his wife and shadowed by the servant girl, who placed wildflowers on the sod above him. Yet Alice Downs, with her sweet Irish lilt and soft curves, was his curse. He went after her with a vengeance, his bent, smoky shade pounding out tunes only she heard, sometimes in the small hours of the morning when the dining rooms were deserted. Sleep was hers no longer.

One evening, Alice ran to the piano when she saw Lyle playing it despite the crowds in the room. He rose up like a clawed serpent and wrapped his hands round her neck. A dining patron, Pendleton Hunter, rushed to the girl's rescue, pulled the ruffian away, and stumbled back in astonishment when the man seemed to melt into the woodwork. Alice screamed, "Leave me be!" and other patrons, who had seen nothing prior to this moment, mistook Pendleton for her attacker. How could he explain? He was an upright citizen, not given to altercations of any kind, especially not assaults on servant girls. His explanation left tongues wagging for weeks. The editor of the *Rico News-Sun* poked fun at him with the enigmatic quip: "If Pendleton Hunter lays hold on another phantom, give the man room. It may be a big one."

Alice Downs failed to see the humor. She returned to Telluride from whence she had come.

Lyle Lazelle accosted no one else, but he loitered darkly in his former places of employment, banging out his torment on available pianos. He lingered longest in the shadows of the Hotel Enterprise and broke through time at the lower hall of the Odd Fellows building, much to the distress of the fraternity.

Some spectral San Juan music has no clear link with a corpse or instrument. It simply seems to be part of certain places, such as the mysterious music that came with a sweep of dancing lights witnessed by early prospectors in a ferny ravine near Red Mountain Pass. Those were the days of simple acceptance, and the place was named Spirit Gulch. Men of that era weren't embarrassed by their beliefs.

Arthur Rice, a man from County Down, Ireland, was one of these. In the latter years of his life, he lived in a cabin on his claim in Galena Lion Gulch, on the west side of Red Mountain Creek, less than a mile from Spirit Gulch. He and his wife had raised ten children, and after she died in 1894, he moved to the cabin, delighting in the music of the gulch, which previous miners apparently had enjoyed and still dropped in to hear. The sound was described as "tiny bells," rippling sweet tunes among the wildflowers. For a brief time one of Rice's sons lived with him, but the son was never able to hear the music. Charley simply believed it came from his father's loneliness. Old-timers said it was something that had stowed away in a trunk when the man from County Down left Ireland many years before.

Celts and Saxons were often guilty of bringing supernatural diminutive creatures with them from the Old Country. Cornishmen stuffed countless Tommyknockers in their boots and luggage to insure safety in the mines. Others captured hobgoblins, brownies, or fairies to assist them in their new lives far from home. Most of these creatures were made of music, reveled in it, produced it at the clap of hands. For Mabel Hock and her brothers, San Juan fairy music was their saving grace.

Mabel's father, William Hock, had left England seeking a better life for his family. Settled at last in Ophir, with employment at the Suffolk Mine, Hock sent for his wife Elizabeth and their three children in 1892. Overwhelmed by the harsh vertical landscape and their first terrifying winter of avalanches, the children yearned for the green glades of home.

Ten-year-old Mabel seemed to pine away in the summer of 1893, until her brother, fifteen-year-old Will, began taking her on walks into the high meadows. Somewhere along Waterfall Creek, at the edge of a mossy brook where alpine flowers nodded over the clear water, Mabel and Will discovered the unmistakable magic music of a displaced band of fairies. They listened to the music for hours and returned to hear it the following day. The soft, tinkling sound greeted them again, and a nearby ring of tiny mushrooms proved the fairies had been dancing here all night. The spot became a refuge for the children. Here they dreamed of castles and kings, of rainbow magic and dragon wings glittering in the sun.

As years passed and Will went to work in the mines, Mabel took her younger brother, Arthur, to listen to the fairy music. Later, baby Ernest, who was born in Colorado, would share the secret of the spot. No one ever knew how the fairies came to be in this alpine place, but as long as Mabel was there to listen, they played for her, easing her homesickness for a country that became a dim memory.

While talk of fairy music was tolerated from the lips of children, it was condemned in adults, especially by the clergy, leaving many Irish tales untold. Even now, church ministers discourage their flocks from fraternizing with supernatural entities of the pagan or ghostly variety, no matter how beautiful their music. Except for the Holy One, ghosts have always been particularly unwelcome in churches and talk of them summarily hushed. They have been denounced as "evil," the "work of Satan," or "trick of demons." Nevertheless, even the devout can't help confessing long-secret stories of otherworldly music when there is a willing ear.

An old woman, whose mother grew up in Creede, told how her mother used to hear the soft, sacred sounds, "like the perfect voice of a choirboy," in the Creede Congregational Church, a diamond-paned Gothic gem built in the first decade of the twentieth century. Others whispered (with an apprehensive glance over their shoulders, as if looking for the pastor) of nearly inaudible organ music or "pipe" music or angelic voices singing in a number of San Juan churches. Among these were St. Patrick's in Telluride, First Congregational in Silverton, St. Columba's in Durango, and the old Foursquare Church in Durango.

Only one ghostly choirboy in all the San Juan churches was ever identified with a once-living person: Tom Greatorex, a young Silvertonian whose boundless enthusiasm for life infected all he met. Described by contemporary newspapers as a "natural born gentleman" and "noble soul," Tom was said to possess a beautiful, resonant baritone voice (by some accounts, bass; most likely he sang both, since he was in four-part groups).

As a businessman and artist, Tom traveled frequently to other San Juan cities. Many people knew him and loved him, especially flocks of adoring young ladies.

One terrible night in March 1881, Tom was with friends in Durango when he witnessed a brawl in the town's tenderloin district. Jumping in to assist the ladies, he was knocked down and shot point-blank in the back by a ruffian called Jack Roberts. Roberts fled. From Durango to Ouray, Lake City to Rico, Tom's friends cried for hemp. A reward of $500 was put on Roberts's head, on or off his shoulders.

Because Tom clung to life for a day, then two, then three, his friends built a tower of hope, believing his recovery was certain. His death ten days after the shooting collapsed the tower, grief and shock tolling through the region like a call to arms. The *Dolores News*, under the large bold headline, TOM GREATOREX IS DEAD, poured out "bitter and scalding tears." Businesses in Durango closed. Carriages were draped in black crepe. The "unprovoked" murder, said the Rico editor, made men "wish for but an opportunity to give his assassin a death such as never existed in even Poe's imaginative brain."

A simple hanging might serve as well, and that was the notion of the men who went after Jack Roberts when he was captured in New Mexico. In a passing brief the *La Plata Miner* reported March 26, 1881: "A party from Durango went down after him, but came back without him, and reported that he had got lost. He is thought to have gone to another climate via the limb of a tree." Vengeance done, the book was closed.

In the ever-changing boom days, Thomas Greatorex all too swiftly became little more than a name, a passing story. Except to secret hearts that loved him still. Louisa McMullen of Rico held Tom permanently in her heart. She wasn't surprised to hear his rich baritone in the choir at the Congregational Church in Silverton during her visit with friends there that summer. In Rico, she invited a spiritualist to bring Tom out of the netherworld to serenade her once again. Even though she married Johnnie W. Sommers, "one of the most popular boys in Rico" in fall 1882, Louisa secretly listened to Tom's enchanting music whenever opportunity presented itself. As late as winter 1899 Mrs. Sommers solicited the gifts of Mary Ellen Lease, a Telluride medium, to bring Tom forth for a private candlelight concert shared with her friends, Rosalie Higgins, Nettie Gardner, Lillie Silverman, and Emily Powell. In the long winter nights of these savage mountains, music was needed the most.

The winters themselves produced the eeriest musical phenomenon in the San Juans, a sound old-timers called "the Voice of the Mountains," or "the Voice of the Winter Wind." It is described as a low, melodious moaning or humming, not the howling of the wind across crags, nor the whistling of gales driving snow through shaft houses and abandoned cabins. The sound comes especially at dusk when the spruce boughs are still and the coyotes are silent, a spine-chilling sound like men's voices echoing out of time. Some said it was just the wind. Others swore it was the collective voice of the lost, all those who had perished in the claws of the avalanche, the White Death.

The White Death or White Terror was an eternal threat in winter. Utes were the only people with enough sense to stay out of these mountains at that time. When prospectors came, baritone after baritone was added to the Voice of the Mountains. San Juan winters snatched away hundreds of strong, adventurous men over the years, crushing and mangling their bodies beneath a savage snowpack. Sometimes a victim vanished into the White Terror's jaws so completely he was never found again, or found years later in the August heat, his flyblown corpse sticking out of the vestiges of a dirty snowbank, his voice added to the chorus.

Whistling a descant above this collective chorus is the spirit of Sweyn Nilson, lost in the same heavy, wet winter that claimed Scotty Farquharson. Sweyn was a subcontractor on the mail route between Ophir and Silverton in 1883. A native of Sweden, he was a tall, strapping young man with a "ready smile" and a melodious whistle. He could whistle a trilling rendition of any tune he heard once, or imitate the calls of numerous birds. The Ophir boys always had a place for him at the table. Rico editor Charles A. Jones dubbed him "the Whistling Swan." He was said to whistle to the trees while alone on his treks over Ophir Pass, the mail sack on his back. As he dropped into the Howard Fork drainage, miners knew the mail was near, for they heard his cheerful whistling a distance off.

In December 1883, Sweyn had delivered the mail to Silverton and was ready to return with a full pack to Ophir, but howling winds over the Divide threatened blizzard conditions. His friends in Silverton advised him to wait out the storm. Sweyn refused. He wanted to make sure the folks in Ophir received their Christmas mail. It was December 23, and if he left immediately he would accomplish his task. People were counting on him.

Sweyn was a natural on the "snowshoes" or "long boards," the names used for the long cross-country ski of the era. He knew the route over Burro Bridge, up the Middle Fork of Mineral Creek, and over Ophir Pass in the dark. He was an ox-strong, stubborn Scandinavian, a man who thought of others' needs before his own fears. And so he went.

Christmas dawned. Sweyn was nowhere in sight. All across the San Juans echoed the boom of avalanches and the White Death devoured human lives like a medieval dragon crunching through the massed ranks of a battlefield, spitting out bones and ghosts in its gluttony. Even rescue parties were swept over cliffs while bringing back the injured or dead. Sweyn's friends only hoped he had "holed up" somewhere and would come whistling down the pass after the storms abated.

By December 29 hope was fading. The *Dolores News* wrote, "It is also feared that the mail carrier between Silverton and Ophir has gone down." By

January 3, 1884, there was still no sign of Sweyn. The *San Juan Herald* reported: "It is a sure thing . . . [he] was caught in a slide and killed."

Search parties went out in February and March. The continuing winter storms had claimed the young man who replaced Sweyn, O. G. Dilla, and searchers found his body near Burro Bridge. He was "a victim of unrequited love," having taken the dangerous route without a care to his safety. With the mail of St. Valentine's Day in his pack, he perished in the deep February snow. But no trace of Sweyn, not even a long board or the mail sack, was discovered. As summer blossomed and occasional searches still revealed no sign of the man, rumors circulated that Sweyn had left the area via another route, taking the money and valuables by cutting open the mail pouch.

The idea was an insult to Sweyn's good name. Determined to squash the ugly prattle, his brother Njord "Nils" Nilson, returned from Sweden to search that summer and fall until the snow drove him into Silverton. With a few friends he resumed the search in summer 1885, hunting in the precariously deep and shadowed throat of Mineral Creek that paralleled the upper portion of the Ophir Pass trail. On August 13 Sweyn's partially skeletonized corpse was found in a snowbank, the mail pouch still strapped to his back. According to Will C. Ferril of the *Seattle Post*, the Christmas letters were still readable, despite being somewhat moldy, and "the wax on the currency package had rotted a hole through the greenbacks." One of the letters was addressed to Sweyn himself, a letter he would have opened in Ophir, a letter of love from his wife back in Sweden.

Sweyn's remains were buried in the area where he was found. From that time on, his cheerful whistling resounded across Ophir Pass, another note in the San Juan symphony heard by those with music in their hearts.

Whether it is Tabeguache spirits singing around the communal drum in the valleys near Creede or the bugling of elk in autumn, it is holy music. Whether it is the perfect B-flat of the Big Blue's coyotes harmonizing with the E-flat of the Nellie Creek coyotes or the simple vespers of meadowlarks, it is magical music. Whether it is the young man in Silverton who plays his bagpipes under a starry fall sky at the corner of the Grand Imperial Hotel (since his house is too fragile to hold the pibroch) or the haunting pipes of Scotty coming over the peaks to join the song, it is mystical music, the eternal music of these mountains. It is the soul-talk of the San Juans.

3

THE *U*NHOLY *T*HRONG

As the bridge came into view, Charlie McClellan's fine bay mare balked, tossed her head, and stalled. The string of workhorses he pulled behind snorted defiantly, stomping, whinnying, pulling away. McClellan tried to gain control, but his mare reared and the others scattered, tangling in the rope. McClellan cursed, pulling his mare around. With eyes wild in fear, she backed away from the bridge.

"Come off that horse, you filthy son of a bitch!" a ragged voice screamed.

McClellan wheeled the mare around. No one was near.

"I said come off that horse!" The words hit him as some black cloud smashed against him, nearly knocking McClellan from his mare. He pulled his rifle from the scabbard, yelling for his assailant to show himself.

The frenzied mare reared, throwing McClellan to the ground. The other horses stampeded in confused circles, as if chased by stinging hail,

33

their hooves pounding too close to McClellan's limbs. He yelled, scrambling for the gatekeeper's nearby cabin, and a dark whirlwind engulfed him in its rage. An ugly drunken laugh and vile words spun out of it. A voice challenged, "You can't whip one side of Jim Luce, you Irish son of a bitch!"

"Jim Luce!" McClellan gasped. "You're dead!"

Old James C. Luce had been keeper of the tollgate at the bridge over the Uncompahgre River near Chaffee Gulch when he was shot in March 1881. The bridge was four miles south of the Los Piños Agency (near Colona) on the road between Montrose and Ouray. Charlie McClellan, a Ridgway rancher, was bringing a string of workhorses from Montrose to his ranch in March of 1894 . . . March 5, 1894, the anniversary of the day Luce was killed.

Luce was no more than a dark, vile, shapeless cloud to McClellan, but his fury was potent, his words clear, his animosity packing enough punch to knock a solid man off his horse. McClellan had heard the tales . . . avoid the place on March 5 . . . Luce's ghost . . . the vile curses. McClellan had scoffed, never giving "those schoolgirl tales a thought."

Jim Luce was a crusty old gatekeeper in his day, residing in the low-browed cabin near the bridge. He was a hard drinker, swilling the stuff for breakfast, picking fights with perceived enemies, one of which was the Irish rancher Thomas Herron, whom Luce accused of "taking the tollgate" away from him.

Herron had been instrumental in having the gate removed, but not out of animosity toward Luce. His negotiations were with A. F. Paff, who owned the ground, and the tollgate was no longer of use. Jim Luce was approaching sixty and it was thought he might return to New York, where his wife and adult children lived, to spend his remaining years in peace.

"Peace, hell. New York, hell. I'll show that Irish son of a bitch who's old," was Jim Luce's reply. He bitterly complained to his friend C. S .T. Chaffee for days, blasting Thomas Herron for "playing a mean dirty trick in getting the tollgate" from him. Chaffee tried to convince him to "bury the hatchet, give it up. Tom meant nothing by it."

On March 5, 1881, Chaffee and Luce were at the cabin, Luce drinking his breakfast and complaining again to his friend when Tom Herron rode into view. Luce hurried out to greet him, offering him a drink, and Herron chatted about getting sawdust from the old mill site to use for keeping his ice. Luce said the stuff was three years old, and Herron agreed it was too old for ice. He turned his horse to go back home.

Luce wanted to keep him there, to find some excuse to start a fight, but Herron was too friendly and cheerful. Luce snapped a challenge, a bet. Herron failed to bite. Luce twisted a light remark made by Herron into an insult against himself and Herron begged his pardon, suggesting Luce "misconstrued the point."

Luce snarled an insult. "I don't want to quarrel with you," Herron returned. "We will settle this another day. You're drunk. I don't want anything to do with you."

"You Irish son of a bitch, come down off that horse!" Luce spat. He tried to pull Herron off the horse.

Chaffee attempted to induce the spewing old fellow to go into the cabin, but Luce continued his raving, ordering Herron to be out of there within the next two minutes.

"I'm on the public highway," Herron replied. "I have a right to stay here."

Luce hurled every profane phrase he knew, wrenching Herron from his horse.

"I don't wish to fight an old man," Herron said, but Luce swung at him, cursed him, and yelled, "Tom Herron, you can't whip one side of Jim Luce!"

Herron threw off his coat. Luce grinned. He flew at the younger man, saying, "Now that's right, we'll fight it out. Jim Luce ain't no old man."

Luce was, and drunk, too. Herron knocked off his blows with ease, infuriating Luce, who said he would finish him and rushed into the cabin. Chaffee had gone round to tend his own horses when he heard a gunshot. He ran back to see Herron with a smoking pistol in his hand. Jim Luce was dead inside the doorway of the cabin, a rifle at his feet.

His fury failed to end there. It balled up and blew out of the place, striking whoever came near "his" bridge every March 5 thereafter. Charlie McClellan no longer called the tales of this raving specter "schoolgirl tales." He was a believer after his encounter in 1894 and had "scars to prove it."

Although the original timber bridge has been replaced over the Uncompahgre near Chaffee Gulch, there is nothing to say the inky ball of fury once called Jim Luce is gone. Phantoms who, like Luce, have become the personification of rage pepper these mountains, the savage throng having lost all semblances to men, only "dark shadows" or "hideous tangible rage" left where spirits might have been. Many were killed during the firestorm of their tempers, causing, as was commonly believed, the nightmare anger to remain long after the corpse had cooled and was given over to the worms.

At Alta Basin the jealous rage of Frank Enderich harassed travelers on the roads between Alta, the Bessie mill, and the Silver King Mine. He had no need to wait for the anniversary of his death, as did Jim Luce. He chafed and fumed whenever the conditions were right (whatever they may have been), most frequently in the evening. In the early days his ghost was encountered once or twice, deteriorating to a festering hulk of black vapor in the road by the early 1900s.

Frank Enderich was a young man well known in Telluride, married in 1896 to charming and lovely Anna Woods of Saw Pit. Anna's "cheerful ways" looped many a fellow around her smile, boiling acid in Frank's gut. He took her to live at the Bessie mill near Alta Lakes in 1898, where he could keep a green eye on her. Nevertheless, she soon charmed hardworking and shy Frederick W. Brower, foreman of the Bessie. He moved on to be foreman of the Silver King Mine up the road, but still dawdled at the Enderich cabin, having far too many chats with Anna.

Frank accused Fred and Anna of indecency and "intimacies that are reserved for husband and wife," warning Fred to "stay clear of her." Fred protested his innocent friendship, and Frank threatened him.

A few weeks later, Anna asked for Frank's permission to go boating on the lake with her friend Nora Mooney and Nora's beau, Lu Umstead. Frank granted it, as long as she made it a short affair. At the lake the jolly friends gathered Kinney McLean and Fred Brower, who just happened to be nearby. All five went out in the boat as the sinking sun painted the water gold. By dusk they were strolling back through the woods toward home, Fred and Anna at the end of the single-file line on a narrow path.

Anna's husband sprang out of the woods, firing a shot at Fred. Fred

SOMETHING IN THE WIND

fired back and a brief gun battle ensued, with Frank Enderich dropping flat on his face in the trail. Fred had a shoulder wound. Aghast and shaking, his friends surrounded him and the dead man. Fred begged for forgiveness, saying he had to shoot or be killed. He hurried off to get aid for himself and to call the sheriff up from Telluride.

The coroner's jury cleared Fred Brower of wrongdoing that August 1899, believing he had shot Frank in self-defense. The fury of his failure to get rid of Fred, compounded by Fred's freedom, caused Frank Enderich's jealousy to erupt from beyond the grave, trailing misery through the Alta area, accosting men on the road, enveloping its victims in a confusion of darkness and turmoil, accusing them of trying to steal Anna.

Out in the middle of the Lake Fork of the San Miguel River near Ames, a greasy hornet-headed specter named Jack Ryan cursed passersby from the summer of 1882 until 1884. Ryan had died in the river whilst swimming under the influence, and the authorities billed it "suicide with intent." This rankled the besotted Ryan, whose ghost seemed loath to crawl out of the frigid water, from whence he hurled vile insults at the locals. Someone asked his former partners to "send him to hell where he belongs." The partners, Richards and McDougal, obliged, dropping a charge of dynamite in the drink. The vile gas was seen no more.

Down at Big Bend (near the present town of Dolores) the citizens tried torching the sooty wraith besieging them. First they tried bullets, without result. Fire failed as well, only notching up the phantom's rage a few decibels, and not surprisingly, for the ghost belonged to a Ute murdered in cold blood by one or more of the white settlers. As if murder wasn't enough, the settlers left the body to the flies, bragging up and down the hills about it. "One Good Indian" headlined the story in one paper, referring to General Sheridan's unholy quote. Another reported, "It is high time that some such action was taken to stop the depredations of these impudent rascals." This was in the fall of the same year (1880) that the son of Chief Shavano was killed by a white freighter on the Cimarron, resulting in killings on both sides until the government stepped in. Newspapers screamed against "the red devils," ranted how this "paralleled the bloody reign of terror in France," although this was more drama than truth. Also at this time, the government was busy snatching back those lands granted to the Utes by United States treaty "for as long as rivers might run and grasses grow," with Otto Mears purposely paying uninformed Utes two dollars each to sign a new treaty.

Oddly, only the Ute at Big Bend boiled into a raging specter, his face ashen, his body bloated, a bullet hole through his head. His wrath was terrifying as he exploded through herds of cattle, tore open cabin doors, and ripped off roofing, according to W. C. Carmichael in 1904. Some of the local cowboys attempted to destroy the specter by setting a shed on fire while it was inside. They succeeded only in chasing it down some forbidding gulch where it remained until the waters of McPhee Reservoir swallowed it.

In 1895 a raging phantom described as "a stocky Mexican" savaged a pair of hunters on Lone Cone's lightning-scarred flanks. Sam Peters from Telluride and his partner from Norwood had gone up the Cone after its famous bears. They wound up with ducks and grouse, but one evening while they were roasting supper, a "frightful dark figure" erupted from the smoke of their camp fire, scattering coffeepot, plates, and bedding, "screams emanating from it in Spanish . . . most certainly what were vile insults." Peters fired on the thing, to no avail. It came at him "like a whirlwind," and the foul odor of death and decay choked his lungs, the damp of its black cloud chilled his flesh, and its burning black eyes seared his memory. It disappeared as mysteriously as it had come, "leaving the lads wide-eyed and hugging their Winchesters until dawn."

Old-timers informed Peters he had made the acquaintance of the infamous camp cook of Lone Cone, a Mexican who worked as cook with the Wheeler outfit in 1887. A cowboy named George Sanford killed him over an argument about a saddle. The camp-fire feud gave way to bullets and both men were shot. Sanford's body, however, was given a decent burial, while the Mexican was left in the sage a week. In the end, he was dumped like refuse into a shallow hole, yet word came the following year that "coyotes made trophies of the Mexican's bones on Lone Cone." From that point on he kicked up a fury, dragging the scent of decay with him.

Noxious odor accompanied many members of this incensed mob, even when they weren't left out to rot. At Bachelor, a turbulent camp above Creede, the deranged gaseous husk of Andy Wellington assaulted the family of A. R. Allen. Wellington's last moments in life precipitated the foul haunting. In a rage he attempted to dispatch the Allen family, thus with a shrapnel buckshot load, Allen blasted a cavern through Wellington in defense of himself, his wife, and daughters. The crazed fiend returned after death to terrorize the Allens, a hideous, rank odor oozing out of it. One daughter the specter "struck about the face and head," driving her from the area. In life, Wellington had demanded her for his mate and she rejected him. As Bachelor succumbed to ghostdom itself, the uncorked fiend frothed against the abandoned buildings, its presence drenching the air with putrid fumes.

Some of this wrath and fury in the wind was never identified as belonging to known persons. A small woman in men's clothing, her flesh decomposed and stinking of fire, her eyelids peeling, her skull split, attacked a passerby in rage near the Cedar Creek station east of Montrose in 1901. Similarly, a rash of unknown, furious, rotting, and inky-black phantoms infested the remote gulches of Dolores County from 1880 on. The inhabitants of said county had an uncanny knack for turning up scattered human bones in the gulches. Most belonged to apparent victims of homicide, some with bullet holes, some with crushed craniums. Brought into the *Dolores News* office at Rico, the bones were put on display, and the editor made a notice to the phantoms: "Owner can have same by identifying and paying advertising charges."

One of the unholiest of this unholy throng arrived during the total lunar eclipse of March 1895. Eerie, unusual things were reported in the weeks following, but the night of the eclipse itself pulled the poisonous shade of Sebastiano Tamburo from the bowels of hell. For four years he had lain quietly in his grave, this man of volcanic murderous rage who had shot his wife and himself on April 3, 1891.

Tamburo, an Italian immigrant living near Stoner, had approached his wife after she was granted a divorce, begging her to take him back. Her refusal set his passions afire, and he grabbed her round the neck, pulled her against his chest, and savagely pumped lead into her jerking body as their nine-year-old son screamed. He then downed a slug of strychnine and whiskey and fired two shots into his own breast, dying within minutes.

The woman lingered in agony for eight days and expired. The family's nightmare wounds remained raw, yet were closing with the distancing of time . . . until the lunar eclipse unloosed the bonds of the grave.

According to descendents of one of the woman's brothers, Tamburo's reawakening actually knocked down a tree and shattered windows in the house. He closed his rancid, bone-rot hands around his victims' necks and crushed his mouth against theirs, forcing such vile putrefaction into their lungs that they vomited and fainted, afterward being ill for days. The eclipse that had unloosed him had no power to drag him back, and it is whispered that he still lurks in the dark gulches above Stoner and ranges across the eerie expanse of Taylor Mesa. Some people were rumored to have made circles of stones on the mesa and spread cornmeal in a 1970s attempt to either put an end to his hideous wanderings or to tap into the power of his darkness. Strange stone glyphs do exist on the remote landscape of Taylor Mesa, yet who in their right mind would care to truck with the void that sprang from Sebastiano Tamburo's grave?

Among this raging throng of oily shades were some men who, in life, were good-hearted, temperate, law-abiding citizens. They apparently thundered from their graves only as their good names were despoiled or their property ransacked. One of the latter was Norbert Savignac, a French Canadian who was beaten, robbed, and murdered at his ranch on Wilson Mesa in 1901. He was said to have buzzed like a hornet among the French Canadians there for some time. Another was Henry Huff, whose ghost lost its temper only after treasure hunters started grubbing up his little paradise in Bull Canyon.

Out beneath the broad Western sky, where the hem of the San Juans folds into red rock canyons sacred to the coyote, and tumbles into rainbow gorges imprinted with dinosaur bones, Henry Huff had built himself a ponderosa log cabin in the 1890s. He was a Ute who had been "taken" or "adopted by" the Huff family as a child. As an adult he raised his own cattle and punched cows for various outfits, hunted and trapped coyotes and wolves, and later did some prospecting. Well-liked among the cowboys and considered well-educated by his contemporaries, he was known by most as "Indian Henry."

By 1917 Henry still lived in the remote bottom of Bull Canyon, but he had been joined by a prospecting partner, Clark Akers. The shelves and mesas above were now dotted with uranium mines. At Cummings Spring, less than a half-mile from the Huff-Akers cabin, was the home of Mrs. Laura Foster Keski, her two children, fourteen-year-old Eugene and twelve-year-old Ella, and their stepfather John Keski, a hardworking, hard-drinking, hard-talking Finn whom the children tolerated.

The mother, Laura, did washing for the area miners and offered bed and board to stray cowboys and prospectors. John ran stock and took care of the dusty ranch. Eugene and Ella enjoyed the company of Henry and Clark, both of whom got on well with Laura and John.

Late in the night of May 10, 1917, Laura, John, Henry, and Clark were at the Keski house playing cards and drinking a noxious concoction of "Zanol," water and alcohol, despite Colorado's prohibition law of 1916. The "villainous compound" turbocharged all four of them, and John "declared his wife could throw Indian Henry to the floor," according to the coroner's inquest, since Henry was nearly too drunk to stand up. John bet a quarter it could be done and as everyone was laughing, Laura took up the bet. Henry was knocked to the floor. Again and again, Laura landed him on his butt, Henry taking it "good naturedly at first." As he tired of it, shoving her off, he growled a few insulting remarks and John Keski flew into a rage.

Keski bolted into the bedroom and Henry staggered to a cot to rest, but Clark, fearing Keski's temper, tottered out the door and bumped down the stairs. He stumbled off to his and Henry's cabin.

With a .32-caliber pistol, Keski boiled back into the room, cursing Henry. He pointed at the prostrate man on the cot and pulled the trigger. The bullet sliced through Henry's neck "just under the collar bone, ranging downward and back, breaking the left shoulder blade." The children, who had been in their beds, rushed out at the sound of the gunshot and found Henry bleeding heavily, their stepfather brandishing a pistol.

Ella was sent to tell Clark to get help, while Eugene was sent to hike up out of the canyon to fetch a miner at the Wedding Bell camp, William Sullivan, who had some medical skills. Henry asked for his friend Henry Dange; he wanted him to handle his affairs.

Meanwhile, Clark Akers, blind drunk and shaking from fear, managed to reach the Monogram camp of the Standard Chemical Company, several miles away. They telephoned for a doctor and the Montrose County sheriff. Bob Wilson and Deputy Sheriff Andy Talbert of Paradox arrived by early afternoon with Dr. W. D. Keating of Naturita following. Henry knew of Dr. Keating's rumored dislike for Utes and begged for a different doctor. Eugene and Ella, interviewed in 1980 by James M. Copeland, claimed Keating had arrived with a casket. They further stated that Henry died immediately after Keating gave him an injection, the siblings suspecting the doctor "had administered a purposeful overdose of . . . morphine."

Deputy Sheriff Talbert arrested John Keski for the murder of Henry Huff, placing him under guard at the Monogram camp since cowboys and some miners in the area threatened to lynch the killer of their long-time friend.

By Saturday the Montrose County Coroner, Dr. J. Q. Allen, and Sheriff J. H. Gill arrived, taking charge of the body, calling an inquest at Naturita and sending Keski to jail in Montrose. Allen took $500 in cash from Henry's clothing, and also a gold watch and other property from his cabin.

This gave rumor broad wings. Word spread that Henry had stashed even greater sums of cash around Bull Canyon, in some place in the ground within a day's walk of his cabin.

Meanwhile, Henry was buried on Sunday near Cummings Spring in "a casket of great beauty" covered with flowers from his many friends. A sandstone marker was lovingly carved by the children's grandfather, Jim Bristol, as Eugene and Ella themselves told it.

In the fall of the year during John Keski's trial for the murder of Henry Huff, a carefully laid out story was presented to the jury, this time claiming the shooting was accidental. Popular and flamboyant Defense Attorney C. J. Moynihan so rattled the jury with his rehearsed testimony of Laura Keski and his attack on witness Clark Akers that they returned a verdict of guilty only on a lesser charge of involuntary manslaughter. Despite Keski's own jail statement that he had shot off his gun due to "bad whiskey and bad temper overflowing," Keski was sentenced to eight months. Despite the testimony at the inquest, which was never brought up at the trial, Keski was a free man by summer of 1918.

This was enough to make a ghost rise up in anger, yet Henry Huff failed to appear until the late forties, fifties, and sixties when treasure hunters scrambled into Bull Canyon to mole around for Henry's rumored fortune. Because Henry talked freely with the two friends he trusted most, Henry Dange and Clark Akers, before he died, and because the coroner had requisitioned Henry's cash and valuables, it was more than likely no "treasure" ever existed. The dig-dig-digging, the defacing of his beloved canyon, and the tales that he had been killed by Keski specifically for his money or killed for molesting Laura made Henry's dark foreboding shade fly out of the twilight sky into the faces of "trespassers." This was his canyon. These were his corrals. That was his cabin, hewn by his own hand, where they dug up the floor like salivating badgers.

Henry especially came for those who stayed in the canyon, his anger echoing from the weird hoodoo rocks late in the night. He was a furious dusky form, generally not even recognizable as a human shape, but packing the force of a cyclone in his rage. He nearly sent one treasure hunter, Mark Dana of Nevada, to his death in the Dolores River's muddy water. Dana was digging around the area in the 1960s, and one night "a huge roaring shadow" swooped down on him, battering him with sticks and rocks as he fled stumbling down the stair steps of Bull Creek, pursued, trampled and scratched by the blazing wraith, until bruised and bleeding and pincushioned with cactus, he fell into the Dolores at the edge of the willow flats at the Bull's mouth, puking out his fear.

"I will never forget that thing or that night as long as I live," Dana said in 1979, while living in Denver. He had given up treasure hunting of any kind and at that point was collecting cast-metal toy cars for a hobby. "You had to be there to believe it. It was a nightmare. I really thought I wasn't coming out alive."

The uranium has played out, and the Wedding Bell Mine and other Standard Chemical camps are rotting shadows with skirts of yellow tailings on the landscape. The Keski house is no more than prostrate boards near the spring. All that stands in the awesome silence and otherworldly beauty of Bull Canyon is Henry Huff's ponderosa cabin and his tombstone.

At twilight the tremendous expanse of these deeply convoluted maroon-and-pink canyons echoes with the call of coyotes, song dogs telling a story only they understand. A silhouette on the high ridge above the twisted shapes of wind-worn rock seems to be a man, yet the shadow plays like water against the stars. Is Henry Huff at peace . . . or is he waiting, watching for trespassers?

4

$\mathcal{W}$AITING FOR THE $\mathcal{S}$TAGE

Charley's first passenger remained absolutely mute when she climbed into the coach at Durango. No small talk, no smile; in fact, she refrained from looking him in the eye. She had softly brushed past him, a sweet scent of exotic blossoms trailing after her, and settled into the corner, her face cast downward. She carried no grip, nor had she loaded a trunk. La Plata was her destination, and Charley Cole figured the twenty-eight-mile trip would be a long one for the lady if she continued her icy silence.

He never had a passenger who failed to at least comment on the weather. Before his team pulled out, Charley usually knew the life stories and private dreams of most of his passengers. His insatiable curiosity kept him bound in friendly, prodding conversations.

That silent woman bothered him. She was young, "pretty—more than pretty," well dressed . . . although he knew by her attire and coiffure that she was no woman of virtue. Perhaps a dance-hall girl who had been turned out for drunkenness, Charley surmised, his curiosity filling in the blanks.

As the coach collected more passengers just west of Durango and "a fine specimen of manhood" at Fort Lewis, a lieutenant in his crisply pressed uniform, Charley glanced at the taciturn woman in the corner. He was certain her tongue would loosen up now.

Her eyes never lifted to acknowledge the lieutenant, even though he greeted her with utmost courtesy and a broad grin. Even Charley fell for that grin, thinking "If I were a lady . . ."

Burning up with disgust, Charley mounted the box and slapped his team on toward Parrott City. The day was warm and clear and the dust from the coach and horses left a half-mile long plume behind. As he turned north, the sun hot on his back, he pushed his team into a gallop, pulling into Parrott earlier than expected. He lost the lieutenant but collected a "dandy" of a professional gambler, and, taking him aside, plotted with him to induce the pretty woman to speak before she disembarked at La Plata. The gambler eagerly agreed to the plot.

Thinking himself clever, Charley climbed back on the box and headed his team up La Plata canyon. The river was running clear, the hillsides dressed in green, and the peaks ahead robed in soft blues and browns. Charley heard the voices of a mother and her three sons in the coach praising the scenery. He heard the chatter of a woman's voice and the chuckling of a man: his gambler pleased with—with? The woman must be the redhead with the pinched face, Charley decided, not his mysterious dark-eyed beauty, his silent Mexican princess . . . at that point Charley decided the woman was from Mexico and spoke no English.

That settled, he felt better as he pulled the coach into the La Plata station, the trail dust catching up and overtaking coach and horses. His passengers climbed out, and he watched them one by one, shaking their hands, exchanging chitchat, all except "that lady."

Charley looked in the coach: empty. He wheeled around. Everyone who had been aboard was strolling away toward town. Where did the woman go?

Running after the gambler, Charley asked him if he had seen the dark-eyed woman.

"No," was the reply.

He interrogated the gambler with rapid-fire questions: did you speak to her, did she speak to you, did she get out before you or after you, did she, did you, where is—?

"I thought you meant the red-haired girl," said the gambler and he strolled away, confused and convinced the driver had been in the summer sun too long.

Weeks later Charley Cole picked up the same fare at Durango, failed to get one word out of her the entire trip, and somehow lost track of her after Parrott City, although he was sure she had not disembarked at that place.

Fit to be fried, Charley interrogated his passengers. No one had seen the woman, or if they had, they were unable to explain when they no longer saw her beside them. *Beside them* in the small intimate space of a coach—how did they not notice?

On the morning of August 17, Charley Cole saw his mysterious passenger approaching yet another time. He rushed into the livery and convinced his friend, John "Zap" Zappler, a liveryman, to ride in the coach the entire route, keeping an eye on the woman, no matter what. If she made a move to depart, Zap was to signal Charley by "thumping on the slats."

The day progressed without a hitch and by Parrott City, the woman was still on board as the coach pulled up the river toward La Plata. Zap never thumped the slats, jumping out in the cloud of dust to assist a young woman with a baby. As the passengers ambled away, Charley anxiously inquired after "the lady." She was nowhere in sight. Yet the scent of her delicate perfume lingered inside the coach, proving she had been there.

Zap exclaimed with an oath there was no way to miss her. He had kept his eyes on her the entire trip. Nothing distracted him. He only helped the mother and her babe at the last minute. He was at a total loss to explain when he no longer saw the dark-eyed woman, knowing without a doubt she was still on the coach as it pulled out of Parrott City. Bewildered, the two men took their confusion to a La Plata saloon, telling the story to an enthralled audience.

"Wall, if yez sees her agin," suggested the saloonkeeper, "I would clap a hand around her wrist, 'cause if she is what I 'spect she is, she ain't going to make a sound anyway."

The following week on August 27, Charley Cole and Zap Zappler had an opportunity to catch their bird one more time. The arrangements were the same as they were before. This time, however, Zap was to take the saloonkeeper's advice, boldly taking hold of the woman after the coach left Parrott City.

Zap was no stranger to courage, but the thoughts of grabbing an uncanny, silent woman in front of those other passengers made him break into a sweat. At Parrott City he was so "torn up with apprehension that the other passengers thought he had taken ill," one insisting a doctor be called. Finally, with some hasty but plausible excuses for Zap's pale sweaty countenance and assurances "it ain't no cholera," Charley settled the passengers and headed his team up La Plata canyon. Zap clamped his big hand around the dark-eyed woman's delicate wrist. No sound did she make, nor did anyone seem to be astonished at Zap's bold action.

Short of breath, his heart pounding, his body going cold from fear, Zap Zappler kept his grip on his prey, staring at her, studying her downcast face. She was beautiful, her "nut brown skin smooth and flawless," and her "long black lashes shielding impossibly doleful eyes." A tear fell down her cheek and Zap "felt like a monstrous heel." But he refused to let her go.

At La Plata, the passengers disembarked and Zap remained in the coach. Charley exploded triumphantly at the window. His face fell. No one was in the coach except Zap.

"My God, she's a ghost," Zap stuttered and held up a small bracelet that had encircled the vanished woman's wrist. "My God, she's a ghost." Zap needed a drink.

He and Charley told the tale at La Plata, trying to explain how the woman melted into nothingness without anyone realizing it. "She was there and everyone saw her. Then she was not there and no one knew it. Like a circus dog jumping through a hoop. Take the hoop away and the dog still jumps through where it was."

Nothing could explain the phantom passenger on the coach line between Durango and La Plata City. No one could give her a name. Charley Cole never forgot her, although he had seen her just the one summer in 1885. In the 1930s he was still telling her story in the San Francisco area where he had migrated, a newsman finally recording it. At the end of the tale, with his listeners spellbound, old Charley said he had proof "it happened just as I told you," and reaching into the pocket of his vest, he pulled out a delicate "gold bracelet set with peridot and opal." In the smoke and gloom, the bracelet "seemed to have an incandescent, uncanny light all its own."

Although common in Europe, tales of ghosts hitching rides in coaches, carriages, or wagons were rare in the San Juan. Of the few reported, the ghost invariably was a distraught woman, seen either by the passengers and driver, or only by select passengers. In the summer of 1881, a black woman on the stage line from Silverton to Rockwood suddenly broke into tears, begging the passengers to help her find her "baby girl." They hollered to the driver to stop. Because the woman was nearly hysterical with fear for her daughter, the passengers were unable to discern where she lost the child. The more they questioned her, the more distraught she became, until the driver calmed her somewhat and learned her daughter had not been lost in the vicinity. He promised to get her help at Rockwood and continued down the road. As the coach slowed near Rockwood, the woman simply was no longer on board. One passenger declared her to be the ghost of a woman named Martha who had died earlier that same year in Ouray.

Another weeping woman appeared on the stage between Rico and Ophir, this creature as mysterious as the one who had confounded Charley Cole. She was seen only by Alexander "Sandy" Campbell of Rico whenever he took the stage to Ophir. She "appeared to be a widow," her face hidden beneath a heavy black veil. As the coach pulled out of Rico, she started sobbing. Sandy was somewhat of a gent, and he offered her his handkerchief, which she took. Instead of using it, she crumpled it in her fist and beat her breast. Soon she fell silent, leaving Sandy at a loss for words. As the coach passed the coke ovens, the woman suddenly grabbed Sandy's arm, blurting how she had "finished the man," and was terrified someone would discover her "awful deed," terrified to be sent away to prison or hanged, terrified to kill herself "though wishing it with all my heart." Astounded, Sandy asked, "To whom do you refer?" The woman vanished.

Sandy was a believer in the curative powers of whiskey and after his first encounter with this ghost, which no one else on the coach admitted seeing, he made a habit of carrying a "flask of the most potent" curative with him. It failed to cure him of his visions. It did give him courage, however, to face his friend Tom Hume, who spread Sandy's secret disgracefully. Said the local sheet: "The loudest of these vociferous Caledonians avers the patent medicine generates Campbell's weeping phantasm, not the reverse. Are these not the two same wags who were arrested for disturbing our peace while shooting at phantoms some time ago?" In protest, Sandy declared others had been "witness to this inconsolable apparition" and simply were "not man enough to admit it."

Admitting to seeing ghosts seemed to be no problem for the freight drivers at Capitol City (west of Lake City). When their chum, Jamie Cameron, popped out of nowhere onto the seat of the heavy ore wagons, they welcomed him, enjoying his presence until he abruptly left them at the Pole Creek bridge, three miles east of Capitol City. Cameron had been a freighter in life, running the ore from the Independence mine group down to the mill at Henson. He had to cross the Pole Creek bridge and had a sixth-sense insight the structure was soon to fail under the heavy loads. One morning in August 1889, as he was leaving Capitol City, he told the superintendent this was his last trip "until the bridges were strengthened."

That was his last trip, indeed. The Pole Creek bridge gave way, dumping the horse team into the drink, the heavy wagon being pulled after the horses, crushing Cameron between beasts and timber and ore and burying him in the creek.

For some years after that, his robust shade sprang into the wagons on their way east from Capitol City. He suddenly was seated beside the freighter, his cheerful face no different than he had been in life, but he never was able to stay when the wagons crossed Pole Creek. Always at that point, even if the conversation was a lively one, James Cameron vanished. He may be trying to get across that bridge yet.

Some stage-route ghosts found it impossible to get *into* the wagons or coaches, their faces forlorn as they dissipated into the sunlight. Sometime between 1901 and 1903, Circle Route driver Clint Buskirk was bewildered by a little girl who hailed the coach from the side of the road in Ironton Park. The first time Clint stopped for her, his passengers hollered at him, "Is something amiss?" "Why are we stopping?" "What is going on here, sir?" Clint thought they were a bit brainless since the girl of ten or twelve was plainly in view. He jumped down to speak with her and his impatient passengers yelled all the more.

"She needs to be taken to her father in Ouray," Clint replied. "She says he is sick."

At that point it was his passengers who thought *he* was a bit brainless. Everyone knew Clint Buskirk was one of the crack stage drivers of the region, but he was talking to himself at the roadside. As he turned away from their annoyed faces, he saw no sign of the child anywhere.

After a few identical incidents with the same child in the same spot, Clint realized she was an apparition and tried to pass her by without stopping. That tore him up, for she sadly waved at him with tears brimming her eyes.

A few stage drivers were surprised by the sudden appearance of old dead men of their own profession plopping into the seat on the box with them. One driver on the Tabor & Wasson line through Hermosa Park even claimed to have the famous driver Bill Kelley tag along until the coach reached Hotel Draw. Kelley, ever the gentleman, tipped his hat before slipping away with the wind.

A few coaches were held up by phantom bandits, those powerless, lingering gasses of men who had robbed the same lines in life. These were akin to the neurotic mine ghosts that beat themselves against the void by repeating a last action as if to get it correct before they were allowed to go on. Or perhaps the bandits had enjoyed their avocation to such a degree as to continue it for all eternity.

Billy LeRoy was a frustrated stage robber in life and death. He had a fondness for the red Concord coaches of the Sanderson & Company stage lines, but frequently his timing was off. On more than one occasion his gang's gunfire frightened the horses into running away with the stage before he could rob it. After he was lynched at Del Norte in 1881, LeRoy returned to his previous occupation, appearing with gun drawn to menace the Sanderson stage, or the later Colorado and Wyoming Stage, Mail & Express in the rail-less regions of the San Juans.

The desperado's thin grey shade had no power to stop any stage; one driver, recognizing it for what it was, drove his horses straight through the frustrated Billy LeRoy, laughing over his shoulder at the confused phantom. In Creede's saloons, the driver recounted the tale, mocking LeRoy's inability to separate himself from the clouds of dust left behind by the coach. After the stage lines vanished from the San Juans, rumor had it LeRoy turned his interests to the attempted robbery of red Jeeps along the old stage routes. . . . Watch for a thin fellow waving a long-barreled pistol, but before driving through him, be certain he isn't solid.

One of these red Concord coaches of the Sanderson company acquired some sort of "soul" itself, for in the quiet years of 1910 to 1915 it went wandering over the old routes on its own, with four magnificent phantom horses pulling it. Black, of course. Seen along the road from Creede to Antelope Park or in the Burrows Park and Timber Ridge areas, this coach was a hazy mix of color and shadow, the horses frequently at a spanking trot, their black manes flowing behind, their hooves making no sound against the ground. No passengers rode within and the driver on the box had no face. The mysterious Concord, described as both "beautiful" and "wonderfully terrifying," appeared in the distance, never any closer than several hundred yards. Sometimes it was glimpsed flying through open country, sometimes plodding on the high ridges. Sometimes it waited just beyond a stand of backlit aspen at the end of the day, the sun's golden rays haloing this eerie messenger of the past.

In the 1970s an old woman, Mrs. H. S. Berkeley of Denver, said she believed the "ghost coach" was out collecting the "wandering and lost dead." If that was its mission, it is certain to be at it still.

5

AN OPEN DOOR

Twilight glow painted the snow-covered valley in hues of blue that matched the mood of the frosty air. Mollie snuggled closer to her beau. In the fading silver light of dusk, he seemed a wall of strength on the buckboard seat beside her. The whitewashed, black-trimmed wagon was his. The two trotting horses were also his, and he handled them with skill and ease. Mollie's heart was full of admiration, and her eyes were fixed on his face.

Unexpectedly, she grabbed his arm, crying out, "Stop! Stop!"

Was that a little girl by the road?

Mollie Showalter was a schoolteacher in Pleasant Valley on Dallas Creek, and little children were always at the center of her heart. As the wagon drew to a halt, Mollie jumped down and hurried toward the girl on the far side of the road.

"There is no one there," her beau called. "Mollie, come back."

Despite the half-light, Mollie clearly saw the little girl, a child of ten, her long dark hair matted with frost and soil, straw clinging to her stained frock, her little feet and legs bare, bruises on her face, wearing a hollow-eyed expression of numbing pain. She reached out toward Mollie and the school-teacher gasped, for the girl's fingers were black, the flesh opened and raw.

In the moment of Mollie's hesitation, the child turned and ran. Mollie went after her, calling to her. Mollic's confused and worried beau followed. The child ran to a barn, disappearing through the open door.

Breathless from stumbling through the snow, Mollie leaned against the door, peering into the black maw of the barn. She called out for the little girl several times. She wanted to assure her no harm would befall her.

No response came. There was no sound at all.

By now Mollie's beau had caught up with her, and she pleaded with him to help her find the child. He told her there was no child. He had seen nothing, not a child, not a dog, not a man, not a deer, not even a rabbit. He showed her the tracks in the snow: only her own and his were visible.

Mollie insisted he fetch the lantern in the wagon and while he obliged, she stepped into the dark barn, calling for the little girl. With lighted lantern, Mollie's beau returned to her side, walking with her through the barn. The schoolteacher stopped short near a haystack, a sharp gasp escaping her. At her feet was the girl, curled up like a half-starved an-imal, her eyes closed, her limbs muddy and bruised, and a ghastly mat of dirt, straw, and blood at the back of her head.

Mollie's compassionate heart overflowed as she stooped to touch the child, murmuring, "Poor sweet baby—"

Mollie Showalter's beau was certain she had lost her mind. He angrily snatched the wad of filthy burlap sacks from under her nose and shoved them before her eyes. "Potato sacks, that is all!" he said and, grabbing her by the arm, marched her back to the buckboard and delivered her to her house. "Potato sacks, nothing more."

Mollie knew what she had seen. She wasn't "hysterical" as her ex-beau had proclaimed to all his friends and hers in the days ahead. Someone knew who that little girl was, someone knew where she came from and where she had gone, and Mollie was determined to ferret out the truth.

Mrs. John A. Talbot told Mollie the tale. Mrs. Talbot had seen the same little "waif," lost, broken, seeking refuge in cold dark barns . . . a child called Rose who had been murdered years before.

Mary Rose Matthews was "a very bright child with a sweet, lovable disposition, and one could not help liking her." Her mother had died, leaving the distraught father, who was a Denver policeman, to raise her on his own. Ogden Matthews cherished his "little pet" and did everything in his power to be a good father, but his drinking and depression sank him. He was fired from his job in November 1882. He left "Little Rosie" in the care of his landlady and her daughters while he sought work elsewhere.

Months passed and Matthews failed to return for the ten-year-old girl, "who loved and adored him with deepest affection." The landlady turned the child over to Mrs. Perry, who had close ties to the Sisters of Charity running the St. Vincent's Orphan Asylum in Denver. The nuns took charge of Rosie in April 1883 and, although the little girl with the long dark hair and bright blue eyes was brokenhearted, she became a "treasured helper" and took it upon herself to "look after younger children."

At the end of May, Rose's father returned to Denver, inquiring after her. Mrs. Perry said Rose was at St. Vincent's and the child would certainly be overjoyed to see her father.

Ogden Matthews shook his head. Tears filled his eyes. "I can't. I haven't a dollar in the world to help her. If I see her, I will lose my mind. It would only make her unhappy to see me go again. Tell her I'm sorry. Tell her I will send for her when I get work."

No one ever saw him or heard from him again.

Because of Rosie's "loving and helpful disposition," the orphanage believed she would be easily placed with "a good Catholic family." A couple in Ouray County had applied to adopt a girl of ten to twelve. After consideration and inquiries into their suitability and character, Rose was selected. In July the Catholic pastor of Ouray, Robert Servant, took Rose to live with Michael and Maggie Cuddigan and their infant son, Percival.

Margaret Carroll Cuddigan had married at age nineteen in La Salle County, Illinois, when her first cousin, Mike, who was in his late thirties, charmed her away from her father and reason. He took her back to Ouray County to his ranch on Dallas Creek. His brothers, Patrick and Henry, also had ranch homesteads in the valley, although they associated with Mike only on special occasions, such as the christening of little Percy in summer 1883 and the arrival of Rose that same summer.

Far from the father she loved and longed for, far from the safety of the Sisters of Charity, far from hope and help, little Rosie was devoured by the

55
AN OPEN DOOR

nightmare that called itself Mike Cuddigan. The rage, the drunkenness, the explosive temper, the cruel words and hideous blows of his fist reduced the bright-eyed, beautiful child to numb subservience and vacant-eyed wretchedness.

Maggie did nothing to stop the abuse. She, in all probability, was terrified of Cuddigan's rages as well. Nor did Maggie's brother, James Carroll, who worked on the ranch, lift a hand. Mike's volcanic reputation was feared, yet when he dressed in his "hail-fellow and wholesome" skin, he charmed the stoniest of men and captivated the iciest of matrons. Even his neighbors, who saw the battered and bruised Rose, said nothing to Cuddigan and did nothing to protect her from further assault. Nor did the priest.

One neighbor, L. B. Montgomery, never forgave himself for his silence, for he had known Rose from the day she first arrived. He had seen her as a smiling, eager-to-help, and beautiful little girl gradually being bent . . . then broken. By November he thought she "was acting strangely" and saw her face was badly bruised. She no longer wore shoes; her frock was dirty, her hair unkempt. "She seemed to be very dull of comprehension," he testified, yet he had done nothing to save her.

Dazed and numb, little Rosie was banished to sleep alone in the straw of the barn, old potato sacks her only covering. Cuddigan crept from his wife's side and forced himself on the helpless child in the barn, again and again, hitting her when she cried, burning her when she dared to catch his eye in the kitchen, thrashing her when her dazed mind no longer comprehended his words. Maggie shoved the child out of her sight, struck out against her in her need, and banished her again to the barn. Only over Christmas, when itinerant pastor Robert Servant visited the ranch, did Rose sleep in a bed in the house. After his departure, the barefoot child was ordered to sleep in the straw and Cuddigan again ravaged her.

On Saturday January 12, 1884, Dallas schoolteacher George C. Morrison and John A. Talbot dropped by the Cuddigan ranch, surprised by the stony reception. Morrison inquired after Rosie; she had not been in school that week. The Cuddigans told him she had fallen. Mary Rose Matthews had died. Morrison and Talbot were shown the emaciated, frostbitten corpse, bloodied and bruised about the head and Morrison angrily warned the Cuddigans, "There will be an inquiry." Mike said no inquest would be necessary; Rose had fallen down the cellar stairs. Sunday morning he buried her body in a crude grave on his ranch.

Outrage and suspicion sent George Morrison to Ouray, where he informed Sheriff Charles H. Rawles of Rose Matthews's death, adding he believed it was caused by "barbarous and inhuman cruelty."

Rawles ordered the body exhumed and brought to Ouray. Coroner Hazard and Dr. W. W. Rowan examined it, discovering the child had been raped, starved, beaten, and frozen, with a final blow to the back of her head ending her short life. She had endured severe frostbite for days, the flesh of blackened fingers peeling off, her toes discolored and split. Wounds marked her thighs. Cuts, scratches, and scars marked her arms. At the Cuddigan ranch Sheriff Rawles took into evidence the gunnysacks Rose slept in and found them caked with blood.

On January 17 Michael and Maggie Cuddigan and Maggie's brother, James Carroll, were arrested. They were lodged in the Delmonico Hotel under armed guard and Francis Fitch was retained as their attorney.

But attorneys were useless in Ouray when citizens burned with vengeance. Even as little Rosie's violated body was washed and tenderly dressed by the ladies of the Catholic parish, even as the child was lowered once again into the cold ground (this time at the cemetery), the men of the town discussed "swift justice." A child had been tortured and murdered. David Day, the eternally self-righteous editor of the *Solid Muldoon*, blatantly called the men to act: "The atrocity of this crime is beyond the reach of prosecution," and if the community were to give "the villains the punishment they so justly merit, red tape justice might be pardoned the exclamation, 'Well done, Judge Lynch!'"

Mike Cuddigan in a coward's rage first tried to blame his wife for the hideous torture and murder of Rose. Later he confessed to Sheriff Rawles, but it only fueled the fire. A masked and armed mob overpowered Rawles and took Cuddigan and his wife from the Delmonico. James Carroll they escorted out of town and sent him running, since he had not been at the ranch during the days Rose was murdered.

The other two they dragged north of town, Maggie gasping for the saints to defend her, as her legs buckled and she fell in fear.

"Spare me! I am innocent, God knows I am!" she screamed and begged for the chance to raise her son.

When the mob reached the city limits, they threw a rope around Cuddigan's neck and told him to "say his prayers." He screamed for mercy, sputtered, and trembled "pitifully." No one offered pity. They looped the other end of the rope over the ridgepole of Tom Andrews's cabin and jerked the man aloft. He struggled violently and his face contorted as life was squeezed out of him.

Quickly, a second rope closed around Maggie's neck. The young woman had to be carried to the tree, for her legs would not hold her. Her pleas for mercy fell on deaf ears. She begged. She screamed. She vomited in fear. "But her awful agony did not affect her executioners. They stood by, unmoved . . . turning their heads from her white face and its wild despair."

The mob dragged her skyward and her body swung "convulsively in the air."

Two hours later Coroner Hazard cut the bodies down: death at the hands of persons unknown. The cemetery refused them burial. Mike Cuddigan's brothers, Pat and Henry, refused to claim the bodies (although Henry raised Percy as his own, never telling him of the fate of his parents). Finally, the bodies were buried on a ranch bordering the cemetery, enclosed beneath unhallowed, unmarked earth.

Had it ended there, perhaps the specter of little Mary Rose Matthews would never have been seen. But somehow, some way, Ouray had to clarify to the rest of the state that the grisly lynchings were not a case of revenge, but absolute and raw justice. Mike Cuddigan had confessed. What more did they need? If only the public had seen the violated body of that child. . . .

And Little Rosie was violated again. Once more her corpse was exhumed. This time it was shipped to Denver to the undertaking parlors of E. P. McGovern, with placards and newspapers inviting the citizenry to "see for yourself." By now the remains had to be an indescribably ghastly sight. Having been in the muddy earth twice, in the open air several days, cut open and probed by the examining doctor (he testified to sawing open her skull to determine if the blow to her head caused death), little Rose Matthews was a wretched rotting shell, her flesh blacker, her wounds pulling wider. From 7:00 A.M. to 10:00 P.M. she was the subject for thousands of gawking eyes. Women fainted. Grandmothers wept. Men muttered hanging was too good for her murderers—they should have been "drawn and quartered," or "roasted alive," or "hung head down and pecked to death by geese," as a physician told the Denver *Tribune*. The horrible display had the desired effect: no one condemned the act of Ouray's masked mob. In fact, they condoned it.

One old woman and her daughter, who had been Rose's schoolmate in Denver, knelt beside the "cooling table" and prayed earnestly for "perfect rest and peace on the soul of the murdered child."

How could she rest? Sensationalized, dragged from place to place like a bizarre relic, her remains put on display, not to inspire pity but to settle a point, Mary Rose Matthews fled from the gawking eyes. Fatherless, motherless, the ragged little spirit drifted into empty barns from Dallas to the upper reaches of Pleasant Valley. She was seen at the roadside at twilight, generally during the frosty months, reaching out with her blackened fingers to the hearts of women, seeking the love of a daddy, pulling away at their visible horror to hide again in the darkness of a barn.

L. B. Montgomery was one of the first to see this tragic shade. He carried the weight of his inaction to protect her in her last days, and perhaps this brought the apparition to his barn. At first he mistook the child in the shadows for a runaway. When he approached her and she reached out to him with those blackened fingers, Montgomery recognized Rose. She vanished before he gathered his wits, Mollie Showalter had learned.

Mollie also was told Hans Von Hagen had seen the tragic specter in the barn of his Dallas Divide ranch. Some years later, in 1904, a Denver man, Jerome F. Spellman, was riding through Pleasant Valley and was startled to see a child at the roadside. He stopped to help her in the waning light, but she fled to a nearby barn. Following her, Spellman found her curled up in the hay. He stooped beside her and, as his hand came against her shoulder, she dissolved into the twilight.

Old barns in the valley still shelter the lost child. One area resident reluctantly confessed to seeing a girl at the road's edge one January, whom he followed into the old barn above the creek on the Telluray property. When she vanished in the beam of his flashlight, he was unsure whether to "call the sheriff or a psychiatrist." After finding she had left no visible track in the fresh snow, he "opted for the psychiatrist."

Ghosts in old buildings such as barns, residences, boardinghouses, saloons, bordellos, churches, courthouses, and outhouses are more frequently encountered than any other spooks, especially when the structure is still in use. The traditional "haunted house" occurs in every town in the San Juan region, with more than a fair share in Lake City, Silverton, and Telluride, and an absolute glut in Rico. Well-defined apparitions like little Rose Matthews, however, are unusual, for most haunted buildings have little more than the "feeling of a presence," or exhibit manifestations in strange sounds or scents, a passing shadow, or a door suddenly flying open.

Doors opening and closing and the sound of heavy footfalls are among the commonest manifestations in haunted structures. The fine old boardinghouse at Alta, its face to the awesome view of the Wilson peaks, is subject to a distinct sound in the second story corridor. On rainy days or late nights, one can hear the slow pacing of a man in hobnailed boots as he broods over his domain. He is believed to be the solicitous bull cook who kept the boardinghouse clean and paced the hall at night to keep an eye on his "boys," the miners. This manifestation is so frequent that the place has become a popular midnight spot for occultists who make circles of cornmeal and light candles in an attempt to draw the old bull cook out. He just ignores them and keeps to his pacing.

Other ghostly pacers, stompers, and doorbangers tramp through the courthouse, museum, and bank building at Lake City, several buildings at Ironton, the hospital museum at Ouray, the depots at Creede, Dolores, and Telluride, and the courthouse at Rico, where an ungodly number of spooks have taken up lodgings.

In the late 1800s, Rico was awash in spirits, and a county judge named E. A. Robinson presided over the lot. Robinson used morphine to finish himself off in June 1885, and from that point on banged his gavel and his feet at inappropriate hours in the old courthouse. When the new brick courthouse was built, Judge Robinson quickly took up residence, and soon myriad other phantoms joined him.

At present the retired county courthouse is bulging with spooks, from the top-floor doorbangers to the "Things" in the dreadful basement jail. Dark, cluttered, musty, and dank, Rico's jail cells are full of "Things," desolate, obnoxious as dirty socks, sometimes vicious, always cold, but definitely "Things." Perhaps if a person spends a night in a drafty cell, these "Things" will manifest in form instead of stink and ruckus.

Rico had a unique reputation for hosting spooks in her boom days, most likely due to various editors' friendly attitude toward them, or due to some unknown energy field in the surrounding peaks that sucked them from far and wide. Rico borrowed spooks from Silverton, Ophir, and Dunton and downright kidnapped a few from Telluride and Durango.

Fred A. Huber, an eccentric drunken aristocrat who had a flourish for fancy penmanship, died in Savage Basin of pneumonia in 1901, but flew over to haunt a clothing store (next to the bank on Glasgow Avenue) at Rico, leaving signed notes for the clerk. The spirit from Durango was a "girl of the line" who must have wanted medical advice after death, for she bothered and bewildered Dr. D. C. Gibbs in his offices in the Burly block in Rico. Dr. Gibbs never explained how he came to know who she was and why he had been acquainted with her in her hotter days in Durango.

Rico saloons weren't rowdy enough with the living, thus invitations were sent out to the dead, and these came in greedy flocks. The six-foot-ten-inch hulk called Big Jim Dunnigan knocked over chairs, tables, and fixtures whenever his spook blew into the Rico saloons in the 1880s. The Rob Roy Saloon was tossed by a pack of gaseous fiends under the leadership of Pat McDonald, who had been shot in that place. "Coyote Bill," Ben Ross, and others were recognized among the phantom pack.

For years the ghosts of Tom Wall and "Trinidad" Cummings knocked around John Gault's livery barn and other barns in town— they had been fond of horses and saddles. A Chinese laundryman refused to stay buried after his death in 1883, thumping the walls of the building his laundry occupied as well as the house of Jimmie "Jig" Hume, who had severely beaten him in 1882.

These are just a few of Rico's historical spooks . . . and she has had years to collect more. Telluride might have one haunted building per block, but Rico probably hasn't a building that isn't haunted. True, there are few buildings left in this sagging old village, but they make up for that by crowding more dead folks into them than live ones. Infestation is the word, and if Orkin were in the business of exterminating ethereal pests, they'd have work for decades. Yet, as in the boom days, these creatures are apparently welcome in Rico . . . and more show up each year, probably digging their way out of the cemetery and pounding a path to the 1892 red-stone Dey Building for a party. In 1979 only one spook was mentioned in residence at the Dey Building. In 1989 a half dozen had shown up. By spring of 2000 the place was busting at the corners with spooks, most of which were said to be "ladies of the line."

"Soiled doves," women of the "half world," prostitutes by any other name, have become a favorite ghost in the San Juan. Historically, very few were mentioned. In modern times they are busier than their living counterparts ever were in the days when miners flooded the towns on Saturday nights. Bordellos and cribs renovated into houses or offices are rife with the mysterious sweet perfume of dead dance-hall goddesses, fleeting forms, displaced paintings, eerie noises in the night, the soft brush of fingers across one's lips. . . .

Silverton's Blair Street, Ouray's lower Second Street, Lake City, Creede, all have their share of Sizzling Sally ghost tales, but Telluride wins the prize for the most well defined red-light district spooks.

In the late 1890s a leggy blonde named Zella DuPass haunted the second floor of the bordello run by Ed Shanley at 238 S. Pine. Shanley put up with her since she seemed warm-blooded enough and attracted toms to the house, until a Finn took a tumble with her. . . . The poor man lost his mind when Zella turned to gas in his arms and he found he was hugging himself. Her laughter chased him bare beam through the building and out into Pine Street where the marshal collected the babbling victim from beneath some shrubbery and lodged him in jail. Later at the hearing, the Finn was declared off his tree, but he escaped his escort en route to the state asylum and was never seen again. Zella, on the other shank, went on haunting. In the early 1900s, a live prostitute in the district adopted the name Zella DuPass to attract more adventurous clientele, and she claimed to offer "otherworldly excitement" that could make "even the dead rise." Curiously, "Zella" comes from the Hebrew "Zillah" for "shadow."

Not all bordello spooks in Telluride were women. The notorious Silver Bell at the corner of Spruce and Pacific Avenue was (and still is, undoubtedly) the haunt of an Austrian phantom named Angelo Maconi. Angelo and his buddy, Joseph Mengoni, loved to dance at the Silver Bell in 1901 and had a passionate friendship that broke into testy squabbles. One night in November their squabbling erupted into a knockdown fight on the dance floor, and Joseph, being the one who got knocked down the most, ran off and bought a gun. In the days following he cooled off,

SOMETHING IN THE WIND

repairing his friendship with Angelo. They met at the Silver Bell for a good time one Wednesday night, dancing the hours away.

Witnesses assumed the two Austrians were best of friends again, since the entire time they danced, they were "holding onto each other's collar." Joseph confessed about the gun, how he had purchased it to kill his friend but had repented. They talked and danced and their conversation reverted to the native tongue, suddenly growing louder in the small hours of Thursday morning. Angelo tossed a glass of beer into Joseph's face and "lightly slapped him." Joseph exploded, drew his gun and fired, the bullet passing clean through its target and out the window. While a number of men pounced on Joseph, Angelo whacked him with a chair, but growing faint, he retreated behind the bar. He died later that morning.

Although the miners' union ceremoniously buried him at Lone Tree Cemetery, Angelo Maconi's restless spirit hadn't had enough dancing. In a short time he was back at the Silver Bell, a peaceful shade who popped up between dancing pairs, hovered near the bar or slouched through the doors upstairs. He stirred up a pair of Austrians in 1906 by stealing away with the woman they had been squabbling over. Angelo took her across the room and up the stairs, and the men pursued, but as they tried to grab him, Angelo vanished and they grabbed each other, tumbling into a snarling scuffle at the foot of the stairs. The Silver Bell bartenders were said to put out glasses of beer for Angelo, and his ghost dutifully drank them.

Although modern tales identify the ghost in the Silver Bell (now the Ah Haa School for the Arts) as "Ramona," more than likely the creature who pulls paintings off the walls and dances in the middle of the night is Angelo Maconi.

Around the corner and down the block at 205 S. Pine stood the Big Swede dance hall and bordello run by a well-endowed Swedish widow named Gussie Richardson. She had a porter, coachman, musicians, and lively girls. One was a Canadian beauty named Clara Morris, who drove men out of their skins. A young man named Arthur Powell tied himself in knots over Clara, eventually bucking the ire of Gussie. Gussie chewed Arthur's hide and threatened him with a gun, chasing him out. Gussie then sent for her man, E. W. "Gene" Richardson, and when Arthur returned to the dance hall, he and Gene got into an argument. They both pulled guns and bullets flew. Gene dropped, bleeding, dying. Since no one proved whether Arthur shot in self-defense or not, he was "sent up" for five

63

years. He returned later, looking for Clara, and found Gene's ghost at his neck. The phantom was said to have taken up a protective position at the Big Swede and never left until the place was torn down.

Across the street at 220 S. Pine was another bordello, the brick-built Pick & Gad, now a nest of attorneys. Despite the heavy presence of the law, a one-time madam, the girls, and a musician linger in the woodwork. Audrie Ford, a prostitute, madam, and shrewd businesswoman, built the Pick & Gad in the 1890s on the site where her first modest frame bordello had been. For the most part, Audrie ran the Pick & Gad herself, until she fell for a tom named Jimmie Shane. Shane was a prospector and miner with some talent for painting in oils. He did a full-length nude of Audrie, which hung in the Pick & Gad until sometime after she sold the business in 1910 to Herman Wunderlich and August Ress. In the meantime, Audrie and Jimmie had a baby girl named Nina in 1896. For Nina's sake, Audrie took her man's name and had her friend Marie "Rae" Gilbert manage the bordello. Audrie dropped in discreetly to check on her girls, collect the rents, and keep things under control, licensed, and clean.

In their fading years, Audrie and Jim Shane moved to Cortez, where they lived a quiet life, burying their past in silence. They were laid to rest side by side in the Cortez cemetery. But in 1959, the year Audrie died at the age of ninety-one, she went back to the place she had proudly built and toiled over, perhaps to check on it and the painting her husband had created.

The Pick & Gad was no longer a bordello and the painting was gone. Yet Audrie lingered, the sweet scent of her French perfume drifting through the building, her once-again soft and youthful shape seen at the windows. At night the "presence" of her girls warms the place, and strange sounds, mysterious faint music, shadows moving across the windowpanes, creep into the world of lawyers and light.

Bordellos were places full of the raw energy and passion of life and, all too frequently, death, gaining ghosts easier than banks or laundries. Like them, saloons of these mountain towns gathered phantoms with ease. Most often someone who met a violent death in a saloon soon returned in spirit form. This was the case with the tall, powerful, and handsome half-Ute, Dick Neathery, who was shot dead in Wilson & Hazlett's saloon on Third Street in Montrose. Dick, bullet-ridden, bloody, and wild-eyed, boiled through the saloon's walls after his death in 1888, causing patrons to drink more.

In Creede, the Beaumont Saloon was home to a lunatic one-armed phantom that accosted patrons like a hornet. John Mahoney considered himself "the best one-armed man in town," and in 1904, he challenged Lee Hale, another one-armed man, to a fight. They stepped outside the saloon, where Hale flattened Mahoney with one one-armed blow, proving his one arm was faster and harder than Mahoney's. In fact, it was so hard, Mahoney began to convulse, possibly having hit his head on the sidewalk. He was carried back into the saloon, and he died before a doctor arrived. After that, his mood soured, and he knocked two-armed citizens off their stools and popped bottles from the shelves. Not to be outdone, in sheer cussedness, an unidentified spook at the Sheridan Saloon in Telluride continues his (or her) century-long torment of patrons there.

Other buildings where death was frequent were expected to have ghosts, yet only one known spook, "Dutch George," seemed to haunt Telluride's hospital. San Juan jails, on the other hand, had a surprising number of malignant phantoms. Outside of the "Things" in Rico's cells, many jails have been infested for more than a century.

Durango's jail was haunted by the ghastly shade of a bank robber, Cella Hawkins, who killed himself after his confession in 1883. The worst haunted jail was in Ouray, full of the wraiths of men who killed themselves while incarcerated and thick with the spooks of Ouray's heavy-roped justice system. Add to that the ghost of a drunken John Green who mysteriously was roasted alive in the county lockup in 1883. This pack of unsavory spooks continued to grow until tales about them seemed ludicrous. The *Ouray Herald* mentioned them even as late as 1907, this time when a young man named C. D. Gooch was tossed in among them. Gooch screamed for the sheriff as the ghastly gaseous cellmates descended on him. He begged for the sheriff to keep him company, explaining how he saw men and women with ropes around their necks, burned corpses floating toward him with eyes popped out, and headless bodies reaching for him.

Throughout the San Juan, haunted buildings are so numerous that a lifetime would hardly be enough to catalog all their stories. The haunted houses alone would fill a book. Noteworthy among the historical tales was the residence of Moritz and Pauline Stockder, a quarter mile west of the Treasure Mill up Henson Creek. An Italian shift boss who had fallen in love with Mrs. Stockder shot her in 1902 in a fit of rage. Her husband had fired Frank Niccoli, and Frank blamed Pauline, killing her, then himself. The hideous bloodstains from the two deaths could not be removed from the bedroom floor and a wretched presence filled the room. Moritz Stockder took his small child and left the country.

Capitol City and Ames laid claim to haunted post offices, while Beartown hosted a haunted outhouse, home to the ghost of a drunken miner who froze to death on the spot. Another haunted outhouse contained the wraith of Jim Hamlet at Pagosa who shouted, "I'll get even with you, you dog!" At Silverton, James H. Robin's spirit banged around the inside of the water tank where he died.

Most of these spooks continued their thumping as long as the structures stood, and some carried right on even after the buildings were razed, taking up residence in whatever was built around them. One haunted cabin, however, replayed the scenes of death, then ceased as soon as its mission was accomplished. The long, dramatic tale published in the *Rocky Mountain News* of February 1884 was unique in that the haunting included both the ghostly victim and the living perpetrator.

The cabin, belonging to Charles Herndon, was located near Deadman Canyon south of Pagosa Springs. One day Herndon simply was no longer there, no trace of him anywhere, and yet all his belongings remained in place. Soon miners and travelers heard terrible cries coming from the cabin. Upon investigation, nothing was found to account for the sound. The place gained a dark reputation, travelers avoiding it. Not until a party of men was forced by inclement weather to stay the night was the grisly secret discovered.

Relaxing after chow and telling stories near the stove, the men were startled by sudden darkness, their candles snuffed out. "An unearthly sickly glare taking place of their light" made everything visible in the room. In the center appeared an older man, looking lonely and "dejected." The cabin door opened, and a large man crept up on the older man, whacking him on the head with a heavy length of wood. A terrible shriek pierced the onlookers' ears and the older man fell dead. After prying up several floorboards, the larger apparition shoved the body of the other beneath the cabin. "Instantly the unearthly light vanished and all was utter darkness."

The next day the sleep-deprived party pulled up the same floorboards the apparition had, discovering the skeleton of Charles Herndon. Some months later the murderer was shot in a gun battle, and as he was dying, he confessed to killing Herndon, robbing his body, and burying it beneath the cabin floor. The ghost of old Herndon ceased its shrieking from that time, leaving the cabin habitable ever after.

That was the only haunted house in the San Juan known to give up its ghost. The others, from the humblest of outhouses to the grandest of courthouses, have the energy of their phantoms deeply infused in the heart of their wood and stone, pulsating, glowing, humming . . . and, if within Rico's corporate limits, gathering in strays.

6

THE $\mathcal{S}$WINGING $\mathcal{L}$ANTERN

The freighter hauling a heavy load of timber and ore was flying down the track below Rico, heading toward Durango. A brief stop was scheduled for Rio Lado, where a few section men were to disembark for their bunks at the section house. The train had just passed milepost 70 and the Montelores passing track.

Staring into the engulfing gloom of night, made all the blacker by the deep narrow valleys and canyons of the Dolores River, engineer Tom Quine concentrated on the track where the headlight beam reached. The sky was moonless, and the black-robed mountains seemed to close in tighter, their summits higher.

Far ahead a signal light appeared, like a pinpoint hovering from side to side above the track. Quine strained to see it. It was gone. He shrugged, gave it over to the "tricks of the night." The sound of the train throbbed against the silent forests, the only sound beneath this moonless sky, a rhythmic, soothing tune to the engineer. He took a long draw on his pipe and relaxed, although keeping a vigilant eye on the track ahead.

The swinging signal light suddenly appeared again, just as distant as before. The train had already passed the spot where Quine first thought he had seen the signal, thus he called his fireman to his side. Fireman Ed Slick saw no signal light anywhere. "Tricks of the night." No, there—ahead on the track. Slick saw nothing.

When the mysterious signal appeared for the third time, still the same distance ahead, Quine whistled for the brakeman to slow the locomotive, and suddenly the swinging lantern seemed to be only a short distance away. Yelling for Slick to see for himself, Quine and the crew brought the train to a steaming, squealing stop within yards of the signaler. The crew jumped out, running ahead of the engine to see who was signaling and why.

No person was anywhere to be seen. No signal lantern glowed anywhere on the track or in the trees. Covering the track was a dangerous pile of rock, gravel and debris that had washed down from a small creek. At the original, higher speed of the train, Tom Quine would have been unable to see the muck in time, causing a wreck.

Mysterious signals have so often brought trains to a stop in the nick of time, saving them from dangerous situations, that railroad men accepted them without question. Some unknown force was protecting them the way the benign Tommyknockers and kobolds protected the miners, and they weren't about to discover it by chasing it down.

The Rio Grande Southern railroad (RGS) engineers had innumerable tales of these signal lanterns saving their hides, some believing deceased railroad men held the lanterns, making it their mission to protect their brothers. This narrow-gauge railroad, with its determined organizers, talented construction engineers, and energetic crewmen, was built between 1890 and 1891. A monument to Western ingenuity, it covered the most awesome, vertical, dangerous corner of earth a train might dare to travel. Massive avalanches, rockslides, heavy snows, and savage spring floods plagued the railroad where it pushed into the heart of the San Juan Mountains, along gorges and over passes. The steep grades required switchbacks and high bridges whose precision construction would have made the Romans green, yet in a heartbeat could be toppled by the power of roaring snowfields.

In its days of glory, the RGS had its share of haunted passenger trains and "cursed" engines, but none equal to the famous "Dread 107" of the

Denver & Rio Grande line between Gunnison and Grand Junction. The tales of the RGS were far less dramatic (there was enough drama in the landscape), and the worst of the "cursed" locomotives was Engine 19, which simply had a mind of its own, running away now and again, jumping the track, or crashing down embankments. It was rebuilt and put back to work, only to repeat its bad behavior. Engines 3 and 12 were said to be "haunted" but not malignant, Number 3 having the ghost of Bob Heier, a conductor, frequently showing up on the pilot, and a dead engineer named Al Bickford appearing at the throttle of Number 12.

Passenger trains attracted the majority of hitchhiking phantoms, most of whom appeared to be desperately trying to reach "home," yet were always unable to get past a certain spot.

In the late 1890s and early 1900s a tale circulated of a woman who hurried onto the train at Telluride. As the train pulled out from the depot, she watched fearfully out the window, as if afraid someone was coming after her. Satisfied no one was in pursuit, the woman sat down, but her eyes were "full of dread" or sorrow or "regret," as a fellow passenger described her. Tears fell down her cheeks, and again she went to the window on the opposite side from her seat, craning to see behind. The greater the distance between her and Telluride, the more her face became distraught and fearful. She grew faint, slipping down to the nearest seat, invariably causing some motherly passenger or gentlemanly conductor to ask if she needed a doctor. That terrified her, causing her to shake violently and try to get away from the solicitous passengers. Someone recognized her and spoke her name, and she vanished so "instantly from the coach" that witnesses "wondered if she had been there at all." If no one recognized her, she always vanished in the same manner as the train started into the switchbacks of Anderson.

Those who recognized her said the specter was Mrs. Essie Mentzer, trying to escape her "evil, debauched" husband, Dr. O. F. Mentzer, in Telluride and return home to Chicago. In life she was a "charming and amiable woman," unfortunately married to a dangerous physician whose "peculiarities" were enhanced while under the influence of drugs and alcohol. In Chicago she had divorced him, fearful of his violent temper and secretive behavior.

He ran off to Telluride where no one knew him, pledging to be a "new man" of "temperance and fidelity." Essie's brother and his wife lived in Telluride, and soon Dr. Mentzer charmed his way back into Essie's heart, remarrying her and bringing her to Telluride. His old frightful habits returned within months as he looped into drug and alcohol "sprees," committing "acts that did not meet with general approval." He was feared, "especially by female patients." Essie was certain she had made a grave mistake; she could not continue a life with him. He threatened her, abused her, and she decided to return to Chicago. She purchased her ticket. He purchased a gun.

On the night of October 7, 1898, Essie had her brother Will Munroe and his wife at her house, and Dr. Mentzer was unusually cheerful. Late in the evening, Mentzer asked Will and his wife if they were going to bed. They were and, arising, said their goodnights and left the parlor, shutting the door behind them. Suddenly Essie screamed and cried out her brother's name. As he crashed back through the door, Will saw Mentzer pull Essie against him, a revolver jammed to her temple. The doctor pulled the trigger.

Will Monroe flew against Mentzer in the same instant, throttling him by the neck, disarming him and beating him, kicking him, and dragging him outdoors where he hurled him to the sidewalk. It was too late. Essie was dead.

Her body was embalmed and taken to Chicago for burial, yet her desperate spirit seemed trapped in Telluride. Again and again she tried to escape on the train, only to be pulled back through the wormholes of time, into the jaws of her terrors and anguish.

Similarly, the ghost of Isidor Henschel, known by his comrades in Rico as "Jimmy the Jew," played out his last hours on the line between Ophir and Rico. Unlike Essie, he was actually killed in a train wreck in 1901, when he had hitched a ride on a freighter to save time.

At Rice's Spur, just over the sunny side of Lizard Head Pass, the freighter had stopped to pick up a lumber load. In the process, the freighter escaped back down the hill toward Rico, piling up at Snow Spur, the flat cars helter-skelter, the caboose wrecked, and the body of Jimmy crushed by timbers.

Instead of hitching a ride from Rico to Ophir on freight trains, his ghost, now wearing the uniform of the U.S. Navy, in which he had proudly served, appeared as a passenger on the regular trains. No one ever noticed him step aboard. He was simply there as the train pulled the hill toward Lizard Head. But he faded out of sight at the moment it reached Rice Spur. Isidor Henschel never reached Ophir.

The terrible specter of James McDonald appeared a few times on the same line from Rico to Ophir, his destination, Ophir. He had boarded on the fateful day in March 1892 at Durango, having just been released from the hospital after months under the care of the staff, due to a mining accident in Ophir. He was on his way home. McDonald, a Canadian, left his seat in the passenger car and joined the engineer in the cab, a fatal choice. The engine's plow caught in the frog on the switch at Glencoe and tossed the locomotive into a deadly tumble, steam scalding the engineer, fireman, and McDonald. With his flesh virtually boiled off him, McDonald died in screaming agony. As a ghastly reminder, his tortured wraith made brief but horrible appearances on passenger trains as they neared Ophir.

A far more unsavory phantom dampened the baggage car of passenger trains as they moved into the depot at Telluride. The unearthly groanings attracted the clerk, who nearly fainted when he flung open the door. The phantom was a sooty, grotesque creature, with blood spattered down his chest, his own head clutched in his left hand, dangling by the hair. Intricate tattoos decorated his arms in the forms of female figures, flags, and religious symbols. He was thought to be the man who had killed himself by stretching his neck across the rail at the moment a Durango train pulled into the depot in 1899. The head had been severed. Yet no one could fathom his presence in the baggage car. Was he looking to send the head to someone?

John C. Rice, the mail coach clerk on the Ridgway to Rico run, met a phantom several times at the Ridgway depot while waiting for his train. He first met her in fall of 1896, mistaking her for a normal citizen. She was standing on the platform one cold, grey day, her coat pulled tight around her. Tears were in her eyes and she stared forlornly at the tracks.

John, "a genial, whole-souled young man," inquired if he might help her in some way. She failed to respond. She didn't so much as look at him. Again he spoke to her, touching her arm. The blank stare and total lack of response made him think she was deaf. Her grey face and glassy eyes made him think she was ill. She was pretty—or would be, if the bloom were back in her cheek—and she was young, yet somehow old.

"I want to go home," John thought he heard her say as he turned away to go inside the building. He turned back to her just as the train came rolling toward the station. In the instant the train whistle blew, she was gone.

This girl was believed to be a Telluride prostitute who had set out to go back home to Denver, but had only enough fare to get to Ridgway. Somewhere, in some ravine, she supposedly killed herself in despair or flung herself into the river, her body unclaimed, unmourned; her spirit waiting at the Ridgway depot for the train to Montrose and Denver, waiting in the cold, grey fall of eternity.

Phantoms periodically sprung up along the tracks, causing much worry among the engineer and his crew, since most were mistaken for live persons. One was the ghost of a wee boy who stood in the center of the tracks as locomotives approached Saw Pit. One story says the fireman crawled out on the pilot to push the toddler out of the way and in a flash, the boy was nowhere to be seen.

Among troublesome spooks was a motley pack of gaseous bandits who boarded trains when the engine took on water at the Stoner tank. This was a great spot for train robbers to attack, and at one point actual solid-boned bandits did hold up a train here. The phantom bandits usually numbered four, and only the engineer and his fireman ever saw them.

The Durango-to-Silverton line collected a number of mysterious passengers as well, but none of their stories survived in print. One ghost was said to be a doctor desperately trying to get to Silverton to his dying wife or daughter, yet never reaching his destination.

The Denver & Rio Grande (D&RG) to Lake City boasted a few ghostly section men, and the D&RG to Ouray had a phantom engineer at the throttle of an equally phantom locomotive. This was said to be James O'Neil, forty-five years old, a longtime employee who went down with his engine in 1906 when a cloudburst ripped out the bridge foundation. He was on a night run with a freight train to Ouray and could not escape as his engine crashed through the weakened bridge and plunged into the creek twenty-five feet below. His crew had bailed out in time.

"The night was dark and when with the light of their lanterns they found their engineer was beneath his engine in the raging torrent, the train crew knew he had made his last run." But James O'Neil didn't know.

O'Neil loved his job. He loved his engine. He was seen at the throttle of his machine on dark, moonless, rainy nights, the locomotive running the line below Ouray in absolute and eerie silence.

Phantom locomotives showed up along the old tracks more frequently once these San Juan railroads were abandoned. The only ghostly engine, other than O'Neil's, that ran during the days of glory was the "sky blue locomotive" seen by an Ouray character named Jim Knous. This sky-blue phantom was on the Guston to Chattanooga line, and the straight story, if there was one, is in the grave with Knous, since whenever he saw it he was made 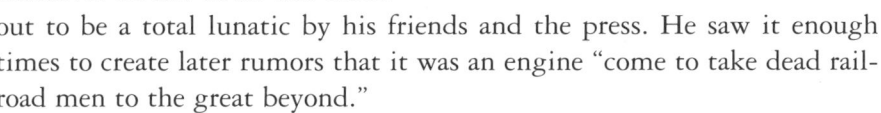 out to be a total lunatic by his friends and the press. He saw it enough times to create later rumors that it was an engine "come to take dead railroad men to the great beyond."

As the golden era of mining declined, those fantastic railroads of the San Juan were sucked away with it, spurs closing, mill lines ripped up, rails used for scrap, eventually none left save the great Durango-Silverton line. Yet tales abound of train whistles echoing along the old grades, of visions of locomotive headlights coming hard through the forests that shoulder grass-grown railbeds, of the sound of wheels clacking out rhythms in such remote places as the switchbacks near vanished Murphy and Gallagher. A few informants mentioned tales of the fleeting glimpse of a train flying across the trestle over the Uncompahgre River north of Ridgway. Fishermen confessed to seeing a hazy train along the Dolores River below Rico, ever so briefly in the fading light. . . .

That era of steam and iron, of great dreams and incredible triumphs, of men and women whose strength matched these mountains, left a permanent mark that will never fade. In the silence of twilight, the soul of those wild days clings like a mist to its lost glory, and mysterious swinging lanterns still signal from the old abandoned tracks and grassy grades.

7

$\mathcal{D}$EMONS AND $\mathcal{D}$ARKNESS

For twenty-four hours of each day the Big Kanawha Mine on Bachelor Mountain whirred and roared, belched and sighed, surrendering its treasury of rich ore. The miners in the Big Kanawha's dusky gullet never knew if scandalous Creede licked her night's wounds in weather fair or foul. Snowstorms might be raging over the Divide or sweet winds tripping through the San Juans, but work in the Big Kanawha continued, undisturbed, to the monotonous chugging and hissing of steam engines, the chirruping of cables through pulleys, and the chittering of ore carts along the narrow tracks. Men toiling in this twilight region for their daily wage were relatively content among the shift bosses and Tommyknockers and kobolds . . . until Neil McQueg invited an unwholesome guest.

Engineer McQueg surely was to blame, reasoned the miners, what with his paying heed to some foggy phantom. If he had not, it never would have assembled its bevy of cousins to come moping and moaning about the mine in a mass infestation. But no, McQueg felt compelled to speak to it—several times—and to go racing after it. This was more than half-interested encouragement. Indeed, it was an engraved invitation: Mr. Neil McQueg, Esquire, requests Your Eminent Presence and the presence of any other Demons you may desire to include, to engage in a general haunting of the premises of the Big Kanawha Mine.

McQueg endured a good deal of joshing from his fellow engineers and miners on account of his vision. In the first few days, when only he was familiar with the malignant spirit, it was knighted as "McQueg's Gas," possibly alluding to a condition of McQueg's brain, and not his bowels. The embarrassed engineer, a straight-laced, "exceedingly serious and erudite Scot" (which indicated irregularity already), was only too re-lieved when his "Gas" went calling on other engineers and a shift boss. With revengeful chuckles, McQueg suggested perhaps his private afflic-tion was to be classified among the communicable diseases. He chuckled into his beer, feeling in the pit of his stomach McQueg's Gas was no chuckling matter.

On Monday, June 23, 1902, Neil McQueg first saw the apparition, believing it was a miner. While McQueg had been standing at the end of the tram, he saw a man less than twenty feet away. He spoke to the man, receiving no reply. He addressed him a second time. There was no reply. "That's an odd fish," McQueg said, and went toward the tongue-tied miner. Gone. Totally gone.

Baffled at such quickness of step, McQueg began a search of the area. There was no sign of the miner. The engineer asked if anyone had seen a strange man about or had been in that section themselves. The answer was negative. After more fruitless searching, McQueg returned to the tram. Upon an instant the stranger appeared out of the shadows. Determined to have a word with this elusive man, McQueg grabbed for his shirt. His hand closed on air. The stranger was gone. Gas indeed.

Shortly after this the Gas was toying with the controls of a hoisting station. In the bottom of the shaft, where Henry S. Jones and other miners were working, a distinct signal to hoist the men was heard. No one in the shaft had given the signal. After some questioning, it was dismissed. The signal sounded again. No one confessed to giving it, and the men returned to work. A third time the signal sounded. Annoyed, Jones checked the switch. Nothing was amiss. He queried every miner near enough to the switch. All swore they had not made the signal. Work was resumed in an apprehensive atmosphere, each man puzzling over the suspect signal.

The following Thursday, June 26, Henry Jones climbed into the skip at the hoisting station. As usual, he began his descent into the same shaft to continue work. The skip jerked and Jones hurtled out, screaming as he fell into the shaft several hundred feet, his skull crushed instantly on impact. His twisted, bleeding body was lying in the precise spot where he had previously heard the three hoisting signals.

Given a moment, the miners connected Jones's fatal plunge and the false signals with McQueg's Gas. Something evil was in the Big Kanawha, and Neil McQueg had invited it. Suddenly no one was laughing.

The Big Kanawha's superintendent, James W. Westlake, attempted to allay the men's fears by telling them the only supernatural creatures in the mine were Tommyknockers (if one chose to believe in such poppycockers), and "Tommyknockers never harmed anyone." (What did he know?) He added very pointedly that Henry Jones's death was, though terribly unfortunate, an accident. Clearly an accident. Accidents occurred in the mine before and accidents were likely to occur again, not, of course, that Westlake would have them, but because mining was a dangerous business. Forget McQueg's Gas, he told them, and recall Henry Jones as the honest, steady man he was. Amen. McQueg's Gas and any other noxious gases were dismissed.

Superstitions were not so easy to put to bed. Westlake hadn't been in the mine. He hadn't heard the signal. He hadn't seen the malignant "miner." He even suggested Tommyknockers were nonexistent. The superintendent's fawning cat, which appeared to be bent on finding Tommyknockers for a meal, was a sufficient annoyance without that excellent gentleman putting down the elfin men. An outrage, to be sure, and a true sign James W. Westlake wanted education.

Although the three occurrences had made a great impression on the men, and Westlake had not, the miners returned to their stoping, tramming, and blasting while the superintendent's cat went among the men, the hoists, and the steam engines in search of a tender Tommyknocker or two. Westlake had employed the large calico cat for the express purpose of keeping the machinery rodent-free. These offending creatures had a talent for gumming up the works when their juicy bodies became entangled in the steam engine or flywheels or belts. The cat, his work his reward, excelled in the business of mouse munching. He was extremely fond of Westlake and showed some affection to the miners. He rubbed their legs during meals at the boardinghouse and brought them gifts of his better rodent specimens. He never produced a dangling Tommyknocker in his teeth, so the miners' suspicions were unfounded, based wholly on the cat's habit of immediately leaping to the spot where someone "rapped on the wall or table."

Only a few weeks after Henry Jones died, the cat went courting disaster near a hoisting engine. McQueg shooed the cat but was startled to see his old friend, the demon, lurking about the engine. As "erudite" as McQueg was, he still mistook the phantom for a miner (Gaelic obstinacy likely had something to do with that). His usual search turned up no miner. He was leaving the spot and the "most unearthly cry or shriek" shook him to the heart. Then the engine jammed. It took McQueg and several other men to remove calico cat jelly from the gears. After a short discussion the men concluded McQueg's Gas had hurled the unfortunate feline into the machinery, perhaps simply for gruesome pleasure or to endanger the lives of the miners.

The strain of not knowing what they were up against began taking its toll on the men in squabbling and animosity. They ostracized McQueg, hurled insults at him, and told him to "shut his trap" about the phantom.

For several days Westlake was markedly cut up over the loss of his cat. He tried to believe the death was another accident, the cat having lost its footing in pursuit of a rat. Yet the men had told him the demon was there beforehand. The demon killed Henry Jones. The demon killed the cat. Westlake refused to succumb to superstition. Accidents were always occurring in mines. *Accidents.* But the superintendent seemed to lose his appetite, and miners noted he was "wan and peaked."

He grew morose with the weight of death and demons on his shoulders, keeping to himself in the mine offices. James Westlake's dark mood overwrought the shift bosses, who became increasingly unnerved by the slightest incidents in the mine. One of them, Lane Pearl, was working alongside other miners when he heard a sound like groaning. Stopping to listen, he realized it must have been coming from a man who was seriously injured. Without hesitation, he went in the direction of the sound. Whoever it was moaned as though he were in excruciating pain, half crying, half choking.

SOMETHING IN THE WIND

The sound died away. Pearl could find no injured man in the section. Satisfied his men were accounted for, Pearl was left with the mystery of the chilling sounds. If it wasn't a miner, what was it? The wind? Lane Pearl knew what he had heard, and the sound was definitely human, a man in great distress. He searched the area thoroughly, thinking the injured party ceased to moan because he had fallen unconscious or died. With an abrupt sinking sensation, James Westlake's name sprang into Pearl's head. He had not seen the superintendent for more than a day. Was it he who was dying in the darkness?

Pearl engaged two miners to help search the section and the moaning came again, this time from a shaft nearby. He descended into the black pit, finding nothing. His anxiety mounted to a point of panic until Westlake was located at the blacksmith's shop, sound of limb, but low in spirit. Although Pearl was relieved to find him, the shift boss realized Westlake's being safe left the mystery of the moaning unsolved. Westlake ordered him to "forget it and get about" his work.

The miners, a superstitious lot to begin with, concluded only the demon could be responsible for the moaning and that it was about to take another one of them. A few still laughed the entire affair into their tankards every Saturday night. They continued to refer to it as McQueg's Gas or Pearl's Gas or the Big Gas and made it all a bit of a gas around Creede . . . until the Gas got up a more active employ.

Many times the demon and its cousins (more than one now, for this occurred in several crosscuts and stopes at once) appeared for an instant and vanished in a whispering mix of evil, spilling foul, choking air into the darkness. Some men fell ill.

By fall, several of the less courageous miners had given notice, demanded their paychecks, and left the area altogether. More followed when trammer Oscar Montgomery had a round with one of the demons. He spoke to a man at the entrance of a shaft, receiving no reply. He went toward the figure. It vanished. Fearing the man had stepped into the shaft, Montgomery investigated the possibility, believing he'd find a broken miner at the bottom. To his relief, no one was there. He made the customary search and questioned the other miners. No one saw any stranger. Montgomery returned to his work. Shortly the demon sprung at him from behind a muck pile, tumbling him backward down a short incline, and he let out a scream.

"That thing pushed me!" he informed his rescuers. "It was trying to kill me. A few feet to the left and I would have fallen a hundred."

More of the men in the Big Kanawha began to believe the mine was truly infested with something demonic. The company continued losing employees while the property manager and the superintendent and other rational persons tried to convince the men the mine was not under siege by malignant spirits. They ordered a complete investigation by a Denver firm and the miners were informed that escaping steam from some machinery in the bottom of the shafts was responsible for the strange occurrences. Perfectly harmless steam, that was all, and when it came forth in volume, it very easily resembled a man or form with the power to dissipate upon an instant. "Steam, gentlemen, so let's be perfectly rational and work as we always have worked."

To many, the steam theory was questionable. Steam had the power to pull the signal, did it? Steam had the muscle to push a man about? Steam had the strength to mush the cat? Those who believed in steam could go ahead and believe. Those who did not went and found a mine to work in where "steam" was less fond of escaping. Of the one hundred men employed, a third had resigned, yet a few returned after the investigators declared the mine free of demons.

In a superior, jocular vein, Denver newspapers reported the Big Kanawha's murderous phantoms as the hallucinations of hysterical, overwrought miners, suggesting the Big Kanawha Leasing Company allowed liquor on the premises. Said one, "If steam can strike terror in grown men, what do they do when Mrs. Mullen boils potatoes?"

The ink on their barbs had barely dried when the evil entities in the Big Kanawha nearly strangled trammer Gus Leingang. He was pulled out of a stope with the life almost gone out of him. His fellow miners "worked him over" until he cried out in gasps how several dark forms "took hold" of him, wrapping loose cable around his neck and limbs, and dragged him to the end of the stope. Steam indeed.

These dark demons spread to the New York and Last Chance Mines, properties connected to the Big Kanawha. Only with winter and the temporary closure of the properties did the plague end. In spring 1903 an apprehensive crew entered the stopes and shafts and crosscuts without encountering any demons.

Unlike the ghosts of dead miners, unidentifiable malicious spirits were considered "demons" whether or not they appeared in human form. Often bad air or the stench of sulfur accompanied them. They rarely inhabited the San Juan mines for prolonged periods, most striking just once or twice. Deaths and accidents at the Palmetto Mine near Rose's Cabin were attributed to the evil work of these entities, particularly during the early years of production when the majority of the crew were men of Gaelic ancestry.

The treasurer of the Eclipse Mining and Smelting Company at Animas Forks became ill after encountering an "enveloping inky shade" in the main tunnel of that mine. James H. Fairchild had gone in the tunnel with the mine foreman out of curiosity. A strange "clinging . . . sulfurous" thing had been reported by a few of the miners and Fairchild, being of scientific mind, probed it with a stick, only to have it sweep around him, making him dizzy and nauseated. After some months he was still unable to shake the illness and eventually went home to Chicago.

During the early Rico boom, a similar entity appeared in the mines on Expectation Mountain west of camp. Each time a new shaft was sunk, the sometimes groaning black form oozed up in the bottom, especially where water was present. Sulphur Creek tumbled down the mountain's flank, giving rise to the superstition among some of the men that demons inhabited the entire peak. In 1881 the black demons of Expectation snuffed out the life of a Swiss man named Frederick Herman.

In 1895 in the Japan Mine at Telluride another of these black, engulfing forms struck the foreman, Henry Brown, causing paralysis. The foreman held no belief in demonic phantoms, but a few of the employees who did abandoned their jobs for fear the same would happen to them.

The heavier the sulfur in the area, the stronger was the suspicion of demon habitation. Some men refused to work in areas with large sulfur deposits. Sulfur and evil spirits naturally fused, and in areas like Guston, where sulfurous slime oozed out of every mine and the scent was strong in the nostrils and sharp in the lungs, the dark fiends of the netherworld didn't confine themselves to mines.

On the road between Guston and Red Mountain Town any strange occurrences (which, oddly, were frequent) were blamed on evil entities. Wagons suddenly lost wheels. Axles broke. Mule teams bolted. Normally gentle horses threw their riders. Stagecoaches overturned. And in 1890 three men jumped from a handcar when the cloudy bulk of a sulfurous demon loomed up in front of them on the track. Of the ten men on the car, only the three who were Irish jumped: Flurry Mahoney, Jack Murphy, and

James Ryan. Mahoney, age sixty-six, hurtled headlong over the edge, breaking his neck. The other two, who suffered cuts and bruises, first told their rescuers they "didn't know why" they had jumped. Later they said they thought a freight train was coming and so they jumped. A few weeks later, James Ryan confessed to roving journalist Fitz Mac that he and the others saw "The Demon." It was a multifaceted, sulfurous creature that seemed to be "a lake of evil" thick as oatmeal, spread throughout the strata of the area, groaning in mines, rattling mills, and boiling out of the rocks now and again like overflow from a pot of hot pitch. The Guston road is still fouled with the sharp scent of sulfur, indicating the demon may be in residence yet and the heavy iron grills bolted over shafts hardly seem adequate to keep such a thing from belching to the surface. Irish, beware.

Being Irish wasn't necessarily a prerequisite for demon visitation, although the frequency of Irish-to-demon encounters cast suspicion on the group. Some said the Irish created their demons; others said the demons were simply attracted to the guilt-ridden Irish. Guilt certainly kept one prospector's demon hovering around his cabin near Wagon Wheel Gap. Keenan was the man's name. Throughout the fall and winter of 1895 to 1896, Keenan was plagued by a "great terrible blue beast with eyes as black as the gates of Hell." The thing thumped against the cabin walls and salivated sulfurous slime down his chimney, frequently killing the fire or making it explode in balls of flame. During the spring thaw, Keenan journeyed to Del Norte and confessed his sins while there. He had taken cash from several totally stupefied miners in a Creede saloon in summer of 1895, and his guilt invited the blue beast out of hell. Upon his return as an absolved sinner, the thing was gone.

Slouching, munching, bone-crunching demons reportedly resided in Goblin Gulch northwest of Creede and in Canyon Diablo, a tributary of Cochetopa Creek, encountered by prospectors and a shepherd in the 1890s.

Whether they are still lodged in these remote places is unknown. It probably takes an Irish prospector to initiate manifestation.

Starvation Gulch and Timber Hill, on the old freight route between Creede and Silverton, were infested with goblins or demons or very ill-mannered ghosts in the beginning of the twentieth century. These were said to be guarding either gold bars buried here by Soapy Robinson and Buster Reede, or sacks of silver buried by freighters who feared an attack from bandits.

In the Robinson-Reede version, Reede was killed in a saloon brawl and his ghost went back to Starvation Creek to protect the gold from Robinson. The freighter tale has the men hiding several sacks of silver when their scouts spotted highwaymen on the road at Timber Hill, which is at the north end of Starvation Creek. The freighters and scouts were gunned down by the bandits, but the bandits were unaware the men had buried the silver. Since that fatal day, the bullet-ridden wraiths of the freighters and scouts have stood guard over the bonanza, driving off all seekers. They degenerated into inky, twisted creatures, more like demons than disembodied spirits.

Several San Juan goblins had originated from ghost stories, traveled "back East," and metamorphosed into lumpy black horrors with hardly a human trait. Suicide was the underlying reason for this. Suicides, although frequent, were impossible to understand, and editors generally condemned the broken man or woman as a "coward," heaping shame on their memory. If ghost stories arose after their passing, the ghosts invariably were hideous, demonic, and dangerous.

One of these was Joseph Papillon, a miner who had built a cabin up Bear Creek above Ouray, a few switchbacks from the Yellow Jacket Mine. An ordinary man not given to excesses, according to reports, he went on a binge in Ouray's tenderloin one Thursday in August 1885 after having had "words" with another man that week. Sunday, August 30, Joe's friend, J. W. Parrott, found Joe's ghastly corpse hanging off the bunk in the cabin, a pistol clutched in the lifeless left hand. Blood caked Joe's features and gaping bullet holes in his neck and nose swarmed with flies and maggots.

The Ouray County Coroner found Joe had been shot thrice, all three bullets entering the neck, two ranging upward, breaking the jaw and lodging in the brain, the third passing through the roof of the mouth and out above the bridge of the nose. The coroner reported, "Two [of the bullets]

DEMONS AND DARKNESS

would have proved fatal," and due to Papillon's "protracted spree" the "testimony . . . pointed conclusively to suicide."

None too surprisingly, some of Joe's friends disagreed. How did the man shoot himself three times when two of these bullets lodged in his brain? Was he so drunk he didn't know he was dead and pulled the trigger again? And rumor had it Joe was right-handed. Although he was buried and the noise of life rattled on, Joe refused to rest in peace. His cabin became inhabited by a malevolent presence so terrible that no one went near the place. No form was ever seen, only felt or heard, and the hideous groanings ripped at the nerves of even the soberest men. Draped in this ghastly pall, the cabin rotted into the earth, its roofless remains still visible beside Bear Creek, still infused with sickening dread and torment.

Like Papillon, Andrew Emerson, a Swedish miner at Ames, became a gruesome, demonic entity after he killed himself in an abandoned stope in the San Bernardo Mine on April 10, 1903. He had $485 in cash, had just eaten a hearty supper, and was in good spirits, yet he went into the stope with a stick of dynamite, laid himself on the ground and, slipping the dynamite beneath his head, lit the fuse. His body was found with only remnants of his jaw and cranium attached. His spirit, or something that had metastasized out of it, became an utter terror in the stope, especially to Frank Fox, who had been Andrew's friend. An inky headless wraith, with tatters of flesh and bone protruding at the shoulders, darkened that part of the mine until the stope was blasted shut. The thing was no longer visible, but its hellish groaning continued from behind the rocks.

Some paranormal researchers suggested what seemed to be the ghosts of Emerson and Papillon were actually some sort of demonic entities, something that may have swallowed the men prior to their deaths, or "usurped the energy" of their lives. These sinister dark spirits drove some men to madness and a few to self-destruction. Logic might say the men were already insane and their private demons only in their heads. Yet the victims were often ordinary, hard workers, stable in their employment, well liked by their friends, and generally described as "sober," "moderate," or "inoffensive."

Fritz Pank, a saloonkeeper in Telluride, was continually tormented by the whispering of fiends in his bedroom and the transient reflections of their hideous forms in his mirrors. First he blocked his ears with cotton and removed the mirrors. His friends began to think his "mind was affected by the fall in the Smuggler." Fritz had suffered a head injury in the Smuggler Mine in 1888, before turning to a less dangerous business, making a fair success of the saloon. Fritz confided to Frank Stillwell, the saloon's piano player, that "spirits had got into" his stomach. That evening he went up to his room at the rear of the saloon and put a bullet through his belly and two through his chest. His friends told the coroner Fritz "was out of his mind."

A honeymooning couple in 1902 in Lake City encountered a nightmarish apparition that nearly made both of them "go out of" their minds. Inger and Clarice Anderson of Chicago were boating on Lake San Cristobal one afternoon in May, lazily soaking in the glorious blue and green scenery, their boat drifting while they relaxed in one another's arms. Clarice was startled to hear cries for help and, jumping up, saw what appeared to be a man in the frigid water in the middle of the lake. Inger was a powerful young Swede who spent many hours rowing and sailing on Lake Michigan, and without hesitation he set out for the man. As their boat closed in on the victim, both Inger and Clarice thought his face and arms were loose strips of flesh, his eyes missing. In his shock, Inger stopped rowing. The man sunk. Clarice urged Inger on, thinking what they had seen were weeds across the man's body, just making him appear already dead . . . long dead.

Arriving at the spot, the couple saw a struggling body beneath the water, pale limbs reaching upward. Clarice held onto Inger and Inger hung over the gunwale, grabbing for the drowning man. Out of the water surged a mangled, nonhuman thing, eyeless, a gaping slash of mouth, its flesh in ragged ribbons, the bones and sinews exposed where the flesh was completely peeled away. It pulled Inger overboard, beneath the now choppy water. Clarice screamed. Inger propelled himself in terror back into the boat, soaked to the skin, gasping for air, violently shivering with cold and fear. Clarice saw the thing again and struck it a fierce blow with the oar, once, twice, three times, Inger joining her. When they stopped, collapsing in the boat, a tangle of driftwood knocked against the gunwale. . . . "No!" they mutually agreed, that Thing was not driftwood.

When they told their story, one of their listeners suggested they had seen a ghost: it was the twentieth anniversary of the drowning of John F. Hogan in that very lake. Poor John was a strong young man of twenty-two when he went down in 1882 . . . pleasure sailing . . . the boat capsized with him and two friends aboard. They all clung to the overturned boat in that icy water, but John believed he could swim to the island. He disappeared without a sound. They found his body the next day . . . rigid . . . in the position of a man about to make an ordinary swimming stroke.

The Andersons shook their heads. The Thing was something evil, not the ghost of a drowned man. In fact, the Thing might have even pulled John Hogan to his death. A water demon lurked in Lake San Cristobal and they weren't staying around to find out what it could do. They cut their honeymoon short, leaving the area that day and returning to Chicago. They never came back to Lake City, but they told children and grandchildren of the water fiend in Lake San Cristobal. Somewhere over the years they had learned John Hogan's death in the lake left his sweetheart, Mary Ann, in eternal heartbreak. The day he drowned he was carrying her letter. Clarice believed the water fiend was specifically after young lovers. . . . Perhaps more honeymooners have this secret dread to tell.

Of the entire slashing, murderous, demonic horde, Tommyknockers "gone bad" were the deadliest. These sawed-off elfin men normally looked after the welfare of miners, particularly Cornish miners, who undoubtedly smuggled the wee buggers past U.S. customs without attracting notice. (Germans did the same with kobolds, who were their mine-safety devices.) As long as they were allowed to keep a few stolen trinkets, had an occasional nip of whiskey left out for them, and weren't insulted, the knockers were loyal to the miners. Knockers warned of impending cave-ins, bad air, and other dangers . . . providing they weren't violated. They could stop a runaway cart or even shield a man during a premature blast . . . providing they weren't abused. Insult, violate, or abuse them, and the knockers became demons, bent on destruction with a knack for accomplishing a high body count.

Most mines in the San Juan hosted beneficial, gregarious Tommyknockers, a variety one might call "run of the mill," the Common Knocker. Two mines, the Forest at Rico and the Virginius in Governor Basin above Ouray, billeted more sinister troops. The tribe in the Forest Mine went beyond mischievous into the realm of sadistic and obscene, a variety of Cesspit Knockers. Those in the Virginius, a virulent infestation, belonged to the variety Satanic Knockers, *Nanus satanus*.

The Cesspit Knockers of the Forest Mine, originally well behaved, became vengeful when one among them had his personal collection of bottles and knick-knacks removed by the mine foreman, Richard Johnstone. The knocker had been filching spoons from the bunkhouse, whiskey flasks, ink bottles, and dozens of his favorite little blue bottles containing Bromo-

Seltzer, not to mention chunks of high-grade ore. The loot was squirreled away in small caches inside the mine, tucked into crevices, secured behind pumping equipment, or stuffed in gear housings. Johnstone thought he had on his hands a deranged kleptomaniac employee with chronic indigestion or, at the very least, a greedy mountain packrat or woodrat (*Neotoma cinerea*). The packrat theory took precedence when Johnstone heard the tapping of soft feet near the caches. Packrats stomped their hind feet when alarmed. The miners informed him the stomping was from boots—that Tommyknockers, not packrats, were squirreling away the loot. "Tommyrot," was his reply. The foreman cleaned out the caches and swore against rats and knockers, warning the men, "I see one, I'll thrash it." That did it. War was declared. Machinery jammed, water hoses broke, candles were constantly snuffed out. Even pie cans were stolen, which was unheard of as a knocker habit. Men on ladders were doused with water (the Forest was a very wet mine), causing them to lose their footing. Sometimes while they were asleep, the men had their clothes stolen, and they were forced to go searching for them in their saggy long johns or bare beam. Richard Johnstone's clothes wound up in the outhouse, and his embarrassment led to accusations against two of the Welsh miners, Tom Watson and Davie Conway, who were the only ones untouched by the knockers. Watson and Conway denied complicity with the wee Cesspit Knockers, but offered to "go down to Clarkes Brothers and buy Johnstone a new suit of clothes." The snickering Welshmen tossed the story around Rico how Richard Johnstone was as "fragrant as a backhouse," thanks be to Tommyknockers.

In June 1897 Johnstone was climbing a ladder in a wet raise and the knockers spit on his candle, plunging him into darkness. He was too wet to relight the wick and so attempted to go back down the ladder by feeling his way. Missing his footing, he bounced down the raise forty feet, whacked into a cross timber, which slowed his fall, and tumbled to the bottom. Knocked insensible, amazingly without a broken bone, he staggered to the mouth of the tunnel, muttering curses on the Tommyknocker race. During his recuperation knocker activity ceased, only to become more obscene on Johnstone's return, with buckets of water, slurry, and slops raining down on the miners after their lights were snuffed out. All Richard Johnstone could do was order more pumps, extra sweet soap, and curse the darkness.

At the Virginius the Satanic Knockers were far more sadistic, the sinister pranks degenerating to cutthroat activities with fatal results. The infestation was so massive even fumigation would not have dampened it, and in later years Cornishmen refused even to seek work at this mine. Cornishmen were in the minority to begin with at the Virginius, a large heavy producer on the frigid northeast breast of the St. Sophia Ridge. Perched at 12,200 feet, the mine was assaulted by howling winds and long winters, deadly avalanches and treacherous roads. The first Cornishmen to work here brought in the Tommyknockers for their own safety. However, the Swedes and Italians poked fun at the Cornishmen, claiming to trap Tommyknockers in their lunch buckets, boil them for supper or render them for bootblack. Too much abuse . . . and the knockers became ugly.

In addition to their usual nasty pranks, the Virginius knockers broke beams, caused cave-ins, battered and bruised men month after month. They were blamed for most deaths (of which there were many), especially the mysterious and gruesome ones: Frank During, Edward Holden, Maurice Fawcett, Lorenzo Mattivi, James Welsh, Alex Olivetti, Patrick Conley, and five at once in an eleven-hundred-foot drop.

On Sunday morning May 15, 1887, the knockers were blamed for hurling a four-pound piece of iron down a shaft eighty feet, where it splattered Frank During's brain, knocking him another twenty feet farther. He died that afternoon. Less than two months later on Friday, July 8, they blasted Ed Holden clean back to Iowa for burial. September 29, 1890, the knockers were toying with the hoisting signals (a favorite evil which was repeated almost weekly in this mine), sending the cage to the eighth level when it was asked for at the tenth. In the dim light Maurice M. Fawcett pushed a loaded ore car into the space where the cage was supposed to be, the weight of the car pulling him into a hundred-foot plunge. "Carelessness" was the unfair verdict against the mangled twenty-five-year-old corpse, but many miners protested, claiming the Virginius was unsafe, full of bad Tommyknockers, and warranted an investigation from the state mine inspector.

As the body count increased, so did the population of the workforce, now more than two hundred men. The knockers were delirious in their bloodthirsty joy, for their activities doubled. After a rash of accidents in 1894, which left an Austrian named Lorenzo Mattivi dead and a number of men injured, including hoisting engineer John McHugh, who half-drowned in a May water burst on level 11 (he died some months later from pneumonia), several Cornishmen walked off the job. Again, miners called for a state inspector, without success.

The following year at the stroke of midnight on November 18, James Welsh exploded, and four miners near him were injured. Welsh had three sticks of dynamite in his hip pocket, "but how it was caused to explode is the mystery," said the *Ouray Herald*. Several theories were afloat, one of which claimed this the work of the bloodthirsty Tommyknockers. Surprisingly, a Swedish miner, Charles Rossdel, said he saw "the villainous little men" running from Welsh's horribly mangled corpse. Rossdel left the Virginius the next day, seeking employment at the Smuggler over the ridge.

The Virginius Mine's reputation had grown black, and hardly a Cornishman could be found there in the 1890s and 1900s. Although they had left, apparently the villainous little men had not, for accidents among Swedes, Norwegians, Finns, Austrians, and Italians increased. The knockers took advantage of the immigrants' difficulty with English, and the American boys blamed the accidents on the language barrier, an underlying hostility infecting the workforce.

On December 18, 1896, five miners crowded into the cage for their descent into the main shaft of the Virginius. Charles Anderson, John Antas, Charles Swanson, Louis Jackson, and Gabriel Rusk, all natives of Norway and Sweden, joking in their usual jovial manner, gave the signal to trammer Albert Anderson to pull the chairs supporting the cage.

No one signaled the hoisting engineer, but instantly as a bolt of lightning, the cage dropped, the young Albert speechless in horror as he saw the faces of his fellow countrymen shot with fear. The cage was sucked down eleven hundred feet, crushing the life out of the five men.

An inquest revealed the "reel or drum of the hoisting engine" was "disconnected from the engine at the time when it should not have been" and that the brakes "were not sufficient to hold the cage without the assistance of the engine." The jury held the mine foreman at fault for putting Albert Anderson at the cage, claiming the young man could "hardly speak the English language" and was "totally incompetent to fill so responsible a position." And most of all, they condemned the hoisting engineer "for having his engine disconnected when he knew it was time for the men to go down in the mine." The distraught engineer swore he hadn't disconnected the engine, not on God's green earth would he have done such a thing, never.

Then how did it become disconnected? Everyone in that cursed mine knew. The Tommyknockers had gone bad.

8

THE $\mathscr{S}$HADOW OF THE $\mathscr{R}$OPE

Guttural, low, menacing, the accusing words dig into his ears and he awakes with a start at the sound of his name sliding slowly across the darkness, "James . . . James . . ."

With cold shaking hands and pounding heart, James fumbles to light the lantern. Light will dispel the terror. . . .

Yet as the flame flickers to life, it plays over the ghastly face of a dead man, a hanged man, his bulging eyes rimmed with blood, his face swollen, contorted, with the knotted veins purpling, as in the last throes of death. He hovers inches from James Bell's bed, and James cannot scream. Nor can he take his eyes away. His heart pounds in pain against his ribs as if to burst through them. The hideous phantom has been creeping into his sleep and into reality for several months.

Fearing for his sanity, James Bell flees Lake City and tries to start a new life at the San Juan and New York Mining and Smelting

Company in Durango, only to be pursued by the wraith until his nights become unbearable.

In desperation he writes his friends in Lake City and, to his horror, they tell him the same hideous phantom has been seen and heard by the schoolchildren when they are near the Ocean Wave Bridge. George Betts is scratching out his revenge, dragging like a rock at the souls of those who hanged him, clawing after their children from his portal in the half-world.

James Bell, perhaps overcome by remorse for his part in the lynching of George Betts and James F. Browning on April 27, 1882, had invited his phantoms. In one letter to his sister Cornelia in Atlanta, he wrote, "I can no longer accept what I did. I shudder and shrink at our righteous zeal that fired our blood to so violent a climax as to kill these men. How can I forget how Mr. Browning begged for our mercy. What if I were him and I asked for mercy and none was shown. Sometimes I want to cry because I cannot undo what we did. I do not know how to accept it, as you say, with stalwart heart that what was done is done."

James Bell was not the only man tormented by the wretched wraith of George Betts. Others, who had no misgivings, who firmly believed the lynchings were justified, were startled in the night by the sudden appearance of Betts. He wandered the streets, poked in at windows, groaned from the fatal bridge over the Lake Fork River near the Ocean Wave Smelting Works. And he terrified schoolchildren, who had no part in his death.

Betts and Browning were proprietors of the San Juan Central, a dance hall and saloon on Bluff Street at the head of Second in Lake City. Although their establishment was successful with its billiards, whiskey, and scantily clad, dancing girls, the two were habitual kleptomaniacs, storing their stolen goods like jackdaws in a secret space beneath the saloon office floor. Their nasty habit led to the shooting of the Hinsdale County Sheriff while they were executing a burglary.

On the day before Sheriff Edward N. Campbell was slain, he and his wife, Ruth, were preparing for the coming IOOF lodge celebration. She was overcome with a terrible premonition that something dreadful would happen to her husband, and tears filled her eyes. Campbell cheered her and brushed aside her superstition, going out that night with City Marshal Clair Smith. They had a thief to catch.

William Luckett, furniture dealer and coffin merchant, had reported someone had burgled his vacant cottage on the flats east of the river. Bedding had been removed and other items disturbed in such a way as to indicate the thieves intended to return. Sheriff Campbell and Marshal Smith determined to wait in the house to see if the burglar would return. At one o'clock in the morning their vigil paid off. There was a noise at the kitchen door. Both Campbell and Smith, with guns drawn, waited in a hall doorway, Campbell standing and Smith crouching at his feet, according to the Lake City *Mining Register.*

The kitchen door opened and one dark figure struck a match to reconnoiter, revealing to Campbell and Smith the intruders were two armed men. The instant the match flickered out, Campbell demanded, "Throw up your hands," and fired at the shadows.

The intruders returned fire. "Oh I am shot!" Campbell cried out and slumped against his deputy, who eased him to the floor. Smith raced out after the intruders. Unable to see which way they had fled, he quickly returned inside and found Sheriff Edward Campbell dead.

Marshal Clair Smith swore that Campbell had been murdered by George Betts and that with Betts was his partner and accomplice, James Browning. Smith had seen both men clearly in the light from the match. He was the sole witness and his testimony was adamant.

Citizens were aroused and a posse dispatched to bring in the accused man. Betts was arrested on the east side of the river as he was walking toward town. He was carrying a .44-caliber revolver that had one spent cartridge in the cylinder. The slug taken from Campbell's body was a .44.

Browning was arrested at the dance hall, his gun confiscated and found to be a .38 caliber. Although he had not fired the fatal shot, he was considered an accessory to murder. Both men had been suspected of several burglaries around town and feeling was against them.

An angry crowd threatened to torch the San Juan Central, prompting the lawmen to station guards around it. At the same time citizens screamed for the neck of Betts, a "graceless scamp as ever insulted the ground of Colorado," the "bawdy house pimp, a thief and a blackguard." The cry for Browning's blood was less vehement, for he had many friends and "respect outside of his questionable calling." The mood of the crowd, punctuated by a chorus of "let them dance at the end of a rope," sent Marshal Smith to call on the assistance of Captain Mullin of the Pitkin Guards. Men of Company C, First Regiment of the Colorado National

Guard, armed with rifles, were mustered to the jail to protect the two accused men from the mob.

Betts and Browning were both manacled in their cells, waiting out the hours of Wednesday afternoon while the good men of Lake City, fanning the flames of righteous anger until they warped into hatred, screamed for blood. Other Lake City killers had waltzed through the court unpunished in a blatant demonstration of the impotence of Hinsdale County justice. If Lake City citizens wanted justice, they must knot the rope themselves and "hurl the murderers to hell."

In the hour before midnight, a large body of armed and masked men rendezvoused near the dead sheriff's house, James Bell among them. They marched to the jail, where a crowd of spectators awaited their arrival. They overpowered and disarmed the guards and sledged open the doors of the jail.

"Don't hang Jimmie!" a few spectators screamed, Browning being guilty only of burglary and not murder.

Their pleas were met with fierce contempt. Browning was Betts's accomplice and deserved to die.

He was taken from the cell first, dragged out by the manacles securing his wrists. A big man, Browning fought against the mob, his head and shoulders lowered, plunging into the force of them, while they attempted to secure a heavy, knotted rope round his neck. He bucked and twisted away from the rope five times like a tiger, shouting out for his friends, begging not to be hanged, but his attackers overpowered him. "For Christ's sake, gentlemen, don't kill me!" he said, as the rope was finally secured around his neck. "Have I no friend here?" he asked. The rope was pulled taut. Likewise, a rope was fastened round Betts's neck, and he was led out of his cell.

Betts calmly asked for a chew of tobacco as he glanced past the masked men in search of his friends. He was told no one was going to save him; he had no friends in this crowd. With a hissed curse at his captors, he fell silent.

The crowd marched Betts and Browning to the Ocean Wave Bridge and, along the way, Betts asked if his friend Harry was among them. He wanted Harry to make certain the news of how he met his death never reached his mother. Harry wasn't present. They would pass word on to him.

"I want my body taken down and conveyed to the house," Betts muttered, meaning his dance hall, according to the Lake City *Silver World*.

Some of Sheriff Campbell's friends shouted at the two doomed men as they passed, and a woman from the San Juan Central pressed into the crowd, begging for someone to stop the hanging.

The condemned men were led to the timbered bridge, where the loose ends of the ropes were slung over the cross beams, one man at each end of the bridge. Again, Browning asked for mercy, saying, "I don't want to give any man away, but Betts did the shooting. You are hanging an innocent man." The stone-faced Betts shuddered.

"Up with them!" a masked man ordered.

The crowd of executioners hoisted the ropes, pulling Betts and Browning five feet off the ground, then jerked them all the way up, within inches of the beams, and fastened the ropes to the side of the bridge. As George Betts strangled to death, his strong young body quivering against the crushing noose, his face went purple, congested with blood, and his eyes and nose hemorrhaged. James Browning vainly fought against the rope, grabbing at it with his manacled hands, once, twice, slipping into darkness on the third attempt, his face pale and tongue protruding. The hideous sight left the onlookers in stark silence. James Bell told himself justice was done.

The corpses were left hanging until the coroner's jury officially pronounced Betts and Browning had died by unknown hands. More than likely some of those "unknowns" were members of the jury. Usually lynchings were carried out by the most upright and prominent citizens of a town. As with the transplanted English gentlemen of Georgetown who lynched a poverty-stricken Swiss man in the heat of anger, then came to regret it in the accusing light of day, many of the good men of Lake City came to hate their act of vengeance. For some it was a source of shame. George Betts and James Browning were, after all, fellow businessmen, deserving of a court trial in the modern year of 1882, when hemp justice had no place in a civilized town.

But it was too late. The two men were dead, buried in the city cemetery by their many friends and associates, mourned by their dance-hall girls, a stone erected in their honor. Nothing could bring them back.

Except George Betts's curse. He slipped the bonds of the grave before the month of May brought muddy water down the Lake Fork. His ghastly shade, marked with the hue of death, appeared at the bridge and again at the dance hall.

THE SHADOW OF THE ROPE

Perhaps it was the hidden guilt of the citizens that brought him back. Or perhaps it was the appalling way he died that haunted the minds of Lake City's best. It was uncommon for a hanged man's face to congest and his eyes to hemorrhage. And Betts's stiffening corpse with its staring eyes and purpled face "grotesquely slubbed," as James Bell described it, was left swinging in the daylight breeze where women and children were forced to view it as they passed the bridge.

At first James Bell tried to dismiss the visitations of Betts as nightmares. As they became more frequent and more distinct, Bell thought otherwise. To Cornelia he wrote, "I am now convinced the voice of Betts is not a mere dream. I believe he is here in the room calling to me in the dark. I have seen his face when I have my own eyes open very wide." He slept with a lamp burning, but found it only intensified the hideousness of the wraith and, when the phantom slipped away like vapor, the lamp cast the long shadow of the knotted rope high on Bell's bedroom wall.

Although he fled Lake City, Bell failed to shake off the wraith and the shadow of that rope. The hanged man clawed his way through the veil of the netherworld nightly. At this time Bell learned from his Lake City friends that one of George Betts's dancing girls had cursed those who hanged him. "George will come for you all," she said, "until not one of you is left to tell about it."

James Bell, a strapping young Southern gentleman, began arriving at work pale and sick each morning. His employer, Mr. Porter, feared he was anemic. Believing if he got far enough away Betts would no longer torment him, Bell decided to return to Atlanta "for a spell." He never came back to Colorado.

George Betts continued his malignant loitering at the Ocean Wave Bridge until eventually he seemed confined to that spot. Older schoolboys contrived to bring a girl to the bridge on a full moon night in hopes she would be terrified by Betts's purple face and rush into the expectant youth's arms for protection.

James Browning, on the other hand, was never as ghastly a ghost as his old partner. Nor did he haunt the bridge. He appeared dressed in his best suit, with the old lark in his eyes. He banged around the halls of the courthouse and erupted through the upstairs courtroom as if demanding a fair trial. In the blackness of the Luckett house, when he and Betts were told to throw up their hands and were fired upon, he had no idea who was shooting at him—lawman or thief. They knew Luckett was gone. Returning fire and running seemed the best option. Premeditated murder? Browning's wraith, angered by his harsh sentence, is angry still, knocking around in the courthouse today, an unsatisfied whirlwind, a late-night thumping, a thief of documents who toys with the lights.

All victims of Judge Lynch didn't have the privilege of returning the way Betts and Browning did, yet lynching victims did far more haunting than did the innocent victims they themselves had dispatched. Sheriff Edward Campbell stayed peacefully in his grave, his young widow and six children never tormented by his ghost. Likewise did James K. Prindle, shot in cold blood by the gambler Henry Read Moorman at the Coliseum theater and dance hall in Durango. It was Moorman, lynched by Durango's Committee of Safety on April 11, 1881, whose twisted shade groaned in the boughs of the fatal pine tree.

A group of nearly three hundred masked men dragged Moorman to the massive pine in front of Durango's fledgling post office and strung him up. They left him hanging in the moonlight with a warning that should anyone cut down the body before daybreak, they would meet the same end.

The editor of the *Durango Record,* Mrs. C. W. Romney, a lively widow in her forties, although aghast at the sight of the corpse swinging in the moonlight, seemed to condone the act. She wrote, "The Powers that Be have promulgated the law . . . they have sealed with the seal of death the fate of future offenders."

Moorman's dark energy remained in the pine until the tree was cut down, perhaps as a warning to "future offenders" or a reminder to the guilt-stained law-abiding citizens who knew in their hearts lynching was akin to the lawlessness they purported to despise.

Betts, Browning, and Moorman were lynched in towns where the press cheered the act of murder by the citizenry, defended it, and concluded with the sentiment that the town was glad to be rid of such unsavory characters. Often the editors painted a portrait of the lynched man in ugly scrawls and harsh shades in an effort to convince the public he was less than human, meriting the execution. If he were less than human, then stringing him up in so inhuman a way was nothing worse than the extermination of rats or insects.

These men weren't rats or insects. They had been popular businessmen with half the town patronizing their establishment—editors probably among them. No one sullied them then. Betts had a mother he wanted to protect. Browning had a wife whom he loved dearly and friends who considered him "manly and honorable." The two had paid for the funeral of a young man who had died alone and far from home while rooming at the San Juan Central. After the newspapers printed condemnations of Betts and Browning, many of the lynched men's friends protested, but neither paper published a retraction or softened the blows. Is this what brought them back in spectral rage?

Larger cities condemned lynchings outright, no matter how guilty the criminal. Justice in a civilized world was dispensed through the courts, *after* guilt was proven, Denver pointed out to her uncivilized sisters in the San Juan. The San Juan editors sent burning replies in the press, telling Denver, "vigilance committees are always right."

Some editors went another step further, turning the mob's brutal "justice" into jolly entertainment. Perhaps this was why Lee Quang's ghost groaned in the dark streets of Ouray. The *Solid Muldoon*'s ink grinned in delight, reporting how the "vigilance committee" dragged this son of China from the law officers "and shot [him] to death under their very noses."

The man was in the laundry business in Ouray since the late 1880s. In August 1891 he was accused of molesting an eight-year-old girl, her mother supposedly catching him in the act. The paper reported his action was "really too loathsome to mention," and that he was suspected of evil deeds before, "positive proof" simply lacking. If Lee Quang were suspected of being such a "brute," then why did the child's mother send her down to the laundry on her own? The truth was, there was a strong undercurrent of hatred for the Chinese, just because they were Chinese. Several mining towns campaigned against them, driving them out.

After the cold-blooded shooting of Lee Quang in the street, beaten and surrounded by a rough mob of the "best" citizens, The *Muldoon*'s David

F. Day didn't even bother to defend the action to the rest of the state. Instead, he chortled in print, "It was a Chinese picnic . . . one Chinaman, three pops and a hundred or two unknowns." Men from Marshall Basin had come over the pass to town that night and the *Muldoon* reported, "This was the first visit of the boys for many moons, and the entertainment was great. At 8:00 P.M. a Chinaman was wafted to the unknown hence."

Ouray was proud of its "record for speedy and unwritten justice," the *Muldoon* being the first to call for lynchings even for cattle rustlers. Proof of guilt was not required. Said the editor regarding Lee Quang's death, "Our people are always right and the *Muldoon* is always with them." With them, at the head of the mob, urging them on.

Lee Quang's ghost was a terrifying, bloody entity, more like a corpse than a spirit. In the dark of night, men, and sometimes women and youngsters, stumbled into it, over it, or were grabbed by its cold, lifeless fingers, a hideous groaning rattling its throat. "The stiffened corpse of a Celestial dropped out of the bushes into the arms of two astonished gentlemen while they were going up Second Street last week. Upon investigation the officers could not discover any dead Chinaman. This is the second incident of this kind and Ross contends these walking corpses are some species of phantom. They don't call him Mossy Ross for nothing."

Not all victims of "unwritten justice" hung around to haunt the site of their demise. Some simply reverted to their former occupations and gave up worrying about the consequences. Brabant Billy, William E. Thomas by birth, was a talented horse thief who pursued his trade with Hank Black (alias Andy Lowe), Hugh Angel, Indian Joe (a half white, half Apache), Tommie House, and a few other rustlers in the San Juan in the 1870s, according to the Pueblo *Chieftain*, having engaged in cattle rustling since 1875 from Saguache to Pueblo. Brabant Bill earned his name when he slipped away with a fine sorrel Brabant or Belgian draft horse from the Pueblo area and sold it to a farmer in the Paradox Valley. Bill and his associates used the old Ute trail through the San Juans when transporting stolen livestock, consequently giving it the name Horse Thief Trail.

In the summer of 1879 Bill and crew waltzed off with several horses from the Galloway ranch in Antelope Park, Hinsdale County. James P. Galloway was informed the rustlers were spotted in Alamosa. He went there himself and apprehended Bill, who, overwhelmed with guilt, signed a confession. Determined to deliver the thief to Hinsdale County for proper trial and certain execution, Galloway shackled his prisoner with a "side-line" chain attached at Bill's left wrist and left ankle.

Jim Galloway rode back over the Ute trail with Bill on a horse ahead of him. An amiable fellow, Bill engaged in casual conversation, slipping in questions as to the distance left to Lake City. Jim suspected Bill was "watching for a chance to escape." He kept a close eye on his prisoner and kept his pistol at the ready. Concerned for the state of Bill's soul, Galloway informed him a noose was surely waiting for him in Lake City and there was no escaping it, so he best say his prayers. Galloway was willing to see the man hanged; he just didn't want to be responsible for him cooking in the sulfur regions.

Sulfur and contrition were the last things weighing Bill's mind, but he certainly was opposed to hemp neckwear. As Jim stopped in the hills about seven miles above town, Bill knew his only chance to save his neck was now, with Galloway dismounted, never realizing Jim was willing to have a good excuse to finish him. Bending low behind a bush, Bill spurred his horse into a reckless gallop. Galloway warned him to stop, leveled his gun, and put a bullet neatly through the back of Bill's neck. The coroner's jury, summoned from Lake City, ruled the killing was justified, and Bill was unceremoniously buried beside the trail where it wound through the trees below Hill Seventy-one.

Bill loved the location but not the inactivity. He danced about briefly when a bear tinkered with his bones that winter. The following spring he was reinterred beneath a pile of rocks nearby. Rocks held him in place no better than dirt. In summer 1880 he was seen along the Horse Thief Trail with a string of workhorses and reported by a rancher who didn't know he was dead. In the fall of 1881 he was spotted galloping away with a horse from the Sparlings ranch and another from the Stone ranch. A few years later he was seen on the ridge near the Bridge of Heaven just at twilight, leading several horses and mules out of the Uncompahgre Valley. Cowboys chased the phantom and discovered that his track and that of the animals virtually vanished after a bend in the trail. The following day the reportedly missing horses were found in their pasture undisturbed. The cowboys were accused of using the ghost to go on a lark.

Suffering such disrespect caused them to guard the sightings of Brabant Bill among their own kind and word spread from ranch to ranch across the San Juan, a tale shared over a pot of smoky beans. Cowboys in

Antelope Park and the Uncompahgre and Paradox Valleys particularly blamed livestock disturbances on Bill. If horses suddenly bolted or a herd of them were stirred up for no visible reason, "that was Bill," as one crusty old sage rider explained. If a horse unaccountably wound up outside the fence, "that was Bill." If a barn was hit by lightning and burned down, but the animals were absolutely unscathed, that was Bill, too. Somehow he saved the horses he loved.

Bill became a mysterious shadow along the Horse Thief Trail and among some cowboys of the San Juan, he gained an odd sort of respect in death, a respect he never enjoyed in life.

Unlike most criminals, whose wraiths tear up the air in rage or terrify their onlookers with unearthly groanings, Bill Thomas seems to have mellowed into a gentleman thief among the noose-scarred throng. From the shadows, he still fondly gazes at the finest horses of the valley, so the old range lads say. They know he is there just beyond the dark green spruce boughs. And on a fine, soft evening when the sun slips out of sight and the stars begin to dot the clear sky with silver, one might be lucky to glimpse Brabant Bill on the high ridges of Horse Thief Trail, leading a big sorrel into the twilight.

9

IN THE ᏰOWELS OF THE ᎬARTH

Shrouded in a dark grey pall, the high peaks echo with a menacing rumble. Clouds curl over the top of Tower Mountain and Macomber Peak, stretching long fingers toward the ragged rocky face of Galena Mountain, where the remains of the Old Hundred boardinghouse seem tethered on the edge of eternity. Wind buzzes in the purple-hued tin and tugs at the skeleton porch, a splintered portal to death in the sky.

Cabled into the rock, the tin-clad boardinghouse has stood against storm and wind and snowslide on its perch twenty-three hundred feet above Cunningham Creek for nearly a century. Glass is gone from the windows. A boulder through the roof buried itself in a tangle of bedsprings and grub tables. In the kitchen, rodents gnaw the potato bin.

A few yards away via goat path stands the Old Hundred's tram house, still holding its rusty ore buckets aloft as if ready for the next shift. Built against the mountain, it conceals the mine tunnel's black mouth. The stench of rodents, gear grease, and debris clings to the raw interior. Sunlight splashes through cracks and gaping windows, playing across the purple-maroon of rusted gears and the rich red-gold of weathered wood.

Suddenly the storm blots the sun. A cracking and crashing thunderbolt tumbles a snarling echo down the mountain. No place for shelter on this sharp-toothed terrain, except within the Old Hundred's trembling buildings. On the back of gusts, rain lashes the tram house. Inside, the floors creak and cables chitter against the wind. Clouds embrace the mountain and, in an otherworldly grey mist that steals away the horizon and ground, leaving only the two buildings, there is a strange calm.

Fingers of mist form at the door of the boardinghouse, shapeless, elongating, and seem to be sucked into the tram house, drawn into the back, vanishing down the throat of the tunnel. At first they are only mist, pulled from the boardinghouse to the tunnel as if a current of air were funneling clouds through the ruins. Yet no wind stirs and the rain is now no more than the dampness of clouds kissing the purple tin.

Out of the silence creeps the sound of voices, men's voices, ever so softly . . . men's voices singing a quaint old ditty. Figures are there in the mist . . . a man on the porch . . . two in the doorway . . . several tramping on the path toward the cable house . . . several more in the building, all like shadows in the cloud, mist out of mist. Chatting, whistling, laughing, they all disappear into the tunnel, and those who took shelter here are struck mute, bewildered, unable to move. Only when the storm passes, and the sun floods the glistening rocky face of Galena Mountain once more, do they find speech.

These are the only miners left in the upper workings of the Old Hundred, also known as Seven Level. No one knows who they are—what they are. They are glimpsed only during storms, when clouds descend on the mountain. In 1979 a veteran miner from the Sunnyside said these misty men had been here since the Niegolds sold the property in 1904 and the new owners stepped up production, improving trails, building trams and quarters.

The crew worked alongside these apparitions, apparently accepting the ghostly miners as part of the mountain's guts. Fatalities on the Old Hundred properties were too few to account for the number of shadowy miners. Thus, rumor held that these ethereal men were responsible for the low death rate in the mine, keeping the living workforce safe. Sometimes a miner heard a man summon him by name and as he went to the spot, finding no one there, the hanging wall caved in where he had been previously working.

Ghosts of fellow miners hovering about in the dark stopes and tunnels were the commonest apparitions in the San Juan's boom days. Newspapers frequently gave them mention. Miners accepted them. Few argued against their existence. Most often these phantoms in the bowels of the earth were recognized as once living comrades who had met death in the mine they haunted. The majority of them appeared in the very spot where they had died or were first injured, horrifying spectacles trapped in the darkness for all eternity, an energy of emotion, silent, untouchable.

Among the ghastliest of these was Dominic Iorio, whose specter, with its crushed skull, bleeding eyes, and mangled limbs, appeared at chute 25 in the Liberty Bell Mine on Greenback Mountain, north of Telluride. The twenty-seven-year-old Italian immigrant was killed when fifteen tons of rock fell on him in 1901. Oddly, the man killed with him, David Saunders, did not return as a ghost, perhaps because his body was shipped to Aspen.

The ghost of Fred Ames, another bruised and mangled blue-grey shade, was said to appear on the skip whenever it passed the third level of the Last Chance Mine on Bachelor Mountain above Creede. Ames had been among a half-dozen men who violated company safety regulations by jumping into the skip when it already held its capacity of six miners. The skip tilted, crushing Ames against the timbers of the shaft, killing him instantly on November 5, 1893. From then on, it was believed, Ames's ghost was trying to escape the horrible mistake, jumping on the skip at level 3 and riding to the top, but vanishing before the skip reached the top.

This neurotic tendency in ghosts was a common phenomenon, giving rise to the theory that the disembodied spirit of a man who had been at fault in his own death was doomed to repeat his last painful moments for all eternity, doubling as a reminder to the living that they should not be "so stupid." "He died from his own stupidity" was the comment tossed off by one mine foreman when a Scotsman seemingly blew himself up in the Terrible Mine on December 3, 1890.

High above timberline on the north face of the St. Sophia Ridge, the Terrible lived up to its name. Considered more dangerous than the average mine (except those with bad Tommyknockers), the Terrible was cold, damp, and poorly timbered. On dreaded level 3, William McLaird, a thirty-eight-year-old native of Dumfries, Scotland, was forced to work alone when his trammer was sent to the surface because another man had met with an accident. Several hours later at the shift change, McLaird was nowhere to be seen. The search party found his body in the stope, torn apart by an explosion. The foreman blamed McLaird for the accident. Although he was an experienced miner, "he let either the candle or a match drop onto a box of caps which he was carrying." No one would ever know the actual facts, but doomed to the stope, William McLaird's grisly wraith twisted out those last agonies. When miners' lights fell on the scene, blood ran cold. The ghost staggered forward, its right hand torn totally away, the remaining shreds of its left hand holding back the intestines protruding through the bloody lacerations of the belly, the eyes torn from the sockets and the face ripped open and imbedded with rock fragments and bits of blasting caps. The apparition moved from the blood-spattered site of the explosion and stumbled along the passage with miners moving out of its way, only to vanish at the spot where the poor Scotsman had breathed his last, alone, blinded, terrified.

Before McLaird, the Terrible hosted a less neurotic wraith. The ghost of Johnnie McCabe appeared throughout the mine, mainly among the fellow miners who had known him in life. These men swore McCabe's life would have been spared had the mine foreman, John Frederick Geisel, properly closed up a thirty-five-foot shaft before sending men to work near it.

During the night shift on July 5, 1887, twenty-one-year-old Mc-Cabe, who had been working at the Terrible only four weeks, was instructed to clear away dirt and rock on the shaft covering. Immediately he went to work, although other miners told him the spot was a "death trap." The day shift boss, Dan McNeil, had taken a miner from the same spot to work elsewhere because McNeil "thought the cribbing over the shaft was dangerous." With too much dirt on the covering, the boards gave way, pulling the timbering from the walls. Dirt, rock, timbers, and John Mc-Cabe were swallowed by the murky water in the shaft.

In desperation McCabe's fellow miners tried to save him, but the shaft was too deep, too full of debris and water. They pulled out timbers, screamed for help and still could not find John McCabe in the muck until the following day. His body was taken to the kitchen, where the miners washed it, dressed it, and "laid it out" on one of the tables. Ed Doyle kept vigil over the corpse for five hours, while Foreman Geisel went to Ouray to make arrangements. The rest awaited the arrival of the wagon and Superintendent D. R. Reed.

Talking among themselves, the men learned others had nearly fallen into the same shaft on previous occasions, and anger wrapped around their grief. The shift bosses were aware of the "death trap," so why did Geisel allow work to continue? Many of these miners had been working in the Terrible only a few months, having bailed out of the nearby Virginius because of its horde of satanic Tommyknockers. At the Terrible they didn't blame the knockers (those were still in the Virginius). They blamed Geisel.

The mine was short of timbering, and the foreman was responsible. The mine was run without regard to safety, just profit, and the foreman was incompetent. They heard from day shift boss McNeil that Geisel had personally instructed John McCabe be put to work over the shaft, "since it was not dangerous for a competent miner," although McNeil told him it was. "I wouldn't work there myself," said McNeil. Larry Burns, who had been working the stope with McCabe and John Pierce, told the men that Geisel took a nap while they were trying to recover McCabe's body. Burns said Geisel remarked, "What's the difference? Men are cheaper than timber."

Seething and on the verge of detonation, the miners said they would all go down to Ouray with the body of John McCabe. Geisel threatened to discharge them if they went. He ordered only eight men to accompany the remains, eight he "knew wouldn't get drunk." He claimed too many of them had gone off for the Fourth of July celebrations and production was down for four days. If they went against his orders now "they could take their time and not come back." This unbolted the rage in several, and they quit on the spot, including Doyle, Burns, and Pierce.

The miners brought John McCabe down to Ouray where they "incited an intense feeling regarding the bad conditions of the mine and especially so against Foreman Geisel," according to the *Solid Muldoon*, July 8, 1887. Townsfolk took their side and the Knights of Labor demanded an investigation.

John F. Geisel and his toady, night shift boss Pat Hackett, denied the mine was unsafe, denied they were in any way responsible for the death of young McCabe, even denied that miners had quit because it was too dangerous near the open shaft. Hackett repeatedly replied to the union attorney's questions, "I ain't going to answer that." Superintendent Reed explained Geisel was competent, that he was just "easily excited and if the men don't do just as he wants them to, he is likely to get excited." In the end, the jury foreman declared, "We are unable to determine whether such accident was the result of carelessness on the part of said John McCabe or others."

Before the end of the month, miners at the Terrible were startled to see the shadowy ghost of McCabe hovering near dangerous spots. Unlike the gory wraiths of other dead miners, McCabe appeared alive, just blending into the darkness of the drifts and stopes. At times he seemed outraged, as if trying to tell them something. Other times he seemed to be "protecting" the miners from injury and was credited with saving the lives of Tim Casey, Dick Tremayne, and Matt O'Malley. These men were working a stope on level 2, one of them ahead of the others, on his back in order to check a fracture in the ceiling rock, just three feet above his face. A voice called to him and he crawled out. Down toward the beginning of the stope all three saw McCabe beckoning. They hurried toward him just as the fractured ceiling gave way, dropping several tons of rock where they had been working.

Dead miners made a habit of warning the living of impending disaster. Usually they appeared with no sound or they briefly called out a name to gain attention. These mine ghosts were often mistaken for a living man, for they appeared in ordinary miner's dress without the wounds and gore of death. George Berry's ghost in the Wyoming Mine on Engineer Mountain was said to warn the men against bad air. Hugh Fay, Charlie Proctor, Tom Eversole, and Archie McDowel, killed the same day in 1894 in the Amethyst Mine up Willow Gulch north of Creede, were said to be very active in saving their fellow miners.

These four men died when a raging fire in shaft house number three melted the cable on the skip, causing it to drop into the shaft. The men were climbing up the skip's shaft because the fire had downed the water pumps and water was flooding the ladder in the manway. As the skip came down the shaft it ground the men against the walls, dragging them into the flooded shaft and leaving hair, flesh, and bits of bone and brains in its path.

Months later, the energetic spirits of these men appeared in all parts of the workings, including the assay office, to warn of imminent disaster. The ghosts are believed to inhabit the Amethyst Mine still, despite its silence, and are reportedly seen on occasions among the old buildings.

In the Silver Lake Mine, the warning appearances of Gus Morrison's ghost were said to go unheeded. High above Silverton, the Silver Lake is in Arrastra Basin, an eerie place of drifting white mill dust, chilling sounds, sagging ruins, and piping marmots at the edge of a blue-green lake with no life in its clear waters. In the 1890s it was a booming area with several large producers. Gus Morrison hadn't been working long in the Silver Lake Mine when a cave-in crushed his skull. A few days later he appeared to his fellow miners, again and again, for four days in a row. They ignored the foggy shade until suddenly one of them, John Richards, was accidentally blasted to the next kingdom.

Other mines where the dead came back to warn the living were Camp Bird at Ouray, the Sheridan at Telluride, the Boston at Mineral Point, and the Butterfly west of Ophir. Sometimes the presence of ghosts wasn't so much to help miners avoid disaster, but was a warning of unavoidable death, a sort of premonition. Miners seemed to accept this and continued doing their work despite the unnerving appearance of their summoners.

Bill Ripley, who worked the Nutter and Clark Coal Mine up Burro Creek six miles southeast of Colona, had seen a "fetch" several days consecutively. A fetch is an apparition of one's self seen in the throes of death. Ripley's fetch appeared as if in the moment of a cave-in, and Ripley told his friend, Frank Balken, he thought he was "soon to be buried alive." Balken replied, "Be very careful, indeed." Ripley, who owned the *Ouray Times* with his older brother, must have believed his fate was unavoidable, for he continued to work. On February 27, 1885, Balken discovered Ripley's body beneath fallen timbers at the mine's entrance.

Dave M. Evans of Rico also saw a ghost that he believed pointed to his own death. Evans was in the Vestal shaft when a hazy white miner or "Whiteboots" appeared to him and said, "It is soon your time," causing his heart to "weaken." He discussed his imminent death with his wife, but she refused to listen. Saturday night he told her he wanted his remains buried beside his family in Hunter, Illinois. The next day he returned to work in the Vestal and while re-timbering, fell 368 feet to his death.

Alex Taylor who worked in the Bachelor Mine up Dexter Creek, north of Ouray, saw a summoner ghost as well. He spoke of it to his fellow miners and they ribbed him, ridiculing his concern that the thing meant death. When he saw the summoner, no one else was in the mine. Taylor related that a man went ahead of him into the stope, "stuck his candle into the wall and went to throwing down ore. Soon after he picked up a piece of rock and threw it, seemingly to attract my attention. The rock struck me on the brim of my cap in front, and I spoke to the man, but he did not answer." The *Ouray Herald* of August 15, 1895, reported, "Taylor insisted" the vision was "absolutely true, and could not be convinced otherwise. On the other hand it is positively known that there was no man in the mine." Taylor believed the vision predicted he was to die in the Bachelor, and when he told family and friends, they looked at him sideways. Three days later, on August 10, Alex Taylor's life was crushed out of him in a cave-in.

Immaterial entities who, like Taylor's summoner, had the ability to move material things, frequented the mines and were stronger than human muscle ever made them. Sometimes the ghosts held back tons of loose rock, blocked explosions of missed shot, or even slouched in to assist an old partner with double jacking. In the Sheridan, Henry Wesson's dead partner, an Englishman named Jimmie Prout, appeared with a hammer and drove the steel Wesson was holding. At the La Junta Mine on Ballard Mountain, south of Telluride, Jack Pulver's old partner, Mel Heitahrend, dropped in from the netherworld on many occasions to advise Jack in stoping angles for the best advantage to access the ore. He picked up shovels to remove muck or struck the walls with a pick to reveal hidden veins. Mel stayed a long time at Jack's side, and it was said Mel might still be wandering among the ruins in La Junta Basin, forlorn and weary, waiting for Jack to return. Curiously, Mel hadn't died in a mine accident, but in an avalanche on Ballard Mountain in November 1895.

A number of mine ghosts in the San Juan derived from miners who died in places other than the mine they haunted. The heroic Barney McGinn, "a man of brave heart and iron nerve," died from exhaustion at the Hotel Sanderson in Ouray. In January 1886, avalanche after avalanche swept through the Red Mountain mining district, crushing men and destroying buildings. Barney was one of the unflagging rescuers, digging out the victims two days in a row, and on the third day he tried to get through the dreadfully deep drifts to Ouray to summon more men to help open the road so the injured could be brought down to town. He fought the snow and wind and cold, taking a few moments of rest at the tollgate cabin, and continued on. He never reached his destination. The following day the mail carrier found Barney nearly lifeless in a drift above Ouray. A rescue team brought him to the hotel, but he died that night.

Thereafter, Barney's intense concern for the men of the Red Mountain district brought his spirit to their sides time after time, not only at the Dutton Mine in Champion Gulch, where he had been a shift boss, but also in the stopes of the nearby Genessee, Cora Belle, National Belle, Red Mountain, and Hudson. For years Barney's tireless ghost was as heroic and attentive as Barney McGinn had been in life. Fitz Mac wrote of him, "men speak of Mr. McGinn's ghost with tenderest affection and untold respect." He had been a man who put other's needs well above his own safety, a shift boss whose gentleness, fairness, and strength made him beloved and trusted among the men. The Irish Catholics were particularly ready to canonize him, for he was one of their own, not merely a ghost, but a "saintly apparition."

Barney McGinn aside, such deep affection was generally reserved for the personal spooks mining men dragged from place to place. These were visible to only a select few, usually the miner and his closest friends. Jack Lair, a miner at the Monte Carlo, north of Creede, kept company with the ghost of his brother George, who had died in 1899 in a Henson mine. Jack had conversations with George, took his supper with him, sang ditties with him, and shared jokes. Other than thinking Jack was a bit "off," his fellow miners were accepting of George. Jack went to work at the Commodore and George went with him, and a few of the Commodore miners reportedly became acquainted with the disembodied George.

Hauling vaporous family members down the shafts and along the drifts created no conflicts with management as long as the miner's work was done well and on time . . . except at the Union Carbonate Mine (U.C.) at Rico. With so many spooks flitting around Rico, the U.C. management must have grown nervous. At the mine a sign was posted: "Trafficking with ghosts within these workings STRICTLY FORBIDDEN." Rumor had it a young miner at the U.C. was injured because he turned to say something to the ghost of his granny.

Another distracting private ghost blew into the Lewis Mine, on the headwaters of Bridal Creek above Telluride, in spring 1896. It was unusual, not only because this ghost was beautiful, buxom, and female, but also because she was a personal ghost *not* related to the miner, William T. Hosking. The miserable twenty-nine-year-old Hosking was more than distracted by this presence and his fellow miners made his private ghost a public affliction. Born in England, Hosking had the manners of a gentleman and was too polite to shoo the ghost. In fact, his fellow miners believed he felt sorry for it. This encouraged the gossamer goddess to make more frequent appearances deep in the mine whenever Hosking was at work. In the bunkhouse at night Hosking would call out her name in his sleep—"Trixie!"—startling himself and others awake. Why she haunted him they could only surmise. Hosking was mute on the subject.

All the miners who worked with Hosking knew his ghost—apparently they recognized her themselves, for she was described as being "more handsome in death than she ever had been in her life." One can imagine how they tormented poor Hosking whenever he encountered the spook, for Trixie, also known as May Green, was a favorite girl of the line in Telluride. She had overdosed herself with morphine one morning that spring, staggered into the kitchen of Al Keech's restaurant, and collapsed. No one could save her. Gossips on the line said she killed herself because she was terribly in love with an English tom named Hosking and wanted Hosking to marry her and take her away from the grinding darkness, the grunting pain, the vomiting nightmares of the half-world. . . . William Hosking fled. He quit seeing her, so the gossips said, and she fell into despair. Her Denver relatives refused to acknowledge her in life and death. Her body was interred in a pauper's grave at Lone Tree Cemetery.

Did Hosking's guilty heart bring Trixie's spirit into the bowels of the Lewis Mine? He never shooed the ghost or turned away from it. Was there some misunderstanding and he actually had loved her, loved her still? The mystery remains cloaked in the silence of the empty Lewis.

Over the mountains at Rico, other lovers met deep in the stopes of the Enterprise Mine. Although women were banned from entering mines due to the adverse chemical reaction their presence had on the timbering, not to mention the hungry miners, there were a few exceptions, such as a special tour for "the ladies" or the request of a dying, trapped miner for his wife to be at his side. In the case of the Enterprise, the two miners had been dead for some weeks, and the request came from their fiancées.

Wyant Winkfield was the first of these lovers to lose his life. He was working Friday afternoon, June 12, 1897, in the bottom of a ninety-foot raise, tying bundles of heavy planks on a rope to be pulled up by his partners working the windlass above. As the planks neared the top of the shaft, some broke loose, hurtling to the bottom and pulverizing Wyant's head. The twenty-one-year-old Iowan was killed instantly. His brother, Leslie, who was working in another part of the mine, rushed to his side in horror. As the body was brought out, Wyant's father met the men at the mouth of the tunnel, but they restrained him from uncovering the corpse for the head was "fearfully crushed." Overwhelmed with grief "too terrible to witness," the heartbroken father had to be taken back to town.

Wyant was a beloved young man, popular with the men and women of Rico, but it was his cherished sweetheart, Katie Whinnery, whose heart was torn in two. She and Wyant were to be married on July 4 at the People's Congregational Church. She was still numb with grief when thirteen days later the town was shocked to hear forty-eight-year-old Captain Thomas H. Wagensler was killed in the same mine. Several tons of dirt buried him in the manway where he was re-timbering, and he suffocated before his fellow miners could dig him out.

Oddly, Captain Wagensler was also going to be married on July 4 in the People's Congregational Church. His heartbroken fiancée was Flora Keltow, and in her shock and horror, she "retired to her room, refusing all food."

Strange rumors came on the wind, hushed secrets passed around town: ghosts were seen in the Enterprise. . . . The elegant captain was in his Colorado National Guard uniform, the one he would have worn at the wedding . . . Johnny Muncaster and Fred Bristow had seen him. . . . And Leslie heard from Bill Murphy that Wyant's spirit was wandering among the Enterprise stopes along the Kitchen vein . . . could it be possible?

On the Fourth of July, with all of Rico busting out the fireworks and beer, band music rattling the windows, and miners shooting off guns in a riot of celebration, a group of men from the Enterprise secretly escorted Flora and Katie to the mine. Among the group were Fred Bristow, Leslie Winkfield, Bill Murphy, and Bill Parshall. Like thieves slipping into the king's treasury, they distracted the watchman with rocks tossed against a building, and when his back was turned, they scurried into the main portal.

The Enterprise was a damp and dangerous place, thus the men exercised extreme caution, assisting the ladies as they crept deep into the mine, full of expectation and dread. What if the ghosts did appear? . . . What if they were ghastly and gory—so many miners told of grotesque ghosts. . . . What if they terrified the ladies and something regrettable happened?

A chill fell over the group. Leslie wrapped his coat around Katie's shoulders. Someone did the same for Flora, but she gasped, "He is here!" and sank against the man.

"I see him," Murphy whispered. "Wyant—"

Flora recovered her composure and whispered back she didn't see Wyant. She saw Tom. In that dark and groaning place confusion and fear coiled round them, but Flora suddenly stepped forward and spoke to her captain, "becoming excited or elated." She reached out to the darkness and a "tear coursed down her cheek." Yet she smiled.

At the same time Murphy, Katie, and a few of the others clearly saw Wyant. His fine face seemed eerily "bright." Katie rushed toward him and the men pulled her back, fearing for her safety. "I will always love you," she told him. Turning away, she begged to be taken out of the mine.

Hearts pounding from the excitement, minds reeling from the brush with the mysterious, the women and miners remained in awestruck silence until they reached the mouth of the tunnel. Overwhelming, bewildering, frightening: an indescribable mix of emotions made them stand, gasping for air, half laughing, half crying. What had they seen? They knew it was real, yet each one seemed to see things the others had not. One thing was certain, Wyant and Thomas had reached through the veil of death. Described as "shining" and "bright," the apparitions reflected peace, both appearing strong, whole, untouched by the fatal injuries. The esoteric vision soothed the hearts of Katie and Flora, both believing it meant their loved ones were in a place beyond hurt and darkness, a place where one day they would see them again.

Unlike the ghosts of Wyant Winkfield and Captain Wagensler, who faded from the history of the Enterprise, one mining ghost in Telluride has bounced from basin to peak, bridging time and culture with the energy of blowflies on a corpse. In his quest for the return of his head, it is suspected he has even hitched a ride on the ski lifts, mistaking them for aerial trams (which is understandable, since a man without a head can't see where he is going). For several generations now the headless, angry, wild miner's name has been forgotten, but since only one headless ghost was known to ransack San Miguel County, present-day sightings also point to William Joseph Barney, victim of murder, treachery, and political duplicity. Killing him wasn't enough. His enemies had to abuse him after death.

His story is a tangled web, as tangled as the story of the brutal days of the labor wars that gave birth to it. From the first strike in Telluride in 1901 to the reign of assassinations and disappearances, on into the dark night of martial law, it was said ghosts massed in these hills like mist. No one will ever know how many men (and women who helped them), union and nonunion, were made to disappear in deep ravines and remote draws, for the mine owners' association had control of the town, the court, the jail, 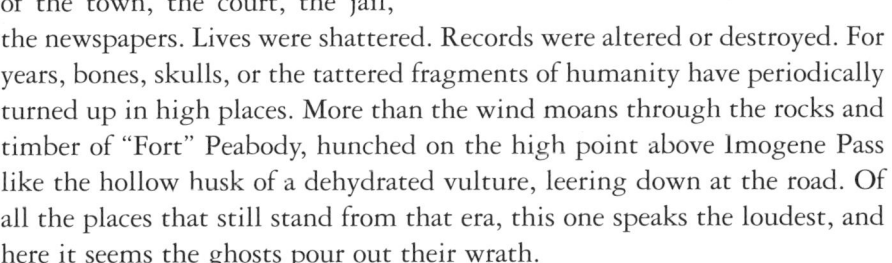 the newspapers. Lives were shattered. Records were altered or destroyed. For years, bones, skulls, or the tattered fragments of humanity have periodically turned up in high places. More than the wind moans through the rocks and timber of "Fort" Peabody, hunched on the high point above Imogene Pass like the hollow husk of a dehydrated vulture, leering down at the road. Of all the places that still stand from that era, this one speaks the loudest, and here it seems the ghosts pour out their wrath.

Fort Peabody was named for the governor in office at the time of the second strike, James Peabody, whom Sidney Lens called "as bitter an anti-union advocate as it was possible to install in the statehouse." The scruffy little roost above thirteen thousand feet was just big enough for the state militia sentries who had occupied it, their guns trained on the pass road below. It remains as a symbol, a reminder, a clenched fist against the unholy time when good men lost their judgment. It evokes powerful feelings of anguish, turmoil, horror, and shock in many who scramble into its sheltering walls today. There is a presence here. Voices come on the gusts through the stacked stones. Lights gleam in the darkness. Shadow and mists play as if seeking a way out of the past. Even the wind-tossed ghost of William Barney has ripped through the guard post like a hellhound sniffing out its lost enemies.

When William Joseph Barney vanished from Telluride on June 22, 1901, Fort Peabody had not been put in place. Years later his ghost attacked the post in savage anger, perhaps because it was so powerful a symbol of oppression. Barney's ghost began its career as a traditional mine spirit, protective of the men he had known. With time and the abuse of his bones and the loss of his skull, Barney gradually evolved into a wraith of wrath and fury, no longer contained in the damp galleries of the Smuggler-Union Mine, but encountered in Marshall Basin, Savage Basin, Turkey Creek Basin, on the Boomerang Hill road, the Imogene Pass road, the boardinghouses at Pandora, Tomboy, Smuggler-Union, and even later in the workings of the Idarado, a headless shadow glimpsed over a shoulder or a terrifying and grisly walking corpse with only a stump of neck protruding from his shoulders.

The ghost of Will, as his men knew him (management called him Barney), was first seen during the nightmare fire that ravaged the Smuggler-Union in November 1901. At that time no one knew where Will had gone, most believing he had simply left the territory in June of that year. He had been a shift boss on level 9, and during the fire, when deadly smoke was sucked into the tunnel and suffocated the stopes and shafts, several men said Will ran up to them, told them to get out, a fire was at the mouth of the tunnel. He grabbed some by their arms, helped one up a ladder. Harry Kangas, Angelo French, Al Floritto, Henry Winklehake, and Peter Beck, all working on the ninth level, were warned or assisted by Will Barney. Later they were told they had seen Carey "Red" Barclay, not Barney. Both men were about the same size and both had sandy-red hair. Winklehake and several others insisted they had seen Will—perhaps he had come back to town and was back at work. Red Barclay was in the ninth level, but they found him dead in a heap at chute 13. Henry Winklehake was certain Will Barney had saved his life; "the man has a face you wouldn't mistake for any other." Unknown to Winklehake and the miners, William Joseph Barney was very much dead.

Will had come to Telluride from Nevada in late summer of 1900, securing employment at the Smuggler-Union Mine. His wife Sarah and their daughter Florence were left at Sarah's father's farm in Larimer County. Will was a strong, hardworking man who stood six-foot-two-inches tall, 210 pounds of lean spring steel, sandy-red hair and mustache, bright blue eyes, and a "ready smile." He shunned confrontation, avoiding situations that might trigger his Celtic ire, because he knew his strength mixed the wrong way with his temper might prove fatal. He was a loyal man, not easily persuaded from his views or his duties.

At the Smuggler, Will was made shift boss over a workforce that labored under the contract system, which had been instituted when the New England Exploration Company purchased the property. Bulkeley Wells, vice president of the Boston company and son-in-law to the owner, Colonel Thomas Livermore, had traveled to Telluride in 1899 to oversee the property transfer. He spoke with the men, assuring them their jobs were secure, but had "words" with a young miner, Vincent St. John, a member of the 16 to 1 Miners' Union, Number 63. The ugly Coeur d'Alene strike of 1892 and the victorious strike for the Western Federation of Miners in Cripple Creek in 1894 were warning beacons in the mind of Wells, who detested unions and union men behind his suave smile and aristocratic bearing. St. John was marked.

Under the contract system, a miner received payment for how many fathoms he mined, a fathom being six feet high, six feet long, and the width of the vein. The width of a vein varied dramatically, and ground varied as well, some veins running through hard, some through soft. Thus, for a miner to earn a living wage, he often had to work twelve or more hours a day when the eight-hour day had gone into effect. If he failed to meet his fathom quota, he received no pay, becoming no more than a serf, owing more at the end of the month to the company than the company paid him.

By May 1901, twenty-four-year-old Vincent St. John had become president of the 16 to 1 Miners' Union. A dynamic, energetic, selfless man who "radiated sincerity and integrity," in the words of James P. Cannon, who knew him, St. John built the local union into an intelligent force of unified men. After repeated requests to abolish the contract system and guarantee a wage of three dollars a day for an eight-hour shift, St. John called a strike.

Pickets were put in place at the Smuggler-Union Mine, its Bullion Tunnel, and at the mill at Pandora. Meanwhile, those men who were nonunion, one being Will Barney, were kept on by management as guards. Fearing trouble from the strikers, mine manager Arthur Collins requested Sheriff Oscar Downtain deputize these guards, so they could legally carry concealed weapons and arrest anyone who might be a threat. Downtain agreed. Will had a reputation for "cool headedness" and "was not given to drunkenness nor discharges of hot air." And Downtain, although a friend to union men, needed all the assistance he could get. Unfortunately, in his fear of the mounting tensions, Downtain was too quick to deputize a few of the other Smuggler-Union guards, such as John Shay and Jack Hyde, who were far less conservative in throwing their weight around than was Will. Hyde developed a dislike for Will, and Will made a point to avoid him.

During the first few weeks of the strike, St. John personally spoke with nonunion men at the mine, asking them to "join their brothers in solidarity." St. John, with his "boyish good looks, simple modesty, astounding courage," genuine compassion for others and unswerving idealism, had an almost irresistible appeal to the miners. Nonunion men daily swelled the ranks of Local 63. The New England Exploration Company hired detectives to join as spies. Charles Painter and his Telluride *Daily Journal* spewed venom on St. John and the union. The *San Miguel Examiner* gave the strikers fair reports, urging the *Journal* to cease its slanderous attacks. Tension mounted.

On June 11 Charley Carlson, a Liberty Bell miner, was walking down the road by the Smuggler-Union company's Bullion Tunnel on his way to town. Jack Hyde stopped him. Hyde made accusations against Carlson, knocked him down, kicked him, and pulled a gun on him, firing twice near his head. Carlson fled to town, reporting the attack to the police, but afraid to swear out a warrant, spoke with the *Examiner* and St. John. That night Will Barney went to town to have a chat with St. John. Will was "fed up" and perhaps ready to join the union men.

Later, at the Metropole saloon, Will came up against Jack Hyde, John Shay, and Shay's friend Samuel Servis, a twenty-three-year-old New York steeplechase jockey who worked as night watchman at the Bullion boardinghouse. Hyde disliked the rumor that Will had been "associating" with St. John and leveled accusations of "traitor" against him. Will's Celtic ire boiled over during the "word scrap" and he pulled his gun, shooting into the floor. Hyde was gleeful and fanned the flames. The saloonkeeper said he would fetch the town marshal. Will growled, "The marshal can't arrest me! I am a deputy and these men are the trouble."

The town marshal did arrest him, bringing him before the police magistrate that night and he was fined for "the illegal discharge of a firearm." Since this was his first offense, the magistrate did nothing further.

That weekend Manager Collins hired fifty scab miners to resume production in the Smuggler-Union and marched them past the pickets with an armed escort. Will was put back into his position as shift boss, retaining his authority as a deputy and thus being required to remain armed as well.

Rumors were rife that Collins was paying one of the union men to keep him informed of St. John's plans. Around this time St. John spoke again with Will Barney, this time at the Bullion Tunnel. Although Will had his wife Sarah and little daughter Florence uppermost in his mind, the injustice and deception and infamy were too much for him to stomach. On Saturday, June 22, Will went down to town to see Vincent St. John, having informed his employer he would return Sunday night.

William Joseph Barney never returned. On Monday the mine foreman Mel Robbins and Sheriff Downtain's payroll deputies, Spellman and Beatty, made inquiries, discovering threats had been made against Barney. Some thought Jack Hyde had made the threats; others thought union men had. Some witnesses claimed to have seen men dragging one man down the railroad track late Saturday night. Another said he had seen a gang of men beating up one man behind Stubbs and Jackway's lumberyard when the victim fired one shot and broke away from his attackers.

Tuesday morning Spellman and Beatty discovered blood on the railroad ties near the lumberyard. They followed a trail of blood down the track to the bridge on the lower end of Spruce Street. A gun, believed to be Will's, was found under the second railroad culvert below the wye. One cartridge had been fired, giving credence to the story of the gang attack. From the evidence, the law concluded Will had been "violently dealt with" and his "body thrown in the river." The river was searched each day without results. When Sheriff Downtain returned to town, he continued the investigation, but nothing more could be discovered.

As days plowed by, tension between the strikers and mine management knotted tighter. Collins put more scabs to work. He armed his scab workforce and hired more guards, threatening the union's power to call for negotiations.

On July 3, a gun battle broke out, leaving one union man dead and two nonunion men dead. In the end, Manager Collins signed an agreement with St. John, guaranteeing a wage of three dollars per eight-hour day. The strike was won. Peace, although strained, returned to Telluride. At this time the still-seething management began a wholesale campaign to destroy St. John and the union. Only now did they publish notices of rewards for "the recovery of the body of W. J. Barney" and for evidence leading to the "conviction of the party or parties who caused [his] death," and they spread word

St. John himself was the murderer. Arthur Collins, newspaperman Charles Painter, and other anti-union businessmen joined the statewide Citizens Alliance, whose blatantly overt goal was "to destroy" the Western Federation of Miners and all its local unions "by whatever means necessary."

In November 1902 Manager Collins was assassinated. The Smuggler-Union was shut down. Shocked by the coldly calculated assassination, even Painter failed to point his ink-stained finger at St. John this time, writing, "local organizations are not responsible." Yet, as the news burned up the telegraph and telephone lines, outraged editors across the state picked up what Painter had started, laying the murders of Collins, Will Barney, and various mysterious disappearances on St. John and his union men.

Bulkeley Wells was put in charge of the Smuggler-Union company. Determined to destroy the union "by whatever means necessary," as the Citizens Alliance had earlier declared, Wells and his business associates "imported" two gunmen, Robert Meldrum and Willard Runnels. Warrants were issued for St. John and other union leaders.

St. John, who had gone to Denver, was labeled a fugitive by Wells and his cronies. They sent Meldrum after him. The Western Federation of Miners sent St. John on legitimate business to Idaho, hoping in his absence his enemies would cool off. Meldrum's failure to arrest St. John prompted Wells to hire Pinkerton detectives to harvest him. St. John's location was no secret, and many Colorado newsmen saw Wells's obsession and the charges as ridiculous, blasting the affair as "theatrical" and "nonsense." Yet Wells persisted.

On September 5, 1903, a second strike was declared on behalf of the mill men, and once again the Smuggler-Union and other large mines in the area were crippled by walkouts and pickets. This strike grew ugly as strikers were arrested, deported, and mistreated. Telluride was turned upside down. When the Mine Managers' Association screamed for military intervention, their new friend in the statehouse, Governor James Peabody, obliged. The state couldn't afford the expense of posting troops, so the mine owners advanced Peabody nearly a half-million dollars.

In November, state troops arrived in San Miguel County. As the situation worsened, martial law was declared. Bulkeley Wells, a captain in the Colorado National Guard, organized a local troop of anti-union businessmen and cowboys. The new, union-hating Sheriff Cal Rutan deputized more gunmen. Rutan had served as sheriff before Downtain and was now back in office, seething with animosity for anyone connected to the union.

Wholesale arrest of union pickets began, and the new president of Local 63, Guy E. Miller, was arrested. Union hall was raided. Homes were searched and raided, and union wives and children were left weeping as their men were shoved onto trains at the point of bayonets and deported. Eventually Captain Bulkeley Wells was put in command of the district—a jackal in charge of the hen coop.

The nightmare seemed endless, but with the wholesale deportation of union men and mass hiring of scabs, the strike was broken, November 28, 1904. Captain Bulkeley Wells was puffed up with self-importance. He had been promoted to general in the state militia and strutted his power in Telluride like a prize cock. His obsession with the charismatic St. John regurgitated during these quieter times, and he put up a reward of $6,000 for the man he termed "the murderer of W. J. Barney."

The Pinkertons were still on the job, and when a small union fish named Steve Adams was arrested and brought to the Idaho penitentiary in 1906, Pinkerton agent James McParland marked him for his showpiece. A confession was manufactured and Adams was told he would be "taken care of" when he signed it. His protest brought threats of certain execution, and Adams signed the document. McParland then informed Wells that Adams had confessed to killing Arthur Collins and to burying Will Barney. Wells, Deputy Runnells, and another Pinkerton detective went to Idaho and secretly escorted Steve Adams to Telluride, so they claimed, and said he showed them where W. J. Barney's body had been buried, although snow prevented them from digging it up. They returned Adams to Idaho in time for his trial on murder charges there.

Idaho failed to convict Adams, and he was extradited to Colorado to stand trial for the murder of Arthur Collins. Wells and Runnells personally brought him from Caldwell to Telluride. In the meantime, Vincent St. John, now president of the miners' union at Burke, Idaho, was arrested. Sheriff Rutan brought him to Telluride, where Bulkeley Wells smugly informed him, "Now you will hang." He was charged with complicity in murders committed in Telluride in 1901 and 1902, including the murder of Will Barney. The only evidence against him was the manufactured confession of Steve Adams. Once again, the charges found no footing and St. John was released. Wells was beside himself.

The *Journal* admitted, "Bulkeley Wells . . . has been relentless to punish such men as . . . Vincent St. John . . ." Wells's personal vendetta was obvious even to his friends. Unable to secure a rope around St. John's neck, Wells used the newspapers to hang him. When Will Barney's skeleton was finally found, Wells personally instructed the *Journal* to print the banner headline that Barney was "brutally murdered by St. John." He claimed a young stablehand named Sam Servis had witnessed St. John and six union men pull Barney from his horse on the night of June 22, 1901, in Gus Roth's livery. He claimed Servis heard St. John say, "Don't kill him here." They then took him out and beat him nearly senseless, then managed to make him walk up the Boomerang Road several miles, where he was shot and his corpse dumped behind a log. A few hours later St. John and Oscar Carpenter returned and threatened Servis to keep his mouth shut . . . and after that Servis supposedly disappeared, most likely "done away with."

Some weeks or months or even years later (the discrepancies were between Wells's version and Runnells's), Will Barney's stinking corpse attracted attention, but only to union men, since no one else on the Boomerang Road to Alta apparently noticed. To ward off an investigation, St. John sent two men up to bury the putrid remains of Barney. One of these undertakers got drunk and started talking, so St. John brought Steve Adams in to move the body lest it be found, or so said Wells.

Adams and union Secretary-Treasurer Oscar Carpenter, according to Wells, then went up to do the reburial. The clothes were removed and shoes cut off, these items being placed in a separate hole from the bones. Oddly, all this burying and reburying was done within a few yards, which made no sense whatsoever if men were bent on hiding evidence from previously known locations.

Deputy Sheriff Willard Runnells, whose version of the Adams confession contradicted several points made by Wells, claimed to be the person who found Will Barney's skeleton. The bones were brought to town and kept in a secure place, no coroner's inquest called. Wells knew a coroner's inquest would turn up the real facts, as other inquiries had proved Pinkerton agent McParland manufactured Adams's confession. The confession was thrown out as evidence in Adams's own trial when he was acquitted of the murder of Arthur Collins, even though Wells and Runnells were allowed to testify about the confession.

In the case of Will Barney, the earliest suspicions fell on Jack Hyde, who was rumored to have help from spies in the Telluride Miners' Union. Pinkerton spies at Cripple Creek knew Steve Adams there, before his appearance in Telluride. Since Barney was already dead a year before Adams arrived on the scene, it was impossible for Adams to know who had killed Will. McParland also manufactured Sam Servis as a witness, for Servis had never actually worked at the livery, but was a Smuggler-Union watchman at the boardinghouse "up the hill." He was also known to be anti-union and a friend of Jack Hyde and John Shay. If he ever made any testimony, it was paid for and probably by management or Pinkerton. Nor did Servis get "done away with" for what he had seen. His wife was in New York, and to her bosom he returned in 1902.

Most astounding, Will Barney brought suit for divorce against his own wife in April 1902, when he was already dead. He was not present in court, but his attorney was. The county judge, J. M. Wardlaw, was in the pocket of the Mine Managers' Association. Likewise, Barney's wife, Sarah, was strangely represented by H. M. Hogg, the expensive and powerful attorney for the Smuggler-Union company. Sheriff Cal Rutan, who knew Barney was missing and assumed dead, who had reward posters plastered from Tel- luride to Durango, was also pres- ent at this extremely mystifying divorce case. Sarah, probably un- der duress, admitted to adultery with a Windsor Sylvester, and the dead plaintiff's case was immediately granted. Sarah and her daughter vanished from Telluride that day. News of the proceedings was hushed. Sarah knew some- thing, and the mine owners didn't want her telling it. Was Will actually alive and his "ghost" not a ghost at all? Was the skeleton Will's or that of some other hapless victim of the mine owners' treachery?

Meanwhile, the ghost popped up at the Smuggler-Union from time to time, with head in its proper position, until Bulkeley Wells confiscated what were believed to be Will's remains for "safe keeping." Will was never properly buried, nor were his wife or daughter informed of the discovery of his bones. Instead, Wells, still obsessed with destroying Vincent St. John (who was now head of the miners' union in Goldfield, Nevada), took Will Barney's moldy skull and loaned it to his business friends around Telluride. Charles Painter, John A. Adams, J. C. Anderson, W. B. Van Atta, and others displayed the skull in their shop windows with a sign proclaiming, "See for yourself! The Grewsome work of the Telluride Miners Union and Vincent St. John." They gladly pointed out a ragged bullet hole on the side, toward the back.

As years turtled by and Wells went to other climes, Will Barney's skull was no more than a curiosity, now forgotten, wrapped in brown paper and stored in an attic. Stories of an angry, headless ghost, "a miner looking for his head," were tossed about by schoolchildren. Miners occasionally ran into the same rampant creature in the drifts and stopes or on the Boomerang wagon road near the remains of the old sawmill.

Around 1939 four young men, George Cappis among them, were playing in an abandoned building at the corner of Pacific and South Fir. George discovered a brown paper sack containing a skull with a bullet hole in the side. George brought the skull to Dr. Joseph Parker, county coroner and beloved town physician. Nothing could be done to discover the identity of the long dead, thus once again Barney's skull became a curiosity, collecting dust on the high shelf in the hospital at the top of North Fir Street. (Dr. Parker's son recalled seeing a skull without a bullet hole that sat on his father's desk in the Colorado Avenue office, but this was most likely a second skull, since George Cappis worked at the hospital and knew the skull he had found was there on the shelf.) For years Dr. Parker left the skull at the hospital; then, when the place was closed down, the skull was again lost, possibly given away as a souvenir.

William Joseph Barney, now consumed by the Celtic ire he so carefully had guarded, will never find his peace. Doomed to his impossible quest, he continues to ride the howling winds, to suddenly appear on the ski lifts for a brief moment out of time, to bang along the deserted stopes and crosscuts in these hollow hills, to stream through the startled tourists at Fort Peabody, forever searching for his head. His wraith is forever angry at those who really killed him, and forever whipped into a frenzy by those who insulted his dignity when they used his remains to dishonor good men.

10

$\mathcal{D}$EAD $\mathcal{F}$ROG $\mathcal{W}$ALKING

A naked moon glares over the Animas River valley, flashing on the water in search of her lost children. Once they were abundant. Once the valley was their marsh. Once their evening chorus rattled the night air like the vespers of totally squiffed monks who had glockenspiels jammed in their throats. Now they are silent.

Yet there is a sharp, raspy call. Then another . . . and another. The hay fields on the banks of the Animas suddenly resound with the din. The dead have awakened. They trample the hay in their onslaught, choke the atmosphere with their staccato call, and assault the rancher's quarters like a nightmare regiment from Calaveras County with "Dan'l Webster" at their head. The rancher spots them floating outside his window, sees their slippery, spotted corpses glinting in the moonlight, their wee arms and legs stiff with rigor mortis, and their webbed hands splayed as if waving at him. He hears their rasping call expand, like sticks drawn rapidly over the riffle of a sluice. The thumping on roof, windows, and walls, coupled with the obnoxious riffling, finally drives the rancher out of his house in his nightshirt, a Winchester in his hands. One blast at the moon silences her dead children.

At dawn the rancher sees dead frogs hovering above his hay field. On closer inspection he discovers the frogs are suspended by means of willow pikes planted in their bowels, the other end stuck in the earth: warning fetishes left by angry spirits.

This ground wasn't always hay fields. Once the Animas River slogged through bog and marsh here, creating breeding sloughs for blue-ribbon mosquitoes, the Striped Chorus Frog, and the Northern Leopard Frog. The frogs were so numerous that the first homesteaders who staked the marshy areas were ribbed incessantly for "jumping sacred croaker grounds" and warned to watch for reprisal from the "great froggie spirit" when the marshes were drained.

The first return on those fields wasn't from spirits, but from hay that fetched $100 per ton that fall. Other ranchers followed suit, and the frogs were driven from the sloughs the length of the valley. In the second or third spring the rumors began: Sackett was hearing frogs, so were Gaines, the Trimbles, and others. Frogs were singing in the hayfields where marsh had been, dead frogs, *ghost frogs*, ratcheting out an eerie sound in the moonlight, hundreds and hundreds of *ghost frogs*.

Frogs, being creatures of habit, might have simply returned to the old breeding grounds despite the absence of water. Or the din might have been spirit related, either to the disembodied variety produced by defunct frogs, or to the windy variety produced by canned cowboys.

Cowboys were responsible for a vast number of gaseous critters roaming the San Juan. The frog story belonged to a bowlegged old range man named Charlie Lewis (retired to Nebraska), who had spent most of his life astride a horse. He noted that the Animas rancher who was assaulted by frog spooks had found the bottom board of a sluice in his hay field. He also pointed out the frogs became increasingly larger after death, eventually big enough to cinch up and ride for bucking bull . . . frogs.

Most cowboy-affiliated spooks had a tendency to grow in time— range grass was exceedingly nutritious. One of the well-known "windies" of the 1880s told of an enormous bull phantom with halitosis so bad it could kill a man a half-mile off. This bull's entourage consisted of prodigious poultry ghosts produced when old Mrs. Fisk rung the chickens' necks. The story had its origins in northeast Colorado, probably on the Iliff ranch, but it traveled to the southwestern part of the state before 1890, most likely in the hip pockets of restless, overripe ranch hands. In southwestern Colorado the bull became an entire herd of phantom cattle running terror across the range.

A cowboy's above-average ability to channel spirits and see visions stemmed from his diet of beans and Taos Lightning and the habitual sniffing of greasewood and cowhide. A man too long in the sage became a confederate of the spirit world. He was never judged by how much he drank, but what he saw when he was drunk. Add to his profession of range rider a Gaelic tribal parentage, and the poor lad saw more spirits than he could bear.

One of those so powerfully afflicted was Will Gordon, a cowboy for the Carlisle outfit that ran herds in New Mexico, Utah, and Colorado. On his religious excursions to the dance halls and saloons of Durango in the 1880s, Will chatted with the departed souls of dead birds, dead monkeys, and a dead faro dealer. Once arrested for shooting holes in floors and buildings, Will claimed self-defense: he was being assaulted by the ghost of a nipping parrot that had belonged to a dance hall girl.

Will was arrested on other occasions for too much familiarity with spirits and free use of firearms in Durango, particularly when he and his fellow cowboys used bullets to make a few strangers dance. His conviction and fine in 1892 produced no change in his habits. In 1894 he was riding herd in the Lone Cone area and shot a bear that was too close to the cattle. The following night the enraged bear's ghost, now pale white and much larger than it had been in life, charged Will, forcing him to unload his six-shooter, hitting a nearby pack horse. The desperate, screaming Will was saved only by the swift action of a fellow cowboy. Known for roping everything from mountain lions to eagles, the cowboy, with calm mastery, swung his lariat, snagged the spirit, spun it round his head, and hurtled it off to the stars. He should have lassoed Will.

Cowboys on the eastern flanks of the San Juan region had more sinister bogies besieging them and their herds. These were a pack of dogs that eventually became known as "The Devil's Curs."

Large, powerful animals "endowed with a larger share of dog reason than is usually given to man's best friend," according to the *Saguache Chronicle,* this pack began as a mere pair of renegade herd dogs in the valleys west of Saguache in the 1870s. They took to culling the herd on their own, under cover of darkness. Together they selected a calf or bony old cow, drove it out of the herd, and shared a sage-side dinner in a remote wash. Three cowboys who set out to exterminate the bandits were lured by the wily dogs into a tangle of greasewood and sage. While the men cursed the snags of the thicket, the dogs disappeared from the maze. Determined in their deadly mission, the cowboys recruited a dozen more riders and set out to hunt the dogs to their doom the following day.

The dogs were spotted running parallel to the main cattle herd, and the men gave chase. With uncanny intelligence, the two outlaws led the cowboys into the greasewood, doubling back beneath the brush, hiding until the party passed, running in the bottom of arroyos, and finally separating to make tracking more difficult. Bud Stowe got a bead on the northbound cur and dropped it with his carbine. The other escaped into the twilight.

With one horse lame, a shotgun destroyed, straps and cinches broken, the scratched and bruised cowboys gave up the chase, satisfied the other dog would not return, especially if they displayed a warning. The bloody corpse of its companion was hung head down on a post.

In the days following, the corpse vanished. No sign of track, no sign of vulture or bear, no sign of maggot or beetle was found near the post. Before summer arrived, two dogs again deviled the herd by night, and no matter how skilled the tracker, no one could bag them. They were the devil's own.

As years passed, other fierce phantom dogs joined the pack, and it ranged from the Saguache drainage south to La Garita Creek. By the 1880s the pack was tormenting cattle and sheep as far away as the flanks of San Luis Peak and had reached the valleys near Creede and Antelope Park by 1894. Encounters with these demon dogs were gruesome, nightmarish. Even sober cowboys, with their sun-roasted, tough exteriors, lost composure recounting their tales. According to the *Creede Candle*, the worst incident nearly claimed the life of Mose Pickett. Mose was a range boss, a big, hard-nosed puncher who, with his horse, was a mobile arsenal of rifles, pistols, shotgun, knives, and half a dozen cartridge belts, a man ready for bear, bull, or desperado. Nothing (except marriage) scared Mose Pickett.

One September he and the boys were out on the range west of Spar City, rounding up the herd. Several nights in a row they had been disturbed by the eerie ululations of coyotes, a weird wailing that was different than the usual coyote calls. On the fourth morning they discovered a calf's ripped-open carcass in the nearby oak brush. Mose and four of the boys set out after the coyotes, believing this was all they were up against. They tracked the animals in circles, through thicket, and over ridge, finally spotting them in a sagey draw in Antelope Park at sundown. Instead of coyotes, Mose was face to face with a pack of powerful and fierce, smoky-grey herding dogs, their eyes yellow, their muzzles smeared with dripping blood, a mangled calf at their feet. Mose raised his Winchester and the dogs flashed into the sage.

Spurring their horses, Mose and the boys surrounded the thicket, closing in, shooting into the brush as they went. They tightened the circle until no spot afforded escape for the pack. They emptied their guns into the defiant beasts, which they saw twisting and lurching between the bushes, with unnerving howls and hideous snarls, a "sound straight out of the bowels of hell." All fell silent. Mose dismounted. He pushed his way through the sage and suddenly roared out a curse. The dogs had vanished. Not one corpse, not one drop of blood, not even fur was caught on the clawing brush.

The men remained uneasy that night, sleeping closer together. They started at every distant coyote's lonesome howl. They jumped up at the sound of snapping twigs or piping night bird. Late in the night, Mose saw eyes staring at him from across the fire . . . first one pair . . . then two . . . then more . . . The pack had come for him. He rushed into the dark with his Winchester and a pistol, screaming curses, blasting the shadows, and shot himself in the leg. Although out of commission for this season, Mose Pickett vowed to "do up" the demon pack the following summer, once recovered from his wound.

Despite heroic determination and good tracking sense, Mose failed to do up the phantom dogs. They continued to toy with him, allowing him to shoot them even at close range, yet just as his fingertips touched the carcass, the dead vanished into the twilight like smoke. The Devil's Curs were destined to stalk the range for all eternity.

Not all dogs from the nether regions behaved as miserably as that bandit pack. Most were the faithful companions they had been in life, still protective, still waiting for missing masters, still trying to save what they had lost.

After more than a hundred years, the speckled black-and-white hound of James M. Hardin continues to guard its master's grave on Leopard Creek, about four miles north of Placerville. Hardin had built a cabin in July 1880 at the creek's edge, just below the settlement of Leonard, and set up selling supplies for the miners on their way to the Telluride area. He had left his wife and young daughter in Denver, but brought as his sole companion the speckled hound. Described as a "quiet, inoffensive man," with no need to carry a weapon, Hardin conducted business throughout the summer and fall, adding liquor to his stock of goods.

On Christmas Eve of that year, Hardin and a Southerner named Joseph Martin were drinking in Hardin's cabin. They stepped outside, and abruptly Martin drew his Colt .45, pointed it at Hardin, and pulled the trigger. Hot lead ripped through Hardin's chest and out his right lung. Rushing out of his own cabin nearby, E. J. Trotter saw Hardin stagger backwards and fall dead. Martin leveled his Colt at Trotter, and Trotter dove back into his cabin, but a bullet struck him in the arm, shattering his elbow. Cautiously, Trotter's friend, Ross, peered out the window and saw Martin calmly strolling back to the cabin where he had been quartered since spring, a distance of three hundred yards.

Martin's cabin mates, John Cavanaugh and D. R. Reed, were threatened at gunpoint while Martin packed his bedroll, "cursing and muttering to himself," according to their later testimony. The Southerner strolled out the door and was never seen again. Witnesses failed to ascertain the reason Martin had coldly murdered James Hardin, except they said Martin "was a hard drinker" and "when in liquor, was very quarrelsome." James Hardin was buried near his cabin.

In the first few weeks after his death, his speckled hound attempted to dig up his corpse, "whining pitifully." Finally the dog gave up and took to lying across the grave during most of the daylight hours. The men tossed him scraps of meat. Many times they tried to coax him from his post, without success. Early in spring 1881 the speckled hound was found shot dead on the grave. Rumor pointed the finger at some of the miners, claiming one of them simply "was annoyed at the dog's stubborn faithfulness" and sent him off to his departed master. Another suspicion fingered Joseph Martin. He was said to have come through the area and shot the hound out of "plain cussedness." With the loud racket of the San Miguel boom, the dog and Hardin were soon forgotten, until Gus Talbot blew down the trail on his way to Rico in summer 1881.

Talbot, staying in the settlement a few days, was captivated by a seemingly stray white hound with black speckles over his hide, a feathered tail, and floppy ears. He inquired of Cavanaugh the hound's ownership, hoping he might take the dog with him to Rico, should it be without a master. Cavanaugh was thoroughly baffled. He asked Talbot to point out the dog in question. Talbot led Cavanaugh to the grave and said, "This dog, sir." On the grave, clearly visible and fully animated, was James Hardin's hound. Although Cavanaugh knew the hound was dead, he told Talbot to take it. Talbot reached for the animal, "his hands passing right through it," upsetting the Rico gentleman to such a degree that he fled for home without delay. The speckled hound remained, year after year. Even after the settlement sank into the earth itself, the hound was said to keep watch over James Hardin's final resting place, a lonely guardian of a forgotten master at the edge of Highway 62.

In Hermosa Park, up Hotel Draw where the old stage stop known as Flag Station once stood, ranged the spirit of a dog called "Shep." Unlike the speckled hound, Shep was not alone. His diaphanous companion was a great grey wolf, the same he had befriended in life.

Shep had belonged to Perly Wasson, a stage-company owner who holed up at the Flag Station a few years in an attempt to keep the Rockwood-to-Rico line operating through the winter. Shep was the only canine in the area, and Wasson thought it an entertaining curiosity when Shep fell in love with the grey wolf. The wolf appeared each morning on the hill behind Flag Station, waiting for Shep to bring him a share of his breakfast. If Shep was slow to respond, the wolf "raised an indignant howl," according to the *Dolores News*. The two spent hours running together through the forests and across Hermosa Park, grace in motion, spirits free. For two years the pair was a stage-line attraction, with Rockwood-to-Rico patrons craning to catch a glimpse of the curious companions. Status as celebrities ended when the wolf began taking down goats in the neighborhood. Perly Wasson, feeling an affinity for the animal, first set out a mammoth-sized baited trap to catch "Big Grey," but failing to trick the wily creature, resorted to hot lead. Wise to Wasson's intent, Big Grey grew elusive. Shep secretly slipped away to run with him in uncanny communion. They began to share goat du jour, and Wasson set out to end their career. He succeeded in March 1884, first taking down Big Grey and reluctantly destroying Shep shortly thereafter, due to the dog's acquired fondness for goat flesh.

Now creatures of light and shadow, translucent and eternally paired, Dog and Wolf became part of the wind, seen by astounded travelers in

Hermosa Park and Hotel Draw. Georgiana Gilbert, a Rico belle and lover of mystery, penned a tribute for the *Denver Republican* after experiencing the "vision" of these two creatures "in perfect union." She saw Wolf on the hill one autumn morning, his fur full of sunlight. He threw back his head and called his companion from the nether world. Dog joined Wolf, trotted into a golden aspen glade and, reappearing on the far side, ran as if never touching the ground. "They are free spirits," Georgiana wrote, "never again to be wounded by mankind's meager perception, nor separated by his cruel misunderstanding. They are the soul of the wind."

If Shep and Big Grey were the soul of the wind, Joseph Castello's scrappy phantom dog was the teeth of the wind. Since 1879 Joe and Snap had gone through freezing and thawing until they were nearly cracked, surviving tent winters, mud-floor cabins, hard-rock mucking, the whiskey and tobacco famine, and the insults of Beaver Aleck. Castello, one of the first trustees of Rico, went everywhere with Snap at his side. Snap liked all whom Joe liked and snarled at all whom Joe disliked, especially Beaver Aleck, a lawyer whose heels Snap assaulted despite Joe's feigned politeness toward the man.

The winters at 8,827 feet Snap disliked most of all, even more than he disliked lawyers. Snap's fur was too short for winter comfort and he had to suffer the humiliation of wearing long johns or a blanket tied around him, causing grown men to point and snigger at him. Thus, when the snow in January, February, and March of 1884 continued to pile higher, closing off roads and blocking transport of victuals, Snap could bear it no longer and suddenly died of humiliation. All of Rico (except a few lawyers) mourned Castello's loss. However, instead of seeking those eternal green shores where dogs "bark out their sadness," Snap remained at Joe's side, with an ever-handy tripping nip on the heels of rude neighbors or a prick of sharp teeth to the posterior of lawyers. At their startled exclamations, Joe simply smiled and said, "Good dog, Snap."

A seeming cousin to Snap was an obnoxious lap dog named Pansy that belonged to Ella Holden, a prostitute in Telluride in the 1890s. Pansy was accidentally poisoned in 1889 (someone mistook her for a rat), but her ghost nested in Ella's bed during her tenure at George Rock's house on Fir Street. If Ella landed an abusive tom, Pansy's ghost evicted the man with snarls and nips, giving the woman the reputation as "Ella the Pincher." Annoyed to the point of homicide by the inexplicable nipping, a vengeful tom set Ella's place on fire in February 1893. Ella escaped. The gaseous pet did not.

Some spectral canines in the San Juan were in the company of equally spectral humans, particularly deceased shepherds. Several stories of a phantom alpine shepherd and his two dogs may have generated from a single kernel, or perhaps dead shepherds simply find it difficult to give up their profession, since the mysterious trio has been seen from San Luis Peak to Columbine Lake.

Earliest tales identify the shepherd as Robert Lewis, who accidentally shot himself when he grabbed his gun by the muzzle in December 1876. He and his two faithful dogs were out with Dunn and Carson's sheep on La Garita Creek.

Later stories say the shepherd was Flavio Fresques, a Picuris Pueblo Indian from Penasco, New Mexico. Flavio and his two shepherd dogs were killed by lightning in summer 1914 at the head of the Big Blue, below Uncompahgre Peak. The lifeless shepherd and his dead dogs were found huddled together between two trees, where they had sought shelter from the savage alpine storm, a lightning bolt having killed all three instantly. In the summer of 1992 a party of Pennsylvania hikers were approaching an "Indian shepherd" and his two dogs in a green bowl above Cinnamon Pass, when both shepherd and dogs seemed to fade into "fractured light" and vanish before their eyes.

High-altitude visions frequently place a dog or coyote-dog near the top of Molas Pass south of Silverton, a dog that "seems to be waiting for something" or is occasionally seen "digging" at an equally translucent prostrate figure, a fleeting vision witnesses think they imagined after it fades. Said to be the shepherd dog of Will Colmer, this creature is believed to be seen in its desperate act of trying to save Bert Rogers, a Silvertonian who froze to death in November 1911 at this spot. The Silverton *Weekly Miner* reported, "the dog had scratched Bert's hands in trying to rouse him and dug up the snow all around the body" and had never for a moment left the young man's side. Somehow the energy of that terrible moment was locked into timelessness, glimpsed only briefly on silent November nights, or the dog is seen waiting in the swirling snow, waiting as still as death, waiting for a hopeful dawn that will never come.

This heroic faithfulness made a dog's friendship nearly equal to a man's, yet San Juaners never lynched a dog thief as they did horse thieves.

In those days men loved their horses more than they loved their wives, which made them overzealous in dealing with those who rode off on someone else's horse. When something is loved so dearly, it is bound to hang around after death, and thus it is no surprise there are far more ghostly horses roaming these mountains than there are ghostly wives.

The most beloved of these horse apparitions was Cyclone, a huge, docile draft horse that has drifted through the pastures near Dallas Divide for more than a century. Cyclone's soft, starred nose, flaxen mane, dark chestnut hide, and thickly feathered legs were unmistakable when he began his career as a specter after Jim Harrison shot him in March 1895 in "an act of mercy." The draft horse belonged to Jim's father, and the old man was torn up with grief, until Cyclone mysteriously reappeared in the pastures, seen only by old man Harrison, children, and wandering cowboys.

Other horse spooks appeared in odd places, such as Samuel Wight's dead horse, which made itself known whenever Wight was about to lose at the faro tables in Telluride. Wight was a professional gambler whose horse, Nell, was shot out from under him after he left with his winnings from a poker game in Texas. Nell made it a point to hang around her old friend, telling him when he was about to lose, but never when he was about to win.

Burro spooks brought better luck. An old San Miguel story tells of a miner whose loyal burro dropped dead and followed him thereafter, a pale white form that brayed at good prospects. The Dead Burro Lode in San Miguel County was named to honor the animal.

Near Rico, another white burro spirit roamed the Silver Creek trail from the creek headwaters to Tin Can Basin in the 1890s. This unnamed, forsaken burro, braying out his sorrow, was linked with the disappearance of prospector John B. Geisel, who set out for Mount Wilson in July 1880. Geisel had a white pack burro, and the pair was never seen again, lost to the winds of eternity.

At Dunton a 1903 fire barbecued Chub Bergwin's barn and sent his old one-eyed burro ranging through the area as a phantom.

Some ethereal pack animals preferred to keep a low profile, their presence announced only audibly. Near the Seventy-Six Mine in San Miguel County, the soft whickering of invisible horses disturbed even sober miners. The sound began after two of Barney Kennedy's best freight horses were swept away in an avalanche in the early part of 1895. On the Mineral Creek road up the south side of Red Mountain Pass, the eerie braying of a

dozen mules was said to splinter the air on April mornings. The unfortunate mules had been crushed beneath a six-hundred-foot-wide avalanche
near Chattanooga in April 1886.

Avalanches immortalized many San Juan residents, including a few
cats, whether cats deserved immortality or not. On Christmas Eve 1883,
an avalanche roared through Brooklyn Gulch above the Saratoga Smelter in
Ironton Park. Ripping through the San Jose Mine property, it flattened the
cabin, injuring Billie Wilson, Joseph Wall, and Christopher Leslie and outright liquidated their lazy old ratter, Old Tom. With spring the miners returned and likewise did Old Tom, lounging in ghostly splendor in the
mine entrance, flicking his tale while packrats frolicked.

A more worthy cat, Prince Friedrich, became immortal when an avalanche in Horse Gulch took John Schnelle's cabin for a wild ride in February 1884. The cabin was perched above Horse Creek, not far from the
Puzzle Mine, and the Prince kept it completely rodent-free, his skill
known all around Rico. No rodent existed he couldn't demolish. Since
Schnelle was in Rico during the cabin's departure for lower elevations, he
didn't find the remains of the Prince until some weeks later. He sadly reported to the *Dolores News*, "All that remains of Prince Friedrich, who was
a victim of this winter's catastrophic slides, is his tail. J. Schnelle will give
it a decent burial." Schnelle should have kept it. Prince Friedrich returned
as an active apparition with the power to frighten the rodent population
into submission, but he no longer had a tail. Without that crowning
plume, the Prince was degraded and refused to present himself to anyone
except Schnelle. "We suspect even the mice are laughing," said the *News*.

The resident mouser of Gray and Mann's saloon in Creede, known to
all the greasy miners in that greasy town, was affectionately dubbed Lacy.
If a glass was left on the bar too long, Lacy padded up to it, sniffed it, put
a paw in it to test for liquid refreshment, then lapped the paw in purred
delight. On June 5, 1892, Lacy was barbecued in the hellfire that destroyed
the entire town. As soon as the saloons were rebuilt, Lacy materialized,
begging whiskey from rowdy hall to rowdy hall, especially in the Gem Saloon. Miners decided to give the inebriated cat its own glass and soon were
in the habit of ordering two drinks at once. Members of the temperance
movement choked on the scene: Creede miners holding a glass of whiskey
in one fist and a glass of beer in the other. They condemned the town as
the most degenerate, immoral, dissolute spot in the state. In their defense,

the miners explained they customarily ordered "one for Lacy" and that it was the spectral cat that did all the drinking . . . and what capacity it had.

Yet on the other side of the mountains, a saloon cat named Bobbie demonstrated complete restraint, her ghost seen only in the mirrors of the Elkhorn saloon in Ouray.

Phantom cats were good companions for lonely miners, but what could a man do at 12,700 feet if he had no cat? Curl up with a ringtail? Phillip Bunt did. Bunt worked at the Senator Beck Mine below Trico Peak and his favorite companion was a "cacomistle," or ringtail *(Bassariscus astutus)*, a beautiful fox-faced creature with more tail than body, the tail ringed with black and white bands. Ringtails were called "Miners' Cats" since they were frequently captured and kept as pets in rodent-infested mine buildings. They outshone cats in their ability as ratters. Bunt's ringtail was so closely bonded to him that they slept in the same bunk, the ringtail contentedly sprawled on its back next to him. One morning fellow miners found Bunt's companion ripped open and half-eaten, probably the work of bobcats or an owl. Knowing how the news would devastate the young, lonely, and homesick Bunt, the miners secretly buried the ringtail. That night they were astounded to see Bunt asleep in his bunk with the ringtail snoring beside him. When one of them touched it to see if it were real, the ringtail vanished like smoke.

High altitude often is blamed for lodging peculiar visions in miners' brains, and thus it well may be a "thing of high altitude" that brought visions of the most unlikely hoofed ghost in the San Juans.

In 1891 a miner named Al McIntosh found a Rocky Mountain bighorn lamb struggling to free itself from a snowslide near Ouray. The miner saved the lamb, naming it His Majesty Snowslide Merry or S. S. Merry, for it sprung and hopped and wiggled in unbounded glee, its little flag tail jittering with utter happiness. S. S. Merry was hand-raised by the children and adults of Ouray, having freedom of the streets and frequent caresses. Though he was "perfectly gentle and docile" with humans, by the time S. S. Merry had reached full ramhood, he gained a reputation for "scrappiness" among the town's canine population. Wandering curs challenged him, attempting to pull His Majesty to his knees and his only defense was to—well, ram them from a full flying mount, sending the boneheaded pests tail-tucked and whining to their owners. In the third year of his reign, S. S. Merry discovered the delicate flavor of garden shrubbery, trimming hedges and roses and flower beds. Complaints forced the town board to order S. S. into confinement, where he was nearly forgotten until William Lamont offered to buy him.

Lamont was a progressive sheep man with royal ideas and he bought the four-year-old bighorn ram to breed to his domestic ewes in hopes of creating a hardier strain. After a few years of decadence among these commoners, his ramship succumbed to the diseases they carried masked in their immunity. S. S. Merry was a creature of the wild with no defense against domestic pneumonia.

Missing the gay, jitter-tailed ram, the miner who had first saved him, Al McIntosh, sparked a thought when Madam Gustaf alighted in Ouray in summer of 1902. Many miners "flocked" to the medium because she was telling them the "hidden secrets" of their mines, drawing the future out of the stars, and communicating with deceased loved ones. Al simply wanted Madam Gustaf to contact S. S. Merry to see if he were happy where he now resided in the kingdom of the dead.

The medium balked briefly, but Al and his brother John put down good cash and were anticipating a good time . . . so the Madam commenced calling on the bighorn to come forth. In the noble experiment Madam Gustaf, unable to speak Ramese, pulled S. S. Merry straight from behind the veil. All hoof and horn and joyful energy, he slipped out of her grasp, bounding out to the red cliffs he had loved in life. Now pure white from nose to tail, Merry became a vision common to late-night revelers and miners longing for the innocent days long passed. Nothing would ever confine him; no man would ever own him. He was a white glimpse, a flash in the sun, a summer vision of freedom on the red cliffs above town; a merry, jitter-tailed spirit mixed with majestic dignity that gave old miners a link to their distant dreams.

Some still look up to those cliffs for the mysterious white ram that leaps and frolics with the wind.

11

A COLD SPOT IN THE CORNER

The rocky hem of Anvil Mountain bounced a glare of sunlight against the window, splashing a warm glow up the alcove frame, hazing the view. From the third-story window at the rear of the hotel, the view suffered little under the influence of glare: nothing remarkable in sparse, tired buildings, weedy hillside, and dusty roads.

The bed sagged and the springs creaked. The toilet had an annoying wheeze. The narrow room was musty, as if too long shut up. If he opened the window, let in the morning air . . . no, he was too tired to get out of bed.

Chuck Morrison slumped into the pillows and gazed at the glow of light on the ceiling. It was nearly noon. Breakfast could be useful. . . . No, he was too tired to get out of bed.

He had been on the road too long, pushing to reach New Mexico from Montana, and wound up in a quiet little town in the San Juans, too tired to go on. Silverton's fine old Grand Imperial Hotel invited him in at nearly midnight, and he dropped into the bed without taking off his shoes.

He considered breakfast again; thought about taking off his shoes . . . too tired to get out of bed.

Something broke the light at the window. A dank draft breathed up from the floor all around the saggy bed, and Morrison sat up. The musty scent changed to something more unpleasant and Morrison thought he heard short gasps or sighs or . . .

A dark shape or shadow partly blocked the window. He could see through the "hole" it made through the glare, as if someone had washed out a shape on the panes. A sound, a chill, an indescribable current or energy all seemed to be in that spot. Suddenly he realized it was the shadow of a man, and he jerked his gaze round the room, instinctively looking for the man who was casting it.

The dark form was inside the room, as if standing in front of the window, and at the same time, it seemed to be on the outside of the panes. Morrison felt chilled.

Eyes, terrible eyes full of pain were gazing past him. The eyes were dark, the hair was black, the bushy mustache was black. The man wore a black hat and a black wool coat, yet he was hardly more than a shadow across the glaring sunlight, a shadow with dimension, a shadow that seemed to absorb light.

He stood with a fixed gaze, twisted by some unseen torment. Morrison was frozen in place, watching the man in breathless fear. After what felt like an eternity to Morrison, the man moved toward the bed, his hand reaching out, his eyes still fixed on something beyond the room. The man spoke, a soft foreign phrase, the tone pleading, and abruptly he was gone.

Morrison forgot how tired he was. He flew out the door, down the flights of stairs, to the front desk. He gasped out his story. Realizing how silly it sounded, he laughed, called himself a fool, but glanced at the ceiling, wondering what really was upstairs.

"Luigi," a girl whispered. "You saw Luigi."

Luigi Regalia had killed himself in Room 28 of the Grand Hotel on November 1, 1890. He had made an earlier attempt on his birthday, October 6, but his landlady came in before he could carry out the act. On November 1 he put on his best suit of clothes, took a room at the Grand, and wrote a letter to his friend Carlo Barsotti of New York. Late that evening he put a gun to his head and, while holding a small mirror in front of his face, pulled the trigger. The bullet slammed through his skull from above his right ear, blowing out the center of his forehead near the hairline, badly fracturing the cranium.

Dr. G. W. Milton, who was in the adjoining room, was startled by the gunshot. He rushed downstairs to get the clerk, Harry Giles, and send for Sheriff May. They found Luigi on the floor in a pool of blood, the mirror and a Smith & Wesson revolver clutched in his hands. Luigi was still breathing. They sent for Dr. Pascoe, who desperately tried to bring the unconscious man back from the brink. At 2:20, in the silent cold hours before dawn, the forty-two-year-old immigrant from Pazzallo, Italy, died. He had been in Silverton nine years, leaving many friends heartsick and confused.

Some believed Luigi had killed himself because of a woman back in Italy. Others thought he had been losing his mind for some time, tormented by voices or "spirits" dogging him, and had used the mirror in his destructive exit to see the nightmare creatures behind him. Frequently he had broken off conversations while an expression of fear and pain filled his distancing gaze.

Luigi's ghost was said to have remained in Room 28 from the beginning, many lodgers and hotel staff startled by its fleeting presence. With time and multiple renovations at the hotel, room sizes and numbers were changed. In Luigi's day, only the third floor was used for guest rooms. Later, both the second and third floors were used, with none of the rooms marked as "28." Despite this, Luigi was still seen, always a dark form that seemed to be a void of light, a shadow full of anguish on the top floor at the back of the hotel.

In more recent years hotel guests have seen Dr. Pascoe as well, a small man marked with desperation, rushing into the room in the predawn hours.

Silverton's Grand Imperial Hotel is too grand to be content with one ghost. In the days when the Hub Saloon occupied the spot where the lobby now is, a lean, scruffy miner with his hat pulled over his forehead would walk up to the bar, demand a drink, and vanish. He was believed to be John Loftus, who was shot dead during a botched robbery. After renovations, John's ghost adjusted accordingly and went on to haunt the bar around the corner in the dining hall.

The dining hall was also said to harbor a ghost or two that rattled through after hours, a mark of the violent days when guns settled any sort of argument or altercation. On occasion, a blithe spirit identified as George Foster, a miner killed in an avalanche on February 10, 1900, who was in love with a pantry maid, bumps across the kitchen, knocks down a pan or potato, then departs with a big grin on his face.

Not to be outdone by the Grand, the Strater Hotel in Durango boasts at least a half dozen gaseous guests. Most of these occupy the fourth floor or the basement. None are as well defined as Luigi, yet they do send a chill through staff members, who refuse to talk about them unless specifically asked.

In the basement once occupied by a saloon and gambling den, rumor has identified the ghastly ghost of a gambler and a few prostitutes. On the fourth floor shadowy figures pass through rooms, pianos are heard in the woodwork and images are seen in mirrors and dim hallways.

Hotels have long been a popular haunt for ethereal guests and the older the hotel, the greater the population of resident ghosts or frequent "cold spots." Yet in the San Juans, a hotel didn't have to be old to attract spirits.

A frightening man in a dark suit, with a raw scar on the left side of his face, visited the Glendale Hotel at Ophir Loop each fall. Out of nowhere on the evening of November 28, he appeared in the second floor corridor or the corner room. Passersby saw him standing at the window, silhouetted by a small lamp in the room. He never spoke. No one knew who or what he was. His vacant gaze "held the darkness of the tomb." Before dawn the next day he would vanish, leaving the room awash with frigid air.

Eventually he must have grown weary of the cold, for when the hotel mysteriously caught fire, the ghost was seen standing unmoved and unscorched at the corner room window, the flames roaring around him. The hour was 4:00 A.M., November 29, 1900. Panic stabbed the village that the fire had killed a man in the corner room, for he had never escaped. Yet no trace of a body was found when searchers combed through the Glendale's charred skeleton.

Poker-playing ghosts at Telluride's American House startled those who happened upon them in Room 17 but weren't described as frightening. In fact, this foggy bunch of fellows was a welcome diversion. They appeared infrequently and only on Thursday nights. All four had British or Canadian accents, and the leader among them was believed to be Canadian Thomas Street, a miner who had died of pneumonia in Room 17 in 1888. Street was alone and far from the people he loved, but a woman named Millie Dwight tenderly cared for him, staying at his bedside until his death. For this reason, it was surmised, Street's spirit got attached to the hotel, eventually gathering a few friends from the far side of death for Thursday night poker.

A night clerk named Tabby Waldman became so familiar with Tom Street and his friends in the 1890s that Tabby was invited to play poker with the lads when things were quiet. One Thursday in 1897, Tabby accused Tom and his phantoms of cheating, yelling at them for "taking advantage of a mere mortal," causing a hotel guest to burst into the room. He found Tabby shouting at empty chairs and reported him to the owner, A. C. Hart, who promptly dismissed the night clerk.

A year later the old pinewood American House was destroyed when the adjoining Windsor restaurant caught fire. Tom Street and his poker-playing buddies took up residence at the Maxwell Hotel, perhaps due to some of his favorite staff being employed there. Or possibly the Maxwell wanted a share in the intrigue and invited or ghost-napped the spooks once they were smoked out of the American, for the same story was told here, except the miners were now more cantankerous.

One Thursday night a man from Missouri checked into the Maxwell and was startled by the appearance of four miners in his room just as he was undressing for bed. They "roughed" him up when he asked them to leave. Suddenly they vanished through the walls, came back in a guffawing fury, tossing blankets, knocking over a lamp, and vanished again. He heard the landlady chastising them, then pleading with them to leave her guests alone. As they flew back through the walls, he frantically grabbed his clothes and pistol and fled screaming from the room, clad only in his drawers. In his panic he crashed through a front window and, trailing lace curtains behind him, he ran across the street to the Sheridan saloon, shouting for protection.

The saloon crowd, already in a state of ferment, broke into laughter at the sorry figure before them. Barefoot and wearing nothing save his saggy drawers, with trousers and vest in one hand, a pistol in the other, the Missourian blurted a fantastic tale of a ghostly mob "looking to do" him. A man in the crowd asked for a shot of whatever the naked man's poison was and the laughter rattled the rafters. The Missourian took refuge in the alley. Shortly, the sheriff's deputies escorted him to the county lockup, bent on keeping him "until he recovers from his derangement and gives an account of himself." He refused to give them his real name for fear the ghosts would hear it.

The average hotel spook generally refrained from tantrums, and most in the San Juan merely appeared as unmoving shadows or hazy forms with climate control. The climate they preferred was anything from icy to frigid. At the Delmonico in Ouray, the depressed wraith of one of the proprietors, George B. Warren, chilled the second floor for eight years. He had killed himself on that floor in 1897, despondent since the death of his wife in 1895. Like the spook at the Glendale Hotel, Warren must have wanted to warm up the place, for in 1905 the Delmonico burned down.

Another cold spot was said to be the ghost of Gus King, who accidentally blew a hole through his belly with a Colt .44 in Lake City's American House in 1884. King, a twenty-nine-year-old German immigrant, was engaged to a Lake City lass who broke off with him "through the advice of friends." He took a gun from the hotel office desk, cocked it with intent to stop his breaking heart, but changed his mind. At that point the pistol discharged, and King died in agony eleven hours later. His unseen spirit descended on the hotel office in frosty remorse.

At the Western Hotel in Ouray, footsteps heard in the upstairs hall are followed by an icy draft and sometimes, on the anniversary of his death, December 27, the tragic husk of John J. Hopkins appears. In the early decades of the twentieth century, John's visitations were frequent, and those who encountered him believed he wanted "something" from them, wanted to change what he could not change.

At the age of thirty-two, John had already lost his beloved wife, Carrie, and in his depression he lost his job as well. He had been a union miner at Silverton, but failed to obtain work there, seeking employment in Ouray. Again he failed to secure a job. His money was running out. A woman in Oregon, Elva Albin, was in love with him, pressing him to marry her. He had promised his dying wife he would never remarry. He loathed hurting anyone, yet saw no way out of his darkness. When he made the decision to "finish it all," he was relieved, even "lighthearted and jovial," and spent Christmas in Ouray after having purchased laudanum in Montrose. On Friday, December 26, he went up to his room at the Western and wrote a letter to his sweetheart, Elva, begging her to forgive him and to find a man "more worthy." He wrote another letter to his mother in Kansas and one to his landlady in Silverton, Mrs. Lydia Parmer. A final note was addressed to whoever might find his body: "Mail above letters for me. An inquest will not be necessary. I take my own life by using laudanum. Being tired of life and unable to get work, I take this way out of getting out of troubles."

Disrobing and neatly folding his clothes across the back of a chair, John dressed in his nightshirt, swallowed the drug and went to bed. His body wasn't found until Saturday afternoon, casting a dark pall over the Christmas holidays. The coroner, W. R. Kincaid, noted an "expression of pain" on the victim's face, "which was drawn as if he suffered great agony."

It was that face full of deep anguish that a Denver woman saw at the hotel a few years later. Pauline Robertson was visiting friends in Silverton, and on her return trip, stopped in Ouray at the Western. She was awakened by a "terrible draft" sweeping through her room and there, at the foot of her bed, was "a young man whose blue eyes were so distraught with agony" that she gasped and sobbed at the same moment. He asked her to help him, reaching out to her, unable to touch her. "Who are you?" she gasped. His reply was a choking, "John—" and he vanished. It was 2:30 A.M., December 27. Pauline Robertson was dazed by the apparition, telling her story to no one, until she was fully recovered and back in the safety of Denver friends. She confessed that when she had first gone to bed in the hotel, she had seen a man's clothing hanging over the chair across the room. She got up to investigate, but in the light, the clothing was no longer there.

The Western Hotel, one of the oldest frame hostelries still standing in the San Juans, keeps its ghosts in a veil of silence, yet sightings of John Hopkins have not ceased. Like Luigi at the Grand Imperial, John's eyes are always filled with an unfathomable pain or sorrow, and in his wretchedness he, too, reaches toward the living for some kind of solace, some kind of hope or warmth no one is able to give.

For many years the faint, cold shadow of a young woman named Maggie McRobbie Little sat in silence in a corner of the Hotel Enterprise at Rico. Maggie had died in the hotel from consumption during the time her uncle and aunt managed the place. Her frail white specter requisitioned a chair in the second-floor sitting room, causing consternation among the flesh-and-blood clientele. The Hotel Enterprise, a three-story frame building erected by John Carr in 1890 on Glasgow Avenue, also hosted the grim piano-playing spirit of Lyle Lazelle.

One unusual hotel guest lingered in the ruins of the burnt-out Belvedere Hotel in Montrose. Built at Selig and Main near the depot, this impressive brick hostelry hosted a gala opening in 1890 and was hailed by the *Solid Muldoon* as "one of the finest hotel structures in southern Colorado." For four years it was a high society spot, a place of balls and parties and grand meetings. Fire struck it one night during the annual fireman's ball and, despite the host of firemen already on the scene, the building was a total loss. From 1894 until 1898 the charred hulk of the Belvedere stood like a ghost itself, its blackened chimneys thrusting against the sky, its arched grand entrance inviting boys to sift through the rubble and play captains and kings in the shadow of the walls. The boys were the first to see the mysterious creature in the northwest corner. She was a girl of six or seven, wearing a plain brown frock and black shoes or boots. She aimlessly drifted through the ruins, softly singing a plaintive song. One boy, Jimmie Bowersock, tried to talk to her. She seemed deaf. She never looked at him or anyone else. Only in the dim blue light of dusk did she appear and if one approached her too closely, she seemed to fade into the shadows. No one had a reason for her mysterious presence. One theory proposed she had died in the fire, unknown to anyone. The mystery remained unsolved, for in 1898 the Belvedere's bricks were used for another building, and the little girl was seen no more.

The historical hotel without a claim to at least one cold spot in the corner is rare in the San Juan, and ghosts of some sort or other are lodged in everything from the New Sheridan at Telluride to the quaint bed-and-breakfast in Pagosa, depending on who does the telling. Management at some hotels prefers to keep the ethereal contents of their closets under lock and key, fearful ghosts might drive away prospective clientele. Others put the word out, even if the annoying flushing toilets are no more than bad plumbing and the cold drafts no more than broken boilers, believing known haunts will attract solid guests. Something like Luigi popping up at the bedside might be free entertainment, more exciting than

HBO, yet rumor has it Luigi and his desperate Dr. Pascoe actually drove a European couple out of the Grand Imperial. (Europeans are inclined to take ghosts more seriously than Americans.) Whether the spooks are advertised or not, whether diligent "ghost busters" or mediums scoop them and their ectoplasm into jars or "put them to rest," the mysterious energy trapped in the woodwork of these old buildings never goes away. Even though a hotel is closed up for years and given over to moths and mildew, the energies of the place linger, if not grow stronger for neglect, as in the case of Ouray's Beaumont.

Nearly from the time of its grand opening in 1887, the Beaumont snared a broken spirit. A well appointed, elegant hotel with a restaurant, it had a large staff of maids, waiters, chefs, and pantry help, many of whom lodged in the second story rooms above the kitchen at the rear of the building. Among the restaurant help was a nineteen-year-old woman named Ellar Day, who had divorced her husband and was struggling to raise her small child. She had joined the staff as a waitress in August, having previously worked in the same capacity at the Delmonico. But she was terrified to take orders to the kitchen.

A pastry cook named Joseph W. Dixon had also worked at the Delmonico, and when he was discharged from that hotel, he blamed Ellar. According to the *Solid Muldoon*, Joe Dixon had been discharged from several Ouray hotels due to his "wicked temperament," and it was "well known that he threatened death and destruction to numerous of our citizens on the slightest provocation." Joe must have been an exceptional pastry chef or perhaps the Beaumont was in dire need, for despite his reputation, they hired him in June.

Ellar's fear of the man was crippling. Finally she persuaded her father, J. H. Day, to "make it convenient to be in the kitchen during meal hours," giving her protection from the ominous pastry chef. In her father's presence, Joe treated Ellar graciously.

On Monday, September 12, 1887, Joe Dixon drank himself into a quarreling mood, frightening Ellar so much she had her father escort her to his house instead of going to her own room in the Beaumont. Tuesday she was back at work. That afternoon, after cleaning up in the dining room, Ellar went upstairs to the room she shared with another waitress, Minnie Percy. Drunk again, Joe intruded on the young women, full of threats and trouble. Ellar's father arrived at her door and found Joe sitting on a trunk and the two women sitting on the side of the bed, Minnie speaking angrily to Joe in defense of Ellar.

Joe jumped to his feet, drew a gun, and shouted, "I will kill the whole goddamned crowd!" He fired at Ellar, the bullet slicing into her. He fired on Minnie, but she dove out the door just as Ellar's father smashed his fist into the chef's back, knocking him down. Day struck him with a pitcher, but Joe sprung at Day, thrashing him over the head with the revolver. Girls in the hallway were shrieking. Girls at their windows on the second floor screamed for help from the people in the alley below. Crockery flew and glass broke. A third bullet aimed at Day burned into the bleeding, staggering Ellar. Then another and another. Day pounded the assailant with a heavy washbasin, driving him out the door as Joe pulled the trigger again and again, the hammer clicking against an empty chamber.

Blood streaming over his face from the cuts in his head, blood soaking his white shirt and apron, Joe Dixon staggered downstairs and, at the kitchen door, was collared by the marshal.

Upstairs, J. H. Day, equally covered with blood, was cradling his dying daughter in his arms. The room was spattered in gore. Ellar Day had four bullet holes in her small body. One in her chest went through to the back, where her father could feel the ball just under the skin near the shoulder blade.

The citizens of Ouray were outraged. Few hours passed before they knew what they must do. Ellar Day had grown up in the town, had been loved by many, had brought joy with her shy smile and kind ways. The incendiary words of the marshal and other leading citizens that Joe Dixon was "a fiend, in human form only, devilish by nature and lecherous in disposition . . . assassin of woman's reputation and the would-be slayer of woman's purity . . . slimy with the ooze of moral leprosy . . ." fueled their thirst for blood and led many to believe Joe had attempted to sexually assault Ellar. For many men of that time, this was even worse than the bullets he put through her, for Joseph W. Dixon was black. Blacks, Native Americans, and Chinese citizens were treated with surface friendship and respect for the most part, but accuse any of them of the least sexual impropriety toward a white woman, and white men became unhinged, their rage volcanic.

From that point on Joe Dixon was referred to as "the black devil" or "black fiend." By midnight, seventy-five to a hundred masked men stormed Deputy Sheriff Myers's house, demanding the jail keys. Since he had none, the mob rallied toward the jail, slamming against the door to break it down, but thwarted in that, set the building ablaze. The mob dispersed as rapidly as the fire team arrived. The fire was snuffed. Inside, Joseph Dixon lay dead across the cot, suffocated by the smoke.

The editor of the *Solid Muldoon* defended the murder as "the inherent right of social organization to protect itself under the unwritten law of nature, and by the swift and extraordinary punishment meted out, to deter others from committing such crimes."

Deluded by self-righteousness, the mob failed to instill good behavior in any other murderer or to slow crime, and also failed to bring Ellar Day back. Knowing she was at her end, she requested baptism in the Episcopal Church, and by Thursday night she was dead. Yet peace did not reign.

The nightmare at the Beaumont shattered quiet hours; otherworldly screams bounced in muffled echoes through the second floor walls, heavy footfalls were heard on the back stairs when no one was seen there, blood spatters reappeared in Ellar's old room, and girls whispered of horrifying specters slipping down dark passageways. Both Ellar and Joe or the intense and terrible energy of their last days became a permanent fixture in the Beaumont Hotel.

One visitor in 1896, Alexander S. Blake of Kansas City, claimed to be awakened by gunshots. He rushed out of his room clad in his nightshirt. "A blood-drenched girl" fled down the corridor and Blake went after her, stumbling into a confused night clerk who assured Blake "no one has been shot. 'But the girl—' said Blake. 'A ghost,' the clerk replied. 'Only a ghost.' And no explanation was offered."

In the sunny years and through the dark years, the place was said to be haunted. Even after it was shut up, left to bats and dust and decay, mysterious lights were said to be seen in upstairs windows . . . muffled screams or the sharp report of a pistol startled passersby. Boarded-up windows, peeling paint, and the hollow-eyed dormers of the top floor all spoke of ghosts, yet no one cared to give word to the tale, for it was too ugly, too cold, too frightening to stir up. Forget it, and maybe it will go away.

More than a hundred years have passed since that tragic day, and now the Beaumont is under restoration after decades in the dust. The ghost stories have been revived, although somewhat toned down and manicured for entertainment during the month of October or as incidentals to renovation reports. Yet the ghosts themselves are unlikely to be any less horrifying than they once were. A theory among some paranormal researchers suggests this "psychic or emotional energy" infused into the surrounding material during a highly charged event, "may actually increase" when a building is closed to human habitation. This is due to the "absence of other human energy, positive or negative, that absorbs, diminishes or mingles and corrupts the psychic energy present." Thus the Beaumont's ghosts may have become more intense after all this time of quiet and smothering dust. Many long decades have passed. No amount of paint or polish will cover the shadows of 1887 . . . or so goes the theory.

Does something lie in wait above the kitchen stairs?

12

GUARDIANS

OF THE ANCIENT WAY

Her harvest basket empty, she hums and weaves. Though harvest time has been long swallowed by thirsty sand and wind, still she hums and weaves. She weaves on the cliff's stone loom, an old woman weaving in the shadows of two towering rocky horns, weaving time and waiting . . . waiting for the scattered seeds of prayer to catch in her silent web.

The womb of a great kiva, empty as the old woman's harvest basket, empty and dry and yearning to receive life, lies at the foot of those towering, ragged pinnacles. Even the sky cannot fill this gaping kiva, though its sandstone lips touch the stars in this high place. No song, no caress of the breeze stirs the tired pinyons. No smoke rises from the ruins. Only the old woman waits, weaving and waiting in the shelter of these imposing rocky columns. They are as tall and as powerful as her grandsons, Poqangwhoya and Palongawhoya, the Twin War Gods. These crags enshrine the War

Gods, hold their memory to the sky, create an image of them in sunrise silhouette. Pillars of stone crowning Chimney Rock Mesa, they are sentinels guarding the valley of the Piedra on the southern hem of the San Juans.

The Puebloans have long called Chimney Rock Mesa a holy place, a shrine to the Twin War Gods, sacred to their grandmother Spider Woman, sacred even in time so distant it is no longer in memory. The powerful presence of the Twin War Gods and the deep wisdom of Spider Woman has always been here and, despite the absence of priests and sacred smoke in the kiva, the Spirits are here still. Their presence pulls one into the silence, draws one into communion with wind-torn symbols and ancient walls.

Chimney Rock Pueblo is a spirit place. It is a place of *piki* bread left for ghosts among the sandstone walls. It is a place where mysterious *pahos,* prayer feathers, are left for the night wind to take away. It is a place where Raven Mother speaks in whispers, a place of one-horned fetishes with power in their souls of clay, a place where Spider Woman waits.

Prophecy, legend, and clan spirits are rooted in the heart of the rock at this ruined pueblo. It is said the presence of supernatural entities cannot be destroyed and anyone who seeks them at Chimney Rock Pueblo can find them. The Twin War Gods listen to the entreaties of ordinary men and women, giving them help in time of need.

Throughout the southern flank of the San Juans are awesome, ghost-filled ruins, crowning high points like ancient monasteries or cradled in maroon and amber canyons, rock born of rock, their evening shadows tracing the form of long-ago farmers coming home.

On a rocky hill above Dolores at the Chacoan ruin known as Escalante, the grey shadow of a small woman with long hair is said to watch over the excavated walls. Sometimes she is heard chanting or singing softly the ancient harvest basket songs. Could she be the disturbed ghost of the woman whose grave was opened, whose bones were snatched out of the protection of Maasaw, now unable to find her way back to the realm of the dead? Some Puebloans say she is. She was a woman of high status, buried with gifts equal to those of a warrior, buried with turquoise and bowls and fetishes to keep her safe on her journey, buried many hundreds of years before, only to be dug up, her bones labeled and numbered and stored in the basement of the museum.

Puebloans say those ancient ones taken from their graves can become lost, their spirits wandering in a sort of starvation. Maasaw is unable to find them, to lead them into the underworld, into Maski. Priests of the

One Horned Society cannot help them. And so it is that many ghosts shadow the southern foothills and canyons of the San Juan region.

Yet long before archaeologists began their probing and excavating, the Utes regarded these silent ruins with suspicion, believing ghosts of the dead or spirits of the sky prowled among them. For the Utes, ghosts were dangerous things to encounter, entities capable of causing illness and death. To be touched by a ghost made one sick. Even to see a ghost caused terrible disease, and ghosts were in every whirlwind or dust devil. Thus Utes kept away from the Puebloan ruins. They told many tales of bad spirits inhabiting the abandoned villages. Among these was a strange place called the "Cave of Ghosts."

A band of nomadic people, here long before the Utes or Puebloans, took shelter in this cave and were slaughtered by their enemies . . . then cannibalized. One version of the tale says the evil ones who did the deed were Coyote-witches, shape-shifters. Another identifies the evildoers as some terrible wind-borne spirits. Ever after, the ghosts of the savaged dead remained crying in the cave, a black chamber littered with bones, high in the cliffs of Animas Canyon. Utes wandering below the mouth of the cave heard strange, dark-wind cries of the dead and fled the place without looking back for fear their eyes might fall on whirlwinds pursuing them. This cave may be the cavern now lost to time but once described in the August 1880 *Rocky Mountain News* as "three miles north of Judge Pinkerton's and one mile east of the Rockwood and Dolores Toll Road. . . ."

Like the Utes, the Dineh (Navajo) stayed away from the ancient Puebloan ruins for fear of meeting a *chindi,* an evil spirit drifting through the shadows. A *chindi* caused great harm, even death, and those who associated with ghosts of the dead or evil spirits were considered witches, two-hearts, skinwalkers, or wolfmen among both the Dineh and Puebloan tribes.

Some of the ancient ruins were particularly dangerous, full of ghosts and lurking evils. Of these, a cliff house in one of the canyons of the Rio Mancos was avoided at all costs by local natives. The place gained its chilling reputation one year when heavy spring rains exposed and tumbled out the grinning skulls of the long dead who were buried in the midden below the ruin. *Yeis* (spirits) and witches were said to inhabit the dark place, guarding their hoard of grave goods and secrets.

White adventurers were only lured all the more by these *chindi* stories, believing "grave goods" meant valuable antiquities for Eastern collectors. In the late 1880s Philadelphian J. S. Gallagher, who was relic hunting in the

Bloomfield area of New Mexico, heard the sinister tale of the Rio Mancos cliff house and, hiring a few local ranch hands, set off in search of the place. His informants claimed the place was full of ghosts due to the treasure they guarded: amulets of gold and silver.

For several days the party's search was fruitless. By the end of the second week, Gallagher spotted a small, multiroom ruin tucked beneath the brow of a cliff in a small side canyon. According to the Philadelphia *Public Ledger*, Gallagher's "keen sense of greed" drew him up the dangerous cliff face where he belly-crawled though the loose rock, debris, potsherds, and human bones of the trash midden to the foot of the dwelling. As evening shadows were lengthening, Gallagher hollered to the cowboys to make camp up in the ruin with him. They were reluctant. "Something" seemed to be watching them. . . . Gallagher called them "gussied-up girls," which replaced their fears with the usual sagebrush bravado, and they hoisted themselves and the gear up to Gallagher.

Inside the sheltering walls of the dusty-eyed mausoleum, heaps of ceiling rubble proved to be covering pots and baskets and clay fetishes. Gallagher's excitement at the initial find erased all fear from the cowboy's brains. They drifted to sleep round their small fire with visions of wealth dancing in their heads.

Somewhere nearby, an owl spoke to the night shadows, his eerie call like the song of the long dead. The Philadelphian awoke with a start. Rising and falling like a descant to the owl song was a low chanting or humming, and Gallagher hastily rattled the ranch hands from sleep. They listened. They dismissed the sound as "wind funneled through the cracks in the walls. Surely."

Softly, slowly, scarcely audible, the chanting stole into their bones. They strained to identify it. Out of the stillness crept another sound, like dancing feet upon gravel or heavy sand. Through the T-shaped doorway, they saw a dark, dancing form on the stone lip in front of the ruins. Its dance was slow, determined, moving closer, closer. . . .

The cowboys grabbed their guns, blasting through the doorway at the bulky form. The shrill twitter of a night bird sliced the air, a flash of its sharp wings cut across the stars. Then silence.

Loud guffaws and jokes broke the hush. A bird, a trick of the darkness, nothing more. How silly of them to believe in Indian tales. *Chindi* nonsense. Superstitious Indians. White men were above that. Go back to sleep.

There it was, in their midst, dropped from the ceiling, out of the smoke of the ceiling, bigger than any of them, firelight casting its ogre shadow up the wall. There it was, chanting, dancing that slow creeping step. . . .

Helpless to move, they stared at the awesome creature, fearful it brought death. Burnt rags of flesh nubbled its huge, bony head and clung like melted and bloodied pitch round the empty sockets of its eyes. The scarred, seared arms were powerful, the shoulders broad and made all the bulkier by a rotting fur robe that hung in tatters to its knees. Was it a *Soyoko,* a Puebloan ogre that gnawed the bones of the dead? Or was it the great dark god, Maasaw, Firekeeper, Guardian of the Dead, Slayer of Enemies? The breath of the terrible Maasaw drained all energy out of a man, breath like an enshrouding mist, sucking power and strength.

Too terrified to scream, gasping for air, the cowboys backed away, threw their gear out of the ruin, and fled, pitching, scuttling, tumbling down to the creek. J. S. Gallagher's greed backed him to the corner where his bundle of artifacts lay, but as he moved to pick it up, the spirit "pressed upon him," popping its teeth like a grizzly. A rattle or rasp-like sound pulsated in Gallagher's cranium, a sound of teeth on bone, and he collapsed senseless against the wall as the creature "moved through him" and into the ancient masonry.

Gallagher fled the area without his cache of relics and never looked back. When he finally stopped running, he was back in Philadelphia, an advocate for protection of the "ruins of this lost and mysterious civilization."

Soyokos, yeis, spirit ogres, ghosts, and dreadful creatures continued to pursue the pothunters of the Rio Mancos, and some, like the Bloomfield rancher named Snyder, were so often in truck with these spirits that the Dineh considered them skinwalkers, witches, and avoided them as much as they avoided these places of death.

The Santa Fe *Gazette* reported Snyder actually unearthed a warrior's corpse in 1882 and that this "bold, bad man sought to increase his earthly goods" by robbing the seated, robed skeleton of its possessions. Undeterred by the *chindi,* Snyder ventured north to search for rumored wealth along the Rio Mancos, apparently breaking into the fire darkness of Maasaw, for he was found half dead, starving, dehydrated, with burns on his face and hands, and babbling of "ghosts." No Navajo would touch him. They feared he would "witch" them.

The witch of the Dineh and the *siants* or *si-a-ci* of the Ute and the two-heart of the Puebloan were all supernatural spirits that wandered in remote and tangled places where they roasted the flesh of kidnapped children. Tales of these evil spirits came from the dawn of time and those places known as witch habitations were avoided.

A particularly deadly *si-a-ci* lurked in the canyons of the Dolores, a bent old freak of the wind described as having a "hairy and wrinkled face with eyes like firebrands." She habitually followed the Utes and watched where they made camp. After they were all asleep, she crept up to the feet of a man she had earlier chosen and lay upon him. In fear, he fled, and the witch grabbed a baby or two and thumped off into the darkness. After throwing the babies on the hot coals of her fire and roasting them "till their eyes popped," the *si-a-ci* tore into their flesh with sharp teeth, saving the bones in a pile. Her pile of bones marked the entrance to her lair deep in the guts of forbidding, dry canyons and she guarded them zealously, for out of them she could fashion another *si-a-ci*.

Strange spirit guardians of the waterways were called *paa-pi-ci*, meaning Water Person or Water Baby. Like the *si-a-ci*, these creatures frightened the Utes. They pulled men under the water, sucking the air out of their lungs.

On the friendlier side was the stumpy, sawed-off *pituku-pi*, a supernatural dwarf who lived underground and gave powers to medicine men for curing people who had lost their souls.

Most of the hot mineral springs of the San Juan were watched over by spirits or were the dwelling places of spectral guardians. The healing waters derived their power from these entities. A tapestry of oral traditions surround the springs, lodging Capote, Tabeguache, Weeminuche, Dineh, Apache, and Puebloan spirits beneath and above the steaming waters.

The great bubbling cauldron of Pagosa Springs, with its otherworldly cone of crystalline mineral deposits towering above the San Juan River, reeks with legend as thick as its sulfurous steam. These "big medicine waters" were a gift of the Spirit, who took pity on his dying people and drew up the mud of the earth where they had danced out their grief, according to one legend. Another said the spring was created over the body of a youth who was bludgeoned and left to bleed to death at the edge of the river. In groaning sorrow, the earth heaved up around him to heal his wounds, and hence he has presided within the spring, passing on the curative powers of the underworld spirits. Yet other tales hold the ghost of an Apache warrior within the waters or the *chindi* of a Navajo slain in a fight over possession of the spring.

Whatever spirits reside in the Pagosa cauldron, early trappers and explorers acknowledged their presence when mistaking them for "demons" or "Old Snag." It was the attitude of the settlers and developers that shoved the ancient spirits deeper into the heart of earth, an attitude that transformed the sacred springs into cluttered "health resorts" where profit was the bottom line. A few whites, desperately in search of the "lost paradise" of their romantic version of the West, sought to communicate with the spirits of the springs in the 1890s. One who claimed success was Emily Farnham. Both Pagosa and Wagon Wheel Gap water spirits "discoursed" with her for several years until they "left off abruptly" in 1901, no reason given.

North of Pagosa on the flanks of Treasure Mountain, a guardian spirit of a different kind hovered over the buried gold of a Frenchman who had been illegally mining in the 1790s in territory belonging to Spain. The spirit was said to be the Navajo bride of the Frenchman, protecting his cache until his return. This 11,908-foot mountain has long been the scene of treasure hunters, prospectors, and fortune seekers searching for the Frenchman's gold.

The Frenchman had led an unofficial expedition into the area, and having discovered rich mineral deposits, set up headquarters in the region of Wolf Creek Pass, on the Navajo Trail. Each summer the group mined the veins and placers, processing the gold into ingots and stashing it in three separate locations to protect it from the Spaniards in whose territory they were trespassers. Their plan was to store the gold until the veins were exhausted, at which time they would depart for France. During the three years they mined, they wintered in the village of Taos and replenished their supplies, but they never brought out any gold for fear word would worm out to the Spanish authorities. Meanwhile, their leader, said to be of a noble family, took the daughter of a Navajo medicine man for his bride.

The third summer brought disaster to the expedition, with many men killed by warring tribesmen. The nobleman's Navajo wife, who had stayed at his side for two years, succumbed to a white man's disease, and he buried her in the forests of Treasure Mountain.

Early snows drove the French party out in haste and more perished from starvation and tribal attacks, including their leader. Eventually the survivors resorted to cannibalism, with only two left uneaten. These two returned to France with their tale of horror and their maps marking out the cache of gold ingots in the distant West.

In 1844 a man named LeBlanc reportedly acquired the maps and mounted an expedition to recover the gold, a treasure so vast it would require "several hundred mules" to pack it out. LeBlanc and his hired Santa Fe guides fell victim to raiding natives before they found the ingots, according to a story in the Central City *Register-Call* of 1935. From that time on, rumors of the cache sent prospectors sniffing at the flanks of Treasure Mountain. Empty graves, dead-end shafts, oddly marked stones, and wood-lined pits all hinted of a treasure real and yet to be found. Many seekers came back with tales of the wraith of an "Indian maiden" driving them out of the forests before they could open the earth. They knew she guarded the treasure, and if they could find a way to destroy her, the gold would be theirs. Her wailing in the winter winds is said to still be heard, the eerie cry of a *chindi,* separated from the Frenchman she loved, cursing his kind and his gold forever.

Like the *chindi,* the ghost of a murdered Apache calls out in dark hopelessness from the throat of a side canyon of the Navajo River, south of Pagosa Springs. A sawmill employee named Thomas Franklin attacked the Apache during a Saturday night brawl in the sawmill village of Amargo in December 1890. Franklin cracked him over the head with a billiard cue and the Apache staggered out of the saloon. Sunday morning the man was found on the road two miles out of town, his lifeless body cut and bruised and stiffening in the sun. The Apaches believed Franklin had slipped out after their brother and "finished him" on the road. In a body of forty or fifty, they rode into town, demanding the blood of Franklin, but Franklin's friends hid him beneath the sawdust piles until the Apaches were pacified by promises from Indian Agent Bartholomew that Franklin would be prosecuted.

In clouded mourning, the Apache's brothers took his remains to Navajo Canyon where the corpse was ceremoniously placed in a deep rock crevice, two of his best horses shot and laid beside him, along with a saddle, blankets, and other earthly possessions. Thomas Franklin's friends, Jeff Crocker and Idris Little of Pagosa, for unspecified reasons, believed that among those earthly possessions were gold coins. Knowing where the Apache's body was, they went in after it a few weeks later.

Their greedy fingers disturbed the flyblown dead, and out of the earth evil powers engulfed them, ripping out their souls. The two were found dead months later, their jaws missing. The spot where the Apache had been laid to rest, now desecrated, became a place of whisperings, a place of madness, the habitation of a dark wind. Anyone who dared to plunder the grave would be destroyed by that darkness.

These ancient guardians of the San Juan are made of eternal mist. They are here until time passes away, the *soyokos* in the heart of the stone, the mysterious chanting of Spider Woman on the night air, the awesome Maasaw dancing his slow dance on the rim of the earth, those beings from before the dawn of time, and those ghosts of the lost. Deep in the darkness of night *chindi* ghost fires burn in remote canyons and on desolate escarpments, fires that the wise will shield from their eyes, fires of the wandering dead, guardians of the ancient way.

13

WOMEN OF THE WIND

Sweet, melodious notes drift on the breeze as if the clear, crisp air it-self were humming a lullaby in this lofty place. Golden fingers of sunlight stretch through the trees on the shoulder of Treasure Mountain, painting the wood of this ghost village in rich copper, brown, and amber. Nothing stirs except sparring chipmunks on a boulder. Majestic peaks rim the horizon, their tireless heights gold in the dying sun's light.

As the long rays draw back, blue shadows of spruce forest and mountain creep over Animas Forks, wrapping abandoned, vacant-eyed buildings in sunset magic. A marmot pipes one quick note from the mill foundations. A bird twitters an answer. Like a small child, the breeze whirls a playful dance through the tall grasses extravagant with wildflowers. And the humming, more distinct now, follows the playful wind.

Is it only the wind? The strange, joyful, toying air tappity-taps across the millwork-trimmed porch of a humble house. It hopscotches in swirls from one clump of columbine to another, then runs up the walls of a sagging house to tickle the tin roof. With a blustering puff, it chases a pair of red-cheeked birds through the gaping bay window of William W. Duncan's two-story house, sweeping the day's dust out the back door.

There, in the trail behind the house, a pirouette of satin and a glimpse of lace parasol teases the last rays of the sun. She is laughing. Then she is gone. Only a moment and the blue shadows lengthen, shrouding even the Duncan house, a soft glow splashing back on its face from the brilliant molten gold now coloring the high peaks.

There, on the high trail above the town, she is back. She is music. She is joy. She seems to be the soul of the wind, as she pirouettes again, the graceful flow of her satin dress sweeping the grass. Her fine hat and lace parasol declare her a lady of elegance; her bright smile, a lady of charm. There is no catching up to her, for she is gone before anyone can approach her, gone as the sun is now gone. The twilight has claimed her.

The "Elegant Lady" of Animas Forks has always been a mystery. Never was she identified as the disembodied spirit of a known dead woman. She seemed to be more closely related to the European "elementals" or "nature spirits," born of the earth itself. Elementals often appeared during the clearing of virgin forests, and when mention of the Elegant Lady was first published in the Denver *Tribune* in 1878, the skirts of Treasure Mountain were gutted and stumped to nakedness. This ravaging of the hillside may have drawn her forth. On the other hand, she might have come due to that lethal combination of high altitude and gold fever, mixed with male longing and the scarcity of female faces.

"Attention ladies!" the newspaper chortled. "Poor Bert Guyler of Animas Forks in the San Juan country has fallen in love with the Elegant Lady. He trips over himself in pursuit of her from the creek straight through the camp. 'She is but a ghost,' so sayeth his brothers. It is an obvious case for the ladies aid societies. The boys are suffering a severe shortage. They will accept relief parcels in duchesse lace or plain muslin."

Bert Guyler was probably Albert Geyler, partner of Albert Brendel who established a saloon business in Animas Forks in 1877. Although Bert blew on to other prospects at the end of the decade, his Elegant Lady remained waltzing through the settlement, as a Virginian named W. B. Lindsay reported.

In the 1890s Lindsay was in the region investigating business prospects for his uncle in Virginia. While strolling around Animas Forks one beautiful summer evening, he noticed several miners tip their hats or nod their heads as they passed a certain spot after leaving the post office. He saw nothing there, "save the indication of a small whirlwind." His curiosity urged him "to inquire of the next of these cheerful fellows why he doffed his cap to the wind."

"It is the Elegant Lady," was his answer. He then "gathered the full particulars," discovering the Lady was "mistress to the whirlwind" and "joyful Queen of Hearts" for the "bachelors" of the community, an unknown spirit that came "like a playful coquette at sundown."

Mistresses of the Wind, those wild and incomprehensible beings of the sky . . . some were beautiful, some were frightening, some were as awesome as angels flashing with beams of light. All were mysterious. No one offered a satisfactory explanation for them, although they tried. The "halo of angels" on top of Empire Mountain near Capitol City was explained away as some sort of "phenomenon caused by the thin atmosphere and particular angles of the sun's rays." The "luminous lady robed in silver" who rose from the waters of the Highland Mary Lakes or flashed across the lakes like balls of light, was written off as the "illusions of four cross-eyed prospectors" who had too little "grub" and "an abundance of whiskey." No explanation whatever was offered for the sighting of a "beautiful Navajo maiden" riding a "pinto pony" in the green velvet hills of Cinnamon Pass. Like the others, she was made of light and summer wind, riding her paint off the edge of the planet and into the stars at twilight. During the construction of the Silverton Northern Railroad (1903 to 1904), the company hired a large crew of Navajos from New Mexico. The "maiden" might have been the ghost of a daughter or sister of one of these men, who, having died in the area or elsewhere, was looking for her kin. But it is doubtful, for the description of her as "luminous" and the absolute mystery of her makes her one of the women of the wind.

These were the spirits frequently called upon by clairvoyants for guidance, and when a medium tapped into a powerful one, he or she could demand high fees. Although the press of the day was more solicitous of ghosts derived from dead bodies, giving them ample space without too many sniggering asides attached, newsmen had an unshakeable prejudice against the mystical spirits consulted by clairvoyants. The ink practically sneered whenever a medium arrived in Ouray County. Surprisingly, the miners ignored the opinions of newsmen and flocked to hear what the Elementals had to say through their mediums.

While Madam Gustaf was ensconced at Ouray's Hotel Wilson in 1902, the *Ouray Herald* reported "a great many miners and mining men" were calling on her to have her "tell them the hidden secrets of their mining property." Her wind spirit was uncanny in her accuracy, and the word spread. One miner, who declined to be named at the time, asked Madam where he could find the "lost lead" of two prospectors who were illegally mining in Ute territory in 1863. These men escaped when Utes discovered them. Going to California, they never had a chance to get back to their tunnel "of very rich gold quartz" high on Whitehouse Mountain. On his deathbed, the last of the pair gave the details of the claim to a young man who in turn told the miner.

Madam Gustaf consulted her luminous spirit, who told the miner "where you lose your stick, the tunnel is hidden." The miner was poking around on Whitehouse near the spring the following year and his cane suddenly penetrated hollow ground. He opened the hole and saw the mouth of a timbered tunnel. At the time of the last article in 1903, the miner had not begun work, thus the wealth of his discovery is unknown. Nevertheless, Madam Gustaf's spirit was accurate.

A prospector named Peter I. Spigt in the Mineral Creek area also had success with the spirit he consulted in locating claims. The best-known mining man who was guided (or misguided) by a clairvoyant in contact with a mistress of the wind was New Yorker Edward Innis. His story has been told and retold since the 1870s, when he first began following the directions of his medium.

Innis owned the Highland Mary Mine up Cunningham Gulch where he built a house with a large veranda known as the White House. Being of Scottish descent, he had an inherent affinity toward the supernatural and wasn't shy admitting it. He firmly believed in the guidance of his medium's spirits, who actually determined the direction the mine tunnel should go. She told him he would find "a lake of gold," which caused him to ignore the rich silver veins his men sliced through. The "spectral arm" of the Elemental pointed the tunnel into "uncanny zigzags," while Innis spent more than a million in development, with little gain. He was also said to have paid the medium handsomely. By 1885, his capital drained, he closed down operations. Yet the Highland Mary did contain rich ore. A 1904 article in the

Silverton Weekly Miner said, "whether the spirits were right or wrong . . . the Highland Mary tunnel . . . is now proving to be the 'open sesame' to a vast area of the best mineralized country" in the San Juans.

Unlike Innis, Richard B. Krueger saw no reason to pay a medium or middleman to contact spirits. Direct communication eliminated misinterpretation, so why not capture one all his own? But where does one net a mistress of the wind? Richard knew precisely.

Richard Krueger was born in the village of Braunlage in the Harz Mountains of Germany, on May 1, 1856. This was the morning after the great festival of Walpurgisnacht or May Eve, when ancient pagans celebrated the advent of spring and witches soared through the midnight skies in orgiastic revelry. Although Richard was a baptized Christian, he was raised on the fantastic stories of the Brocken, the highest peak in the Harz Range and the domain of witches since medieval times. A tract produced in Nuremberg in 1746 stated how the witches' Sabbath took place on the Brocken's summit, where a spring and ancient stone altar consecrated to a pagan god were still used for sorcery and rituals. The illustration of the mountain showed little witches on broomsticks flying high above the altar. To Richard Krueger witches were real, for Braunlage cringed in the shadow of the Brocken.

In 1878 Richard had decided to try his own luck in the goldfields of the American West. Tales of fabulous finds were splashed across German newspapers. His friend Frederich W. Walter had already gone to America, writing him of daily wonders and a life of utter freedom, despite the illusiveness of Lady Luck.

Lady Luck was a huckster. Richard needed a witch. If he could net a witch from the summit of the Brocken, he reasoned, he could keep her captive and make her use her powers to show him where to find gold. On the eve of his twenty-second birthday, the wild Walpurgisnacht, Richard climbed the black Brocken and captured himself a witch, the ultimate mistress of the wind. How he accomplished this feat was never recorded, but he did accomplish it, for he arrived in the San Juans some months later with the witch neatly trussed up in a steamer trunk.

Richard was no lunatic. He was a hardworking, sharp-witted man who just happened to drag a seemingly empty steamer trunk, padlocked several times over, wherever he traveled. Early on, he hooked up with Fred, working in mines at Howardsville, Silverton, and Silver Lake. Every moment of his free time he went off prospecting with the trunk strapped to a burro.

The odd grubstake itched the curiosity of acquaintances, but Richard never told them what was in the trunk. The lightness of it was easy to surmise, since neither Richard nor the burro showed any strain under the load.

Sometime around October 1881, Richard confessed to Fred that a three-hundred-year-old witch was in the trunk and he used her for locating claims. He just hadn't found the "big strike" yet, but he soon would. The witch had to be handled carefully. She was very temperamental. One must use her properly.

Like a dousing rod? A homing pigeon? Poor Fred was beside himself with curiosity. Late one day while Richard was in the bowels of the mine at Silver Lake, Fred used a few bullets to knock off the padlocks, and he opened the trunk. Inside was a heap of nasty rags stained with tobacco and littered with mouse bits and bones and fur. Was Richard feeding his witch cigars and rodents? No wonder she starved to death, leaving nothing save rags all stitched together.

The next morning, as Richard came off the night shift, Fred, who was company cook, and the boys ribbed him about his witch, told him "she looked mighty peaked." She needed her breakfast, they said, handing him a plate full of dead mice. In a panic Richard flung open his trunk, cursing the men for trespassing, for letting his witch out. They guffawed and said she was still there. He declared she was not. They looked in the trunk and gasped when they saw the bundle of rags utterly gone, and Richard lost his temper.

He first accused the men of stealing the rags, of hiding the witch in another spot, and demanded her return. They denied touching the filthy rags, hinting he had lost his mind. His disgust with Fred was most vehement, their friendship severed forever. Some fifteen or sixteen years later it was said Fred Walter died all alone and unforgiven in his cabin on his Lime Creek claim.

From the start, Richard had burned his witch's broomstick so rapid escape via air transport was no longer an option. He still had a chance: she had to be on foot or on horseback. He discovered his burros missing and left immediately to track them.

As weeks passed, Richard unearthed faint clues to the hag's wanderings. An old lady was seen with two burros at Red Mountain. An old granny stopped at Dallas, riding astride a mule. She had many powers and changing burros to mules was easily counted among them. The Dallas witness claimed the granny said she was off for Animas City, and Richard trekked south over the range, finding no trace of her. At Durango he fell ill.

During his recuperation in the home of a Mrs. Hurley in the fall of 1882, an issue of the *Dolores News* out of Rico fell into his hands. His mistress of the wind was in the news.

A long article with the heading "A Mountain Witch—An Old Woman Clothed in Rags Who Continually Roams," described how "the most curious specimen of female humanity" had blown into town. She was "a huge and unshapely bundle of rags surmounted by what might have been in days gone by a black-and-white straw hat" with a "piece of old and dirty mosquito netting" thrown over it. The long-faded shawl around her shoulders was "patched and re-patched." Her "skirt was composed of a mass of rags of every description" with "pieces of wagon sheet, bed ticking, calico, old socks, old hats, etc., held together by some invisible means. An old piece of partly decayed gunny sack was held in place by a piece of baling rope" and hung over her skirt like an apron. "Her feet were encased in rags, wrapped, twisted and turned in every conceivable direction and bound over with cords." Her old face was kindly and intelligent, but "her hands looked thoroughly unhuman, long, bony and claw-like and the scrawny fingers grasped an old tobacco sack."

Charles Jones was completely fascinated by her and attempted to get her story. She was too clever for him. She spun a tale to match his desires. "Such a weird spirit must have a history," Jones's article continued. She claimed her name was "Betty Von Plantz—probably fictitious." She said in her wanderings she had "stumbled upon some gold washings" and the Indians she got acquainted with regarded her "as an oracle of wonderful power and foresight."

She told the newsman she had helped a prospector who in turn had abandoned her, leaving her destitute. Her only companions were four unshod horses she "broke to saddle by her own hand." These animals let no other human touch them, striking with their hind feet at the newsman as he neared. They affectionately rubbed their heads against the old woman and she gave "vent to a burst of laughter that seemed demonic."

Finally "tiring of the crowd her odd appearance had attracted," she crawled upon the packs of one of the horses and sitting astride the lot, she "laughed long and wildly as she started down the street. Who this strange woman is or where she goes is one of the unsolved mysteries."

No mystery for Richard Krueger. He gathered himself, bought a five-gallon milk can with a tight lid, and headed out for Rico via the Mancos and Big Bend route. He found his witch in a creek up the Dolores, magically plucking gold nuggets out of the sand. When she ceased her plucking, Richard pounced upon her and stuffed her in the milk can. From that time on, just to collar unwanted curiosity, he told everyone the milk can contained the old rags and bones of his dead mother. No one bothered to open it.

Krueger's witch advised him to work at the mines in the San Miguel district and later at the Enterprise in Rico, where he moved in the 1890s. He doused the hills with his witch rod, seeking that "big strike." By the time he was thirty-nine, he had moved to Ophir and was employed with the Suffolk Mining Company. It was here he let another man see his witch.

At this point the ancient hag had grown fond of Richard, and her greatest asset was her curative powers. At the Suffolk, Richard met with an accident, getting his hand crushed by a falling rock, the injury threatening his livelihood. The witch gathered special plants and minerals and made a potion that completely restored his hand. Later that year a friend at the Suffolk, Robert Brewster, had his arm caught between the tram bucket and cable, breaking the arm above the elbow. The doctor patched him up and sent him back, but for a long time Rob suffered from pain in his arm. Richard opened his milk can.

"The most marvelous sight unfolded before" Rob's eyes as Richard "hauled to on a wad of rags that seemed endless." Once the rags were out of the can, Rob realized "an ancient woman was standing before him." She muttered and cackled and stirred up a potion that she "applied to the injured limb," and in days Rob's arm was "set aright."

At the turn of the century, forty-four-year-old Richard Krueger had found his gold mine. He lived quietly in the village of Ophir at Hotel Elliott on the corner of Fourth and Granite. He worked with George and William Dolf on the Deadwood lease and enjoyed the company of Mrs. Elliott, her daughter Lizzie, and granddaughter Helen. He continued prospecting, collecting nuggets whenever his witch chose to point them out. She had always been stingy with her vast arcane knowledge of gold.

Sometime before 1908 Richard went out in the forest one day and selected a special sapling, stripping it down, carving it, and setting one end with fine willow twigs, all "bound together with copper and braided horse's hair." Late in the twilight on Walpurgisnacht, he took the broom and the milk can up through the snow to the summit of Lookout Peak, high above Ophir, and he gave the witch her freedom. She flew with a delighted cackle across the sky, disappearing beyond the stars.

For many years Richard Krueger shared his room with a milk can, telling curious children that a witch once lived inside. She liked to eat tobacco, mice, and toads, which he had to supply "fresh and plump," he explained. He told how she had escaped from him in 1881 and wasn't found until Charles Jones of Rico wrote a story about her in his newspaper. He showed the yellowed page from the *Dolores News*, a creased and worn and fragile document he "kept in a pocket book."

The witch was free now, he said. Children asked if she flew back to Germany, to the Brocken, and Richard always replied he was "certain she did not." He believed she preferred the San Juans to the Brocken, for he saw her now and again "riding the back of a wild wind" over Silver Mountain or Lookout Peak, cackling at him as she passed. At the conclusion of his tale to his wide-eyed audience, the soft-spoken miner with the sparkling blue eyes whispered, "If you can find her, perhaps she will show you where to find one of these." He produced a large gold nugget from his pocket. It was "witch gold," and that three-hundred-year-old hag from the Brocken had plucked it from the stream herself.

Scraps and bones of the tale of one other witch who knew where the gold was came from the days when the San Juan was Spanish territory. The story was never written down, and as oral tradition is so old, it barely remains in memory. One dusty fragment said a spirit *bruja,* or witch, was chased out of the Santa Fe area by the padres and flew north up the Rio de las Animas Perdidas, the River of Lost Souls, to its headwaters. She cracked bones and ate hummingbirds in a hidden cave, gathering gold from the streams and rivers. If a man could find her and capture her, she would lead him to fabulous veins of pure gold.

Another wind spirit from the Spanish era was La Llorona, who haunted the San Juan River near Pagosa Springs. Early Spanish settlers in the area warned their children to stay away from the river or La Llorona might capture them or drown them or even eat them.

La Llorona was a spirit rooted in ancient Aztec tradition, deriving from the goddess Cihuacoatl. When the culture of Spain crashed into that of the Aztec empire, Cihuacoatl's story mutated into creepy tales of La Llorona, the Weeping Woman.

Really no woman at all, she was a spirit who took the form of a beautiful raven-haired lady, a doe-eyed Puebloan or Dineh or Apache. At Pagosa she hunted along the San Juan River, searching for children. . . . Some tales said she sought the bodies of her own children who were tossed into the river by a Spanish *capitán*, their father. Some said she actually was searching for living children to drown in revenge for the Spaniards taking her own. Still others said she wanted children to roast, to feed her insatiable supernatural appetite and keep her energies and powers at peak performance.

No matter what her purpose, she was fearsome in her beauty, unnerving in her moaning and weeping, relentless in her searching, and relentless in her path once she set her heartless gaze on a child playing at the river's edge.

Eyewitness accounts of her from the early Spanish settlement days were part of oral traditions passed down through each generation.

By the time Pagosa Springs was platted and built into a town in the 1880s, tales of La Llorona were still being whispered into children's ears on stormy nights. La Llorona was "out there." La Llorona "will come for you."

Whether her victims were descendents of Spain, Greece, England, Iowa, or Pennsylvania mattered not. The Aztec-Spanish spirit had infused yet another culture and another, for she was suckled by the wind and the wind had no bounds.

She came unexpected out of an approaching storm, out of the evening sky, the white tatters of her gown flowing in the gusts, her long, long raven hair in a wild tangle around her face and shoulders. Her eerie weeping rose with the echoes of rolling thunder as she turned over stones and poked into the brush along the river.

Robert Ray knew he was in trouble when his eyes met her relentless dark gaze. The sixteen-year-old Pagosa boy had been hunting ducks below town one fall evening in 1883. As the storm gathered, he turned back toward home, but stopped in fear. A woman in white was at the edge of the river. She turned. Robert's heart stopped. La Llorona was staring into his eyes.

Cursed by an uncanny ability to see spirits since he was a small child, Robert always fled encounters with them. His parents found him a number of times cowering or crouched in a tree, with a frightening tale of ghosts to explain his behavior. This time he was armed.

La Llorona drifted toward him. He raised his shotgun. She came closer. His hands shook and the lightning flashed and crashed and tumbled a deafening thunder over the river. Robert blasted the fearsome creature at that moment, falling backward. Still she came at him and he turned, fleeing toward the trees. In nauseating fear the boy scrambled up a tree, his shotgun lost on the riverbank.

His father and a search party found him the next morning. They would not believe him.

Nor did Ed Maloney's friends believe him when he saw a banshee in Durango. Banshees beckoned the sons of certain Irish families, foretold their deaths, and gathered them in. He feared its nightly harassment so much that he fled to Rico . . . not really a good choice, since that town harbored any and all such spirits. Maloney could not escape it. A banshee always harvested the soul she came for. He died suddenly in Rico in April 1881, a hale and hearty young man. "There is nothing to indicate the cause of death," Dr. A. I. McDonald reported to the coroner's jury. The deceased was in "good health." The banshee simply had come for him.

Of all the frightening, mysterious, beautiful, uncanny wild spirits of the wind, there is one born of the sublime, touched by the holy. She dances high on the flanks of Mount Sneffels, a "blithe spirit," luminous, shining, seraphic. Her diaphanous gown, her long graceful limbs and bare feet, her thick, flowing hair, and her serene hazel eyes are barely visible in the summer sun. Yet her lilting laughter and the "overwhelming joy of her presence" are unmistakable.

Those who are lucky enough to see her experience more than other-worldly awe. They say they are "blessed" or "freed" by her joyful presence. They believe she is a guardian, a guide, a being of wisdom and truth, and they call this mysterious daughter of the wind, "The Angel of the San Juans." Her domain is the vertical green meadows above timberline where columbine, lupine, bistort, aster, paintbrush, and myriad other wildflowers explode in a glorious display. Wind and sun, song and dancing feet play through these tapestries of vibrant color until the sun rides down to his kiva in the distant western sea, splashing the high places with magic light.

In the glow of twilight, in the silence of night, the Angel of the San Juans watches over all from her lofty peak, her star-bright, luminous countenance visible to those who dare to believe.

ℬIBLIOGRAPHY

Books, Pamphlets, Magazines, and Archives

Adams, E. B. *Gio Oberto of Telluride, Colorado*. Grand Junction: Colorado Printing Co., n.d.

———. *My Association With a Glamorous Man, Bulkeley Wells*. Booklet. Publisher and date unknown.

Aldrich, John K. *Ghosts of the Eastern San Juans*. Lakewood, Colo.: Centennial Graphics, 1987.

———. *Ghosts of the Western San Juans*. Lakewood, Colo.: Centennial Graphics, 1988.

Anderson, Inger and Clarice. Family papers, recollections, descendents' reminiscences, correspondence.

Athearn, Robert G. *Rebel of the Rockies*. New Haven and London: Yale University Press, 1962.

Backus, Harriet Fish. *Tomboy Bride*. Boulder, Colo.: Pruett Publishing Co., 1977.

Bailey, Paul. *Walkara, Hawk of the Mountains*. Los Angeles: Westernlore Press, 1954.

Bancroft, Caroline. *Colorado's Lost Gold Mines and Buried Treasure*. Boulder, Colo.: Johnson Publishing, 1961.

Bancroft, Hubert Howe. *History of Nevada, Colorado and Wyoming*. San Francisco: History Company, 1889.

Bates, Margaret. *A Quick History of Lake City, Colorado*. Colorado Springs: Little London Press, 1973.

Bell, James. Private letters. A. S. Walker collection.

Belsey, George. *When to Telluride, to Helluride*. Unpublished manuscript, 1962.

Benham, Jack. *Ouray*. Ouray, Colo.: Bear Creek Publishing Co., 1976.

———. *Silverton*. Ouray, Colo.: Bear Creek Publishing Co., 1977.

Beshoar, Barron. "The Lady Known as Who?" *Roundup*, August 1961.

Bird, Allan G. *Bordellos of Blair Street*. Grand Rapids, Mich.: The Other Shop, 1987.

Blackburn, Edith H. *Land of the Silver Spruce*. New York: Abelard-Schuman, 1956.

Bolton, Herbert E. *Coronado*. Albuquerque: University of New Mexico Press, 1949.

Boyd, Leanne C. *Atlas to Colorado Ghost Towns*. Deming, N. Mex.: Carson Enterprises, 1984.

Brown, John. *The Mediumistic Experience of John Brown, the Medium of the Rockies*. Des Moines: M. Hull & Co., 1887.

Brown, Robert L. *Ghost Towns of the Colorado Rockies*. Caldwell, Idaho: Caxton Printers, Ltd., 1969.

———. *Saloons of the American West*. Silverton, Colo.: Sundance Books, 1978.

———. *An Empire of Silver*. Denver: Sundance Publications, 1984.

Bruns, Roger A. *The Bandit Kings*. New York: Crown Publishers, 1995.

Bulow, Ernie. *Navajo Taboos*. Gallup, N. Mex.: Buffalo Medicine Books, 1991.

Catholic World, various issues.

Coffin, Tristram Potter. *Indian Tales of North America*. Philadelphia: American Folklore Society, 1961.

Colorado Genealogical Society. *Colorado Families: A Territorial Heritage*. Denver: Colorado Genealogical Society, Inc., 1981.

Colorado Historical Association. *Historical Encyclopedia of Colorado*. Denver: Colorado Historical Association, 1968.

Colorado Magazine, various issues.

Colorado Mine Operators' Association. *Criminal Record of the Western Federation of Miners, Coeur D'Alene to Cripple Creek*. Colorado Springs: Colorado Mine Operators' Association, 1904.

Colorado State Archives. County coroner inquest records.

Colorado State Business Directory.

Colorado State Vital Records.

Colville, Ruth M. *Del Norte, Colorado: Gateway to the San Juan*. Monte Vista, Colo.: San Luis Valley Publishing, 1987.

Cooke, Anne M. *An Analysis of Basin Mythology*. Doctoral thesis, Yale University, 1939.

Copeland, James M. *A Cultural Resource Survey of Eleven Shell Oil Seismic Lines in Western San Miguel and Montrose Counties, Colorado, 1979*. Includes a February 1980 interview with Eugene Foster and his sister, Mrs. Ella O'Brien. Houston: Shell Oil Company, 1980.

Cornelius, Olive Frazier. *Pioneer History and Reminiscences of the San Juan Basin*. Unpublished manuscript. Colorado State Historical Society, 1933.

Correll, J. Lee. *Navajo Through White Men's Eyes*. Navajo Heritage Center, 1979.

Creede Camp, Its Mines and Mineral Resources, Its Camps and Business Men. Booklet. Author and publisher unknown, c. 1893.

Crofutt, George A. *Crofutt's Grip-sack Guide of Colorado, 1885*. Boulder, Colo.: Johnson Books reprint.

Crum, Josie Moore. *The Rio Grande Southern Railroad*. Durango, Colo.: San Juan History, Inc., 1961.

Dale, Edward Everett. *The Indians of the Southwest*. Norman: University of Oklahoma Press, 1971.

Danielson, Larry. *Old World Folklore in America*. (Sound recording.) DeLand, Florida: Everett & Edwards, 1979.

Darley, Rev. George M. *Pioneering in the San Juan: Personal Reminiscences of Work Done in Southwestern Colorado During the "Great San Juan Excitement."* Chicago: F. H. Revell Co., 1899.

Daughters of the American Revolution. *Pioneers of the San Juan Country*. Daughters of the American Revolution, Sarah Platt Decker Chapter, 1942–1965.

Davidson, Levette J. *Rocky Mountain Tales*. Norman: University of Oklahoma Press, 1947.

Davie, John. *CWA Interviews*. Colorado State Historical Society, c. 1934.

Dawson, Thomas J. Scrapbooks. Colorado State Historical Society.

De Onis, Harriet, ed. *The Golden Land; An Anthology of Latin American Folklore in Literature*. New York: Knopf, 1961.

Delaney, Robert W. *Blue Coats, Red Skins, and Black Gowns*. Durango, Colo.: The Durango Herald, 1977.

Denver Westerners Monthly Roundup, various issues.

Derickson, Alan. *Workers' Health, Workers' Democracy: The Western Miners' Struggle, 1891–1925*. Ithaca, N.Y.: Cornell University Press, 1988.

Devere, William. *Jim Marshall's New Pianner and Other Western Stories*. New York, Chicago, London: M. Witmark & Sons, 1897.

Dolores County. County Court dockets and records.

Eberhart, Perry. *Guide to the Colorado Ghost Towns and Mining Camps*. Chicago: Sage Books, 1969.

Eddy, Frank W. *Archaeological Investigations at Chimney Rock Mesa: 1970–1972*. Boulder: Colorado Archaeological Society, 1977.

Espinosa, J. Manuel. *Cuentos de cuanto hay: Tales from Spanish New Mexico, collected from the oral tradition*. Albuquerque: University of New Mexico, 1998.

Feitz, Leland. *A Quick History of Creede, Colorado Boom Town*. Colorado Springs: Little London Press, 1969.

Ferril, William C. Scrapbook. Denver Public Library, Western History Dept.

———. *Sketches of Colorado*. Denver: Western Press, 1911.

Fetter, Richard L. and Suzanne C. *Telluride: From Pick to Powder*. Caldwell, Idaho: Caxton Printers, Ltd., 1979.

Field and Farm, various articles prior to 1918.

Flagg, Edmund. *Early Western Travels, 1748–1846*. Cleveland: Arthur H. Clark Co., 1906.

Forest and Stream, various issues.

Fossett, Frank. *Colorado: Its Gold and Silver Mines*. New York: C. G. Crawford: 1880.

Getz, Carol Ann Wetherill. "The Wason Legend," *The San Luis Valley Historian*, Vol. XI, No. 4, 1979.

Gibbons, Rev. James J. *In the San Juan Colorado, Sketches*, 1898. Telluride, Colo.: St. Patrick's Parish, reprinted 1972.

Gillmor, Frances. *Traders to the Navajos; The Story of the Wetherills of Kayenta.* Albuquerque: University of New Mexico Press, 1952.

Glazer, Joe. *Mining Folklore.* (Sound recording.) DeLand, Florida: Everett & Edwards, 1979.

———. *The Labor Movement in Folklore.* (Sound recording.) DeLand, Florida: Everett & Edwards, 1979.

Governor Peabody to the Voters, state government pamphlet, 1904.

Graham, Margaret Weber. Scrapbook, private papers.

Greager, Howard E. *In the Company of Cowboys.* Norwood, Colo.: Greager, 1990.

Great Divide, various articles prior to 1900.

Greenway, John, comp. *Folklore of the Great West.* Palo Alto, Calif.: American West Publishing Co., 1969.

Gregory, Doris H. *The History of Ouray.* Cascade Publications, 1995.

———. *The Town that Refused to Die, Ridgway, Colorado.* Cascade Publications, 1991.

Gressley, Gene M., ed. *Bostonians and Bullion, The Journal of Robert Livermore 1892–1915.* Lincoln: University of Nebraska Press, 1968.

Griffin, H. M. Letters, private papers.

Griswold, Don. *Colorado's Century of Cities.* Denver: Smith Brooks Printing Co., 1958.

Gustaf, Madam Celine. *Days in the Light, A Journal.* Unpublished memoirs, B. A. Burgstram collection.

Hafen, LeRoy R. *Colorado and Its People.* New York: Lewis Historical Publications, 1948.

Hall, Frank. *History of the State of Colorado.* Chicago: Blakely Printing Co., 1889–1895.

Harper, Robert L. *Colorado Mines.* Denver: Carson, Hurst & Harper, 1891.

Hart, Herbert M. *Tour Guide to the Old Forts of New Mexico, Arizona, Nevada, Utah and Colorado.* Boulder, Colo.: Pruett Publishing, 1981.

"The Haunted Cabin." *Rocky Mountain News*, February 1884.

Hayward, Janet R. *Colorado Ghost Towns, Lost Treasures, Forts and Gem Sites.* Republic, Ohio: n.p., 1972.

Hill, Alice Polk. *Tales of the Colorado Pioneers.* Denver: Pierson & Gardner, 1884.

Hill, Nellie M. *High Country Parish.* Silverton, Colo.: St. Patrick's Catholic Church, 1984.

Hinsdale County. District Court dockets and records.

———. Property Records and Transactions.

Holbrook, Stewart H. *The Rocky Mountain Revolution.* New York: Henry Holt & Co., 1956.

"Industrial Warfare, 1894–1901." Pamphlet. Unknown author and publisher, 1904.

Ingersoll, Ernest. "Silver San Juan," *Harper's New Monthly Magazine*, April 1882.

———. *Crest of the Continent*. Chicago: R. R. Donnelley & Sons, 1885.

Jefferson, James Robert Delaney, and Gregory C. Thompson, *The Southern Utes: A Tribal History*. Ignacio, Colorado: Southern Ute Tribe, 1972.

Jocknick, Sidney. *Early Days on the Western Slope of Colorado*. Glorieta, N. Mex.: Rio Grande Press, 1913.

Jones, Charles A. *The Early History of Rico*. Dolores, Colo.: The Dolores Star Press, 1964.

Jones, Gwyn. *Scandinavian Legends and Folktales*. New York: H. Z. Walck, 1966.

Jones, Rev. William H. *The History of Catholic Education in the State of Colorado*. Washington: Catholic University of America Press, 1955.

Journal of American Folklore, quarterly, various issues from 1888 on.

Kayser, Joyce. *Phantoms in the Pinyon*. Washington, D.C.: National Park Service, 1965.

Kendrick, Gregory D., ed. *The River of Sorrows: The History of the Lower Dolores River Valley*. U.S. Dept. of the Interior, 1981.

Kluckhohn, Clyde. *Navaho Witchcraft*. Cambridge, Mass: The Museum, 1944.

Kluckhohn, Clyde, and Dorothea Leighton. *The Navaho*. Cambridge: Harvard University Press, 1974.

Kluckhohn, Clyde, and Katherine Spencer. *A Bibliography of the Navaho Indians*. New York: J. J. Augustin, 1940.

Knights of Labor, various records.

Krepla, Rick. "Edward Innis and the Lake of Gold," *The Denver Post*, Empire Magazine, April 2, 1961.

Kroeber, A. L. "Ute Tales." *Journal of American Folklore*, Vol. 14, 1901.

Krueger, Richard B. Scrapbook, letters, personal papers. Greta R. Nikolaus collection.

La Plata County. District and County Court dockets and records.

Lens, Sidney. *The Labor Wars, From the Molly Maguires to the Sitdowns*. New York: Doubleday, 1973.

Lewis, Charles. Interview, 1979.

Linton, Ralph, ed. *Acculturation of Seven American Indian Tribes*. New York: Appleton Century, 1940.

Lummis, Charles F. *The Spanish Pioneers*. Chicago: A. C. McClurg Co., 1900.

Luzar, Retha Beebe. *The Animas City Story*. Durango, Colo.: The Durango Herald, 1978.

Mac, Fitz. Various articles, *Denver World*.

MacDonald, Eleanor D., and John B. Arrington. *The San Juan Basin: My Kingdom was a County.* Denver: Green Mountain Press, 1971.

Magazine of Western History, various issues prior to 1900.

Marshall, John B., and Cornelius H. Temple. *Golden Treasures of the San Juan.* Denver: Sage Books, 1961.

Marshall, John. *Mining the Hard Rock in the Silverton San Juans.* Silverton, Colo.: Simpler Way Book Co., 1996.

Mason, J. Alden. "Myths of the Uintah Utes." *Journal of American Folklore,* Vol. 23, 1910.

Mathews, Carl F. "Rico, Colorado, Once a Roaring Camp," *Colorado Magazine,* January 1951.

McGrath, Maria Davis. *The Real Pioneers of Colorado.* Denver: Denver Museum, 1934.

McLean, Evalyn Walsh. *Father Struck It Rich.* (Originally published in 1907.) Ouray, Colo.: Bear Creek Publishing Co., reprinted 1981.

McNeley, James Kale. *Holy Wind in Navajo Philosophy.* Tucson: University of Arizona Press, 1981.

Mesa County. District and County Court dockets and records.

Metraux, Alfred. "The Ethnographic Approach." *Journal of American Folklore,* Vol. 59, 1946.

Miller, Nyle H., and Joseph W. Snell. *Why the West Was Wild.* Topeka: Kansas State Historical Society, 1963.

Mineral County. Court records.

———. Property Records and Transactions.

Mines and Minerals, various articles.

Mines and Mining Men of Colorado. Denver: John G. Canfield, 1893.

Mining and Scientific Press, various issues.

Monroe, Arthur W. *San Juan Silver.* Montrose, Colo.: Arthur W. Monroe, 1940.

Montrose County. District and County Court records.

Morgan, William. *Human Wolves Among the Navaho.* London: Oxford University Press, 1936.

Motter, John M. *Pagosa Country: The First Fifty Years.* Pagosa, Colo.: J. M. Motter, n.d.

Nankivell, Major J. H. *History of the Military Organizations of the State of Colorado 1860–1935.* Denver: Kistler, 1935.

Newcomb, Franc Johnson. *Navaho Folk Tales.* Santa Fe: Museum of Navaho Ceremonial Art, 1967.

———. *Navajo Bird Tales told by Hosteen Clah Chee.* Wheaton, Ill.: Theosophical Publishing House, 1970.

Noel, Thomas J. *Colorado Catholicism and the Archdiocese of Denver, 1857–1989.* Boulder: University Press of Colorado, 1989.

———. "William D. Haywood." *Colorado Heritage*, Colorado Historical Society, issue 2, 1984.

Nossaman, Allen. *Many More Mountains, Volume I: Silverton's Roots.* Denver: Sundance Publications, Ltd., 1989.

———. *Many More Mountains, Volume II: Ruts into Silverton.* Denver: Sundance Publications, Ltd., 1993.

———. *Many More Mountains, Volume III: Rails into Silverton.* Denver: Sundance Publications, Ltd., 1998.

Notes on Pagosa Springs, printed publication in manuscript collection at Pagosa Springs Public Library.

Ormes, Robert M. *Tracking Ghost Railroads in Colorado*, a five-part guide, n.d.

Ouray County. Lode Locator records.

———. Court records.

———. Property Records and Transactions.

Paradox Valley, One of the Most Beautiful and Fertile Valleys in the State. Pamphlet. Author and publisher unknown, c. 1890s.

Parkhill, Forbes. *The Wildest of the West.* Denver: Sage Books, 1957.

Portrait and Biographical Record of the State of Colorado. Chicago: A. W. Brown & Co., 1899.

Progressive Men of Western Colorado. Chicago: A. W. Bowen & Co., 1905.

Rael, Juan Bautista. *Cuentos Espanoles de Colorado y Nuevo Mexico.* Santa Fe: Museum of New Mexico Press, 1977.

Railroad Red Book, various issues.

Ramsey, Howard Verne. *My Early Recollections of Telluride, Colorado.* Unpublished manuscript, 1988.

Rathmell, Ruth. *Of Record and Reminiscence: Ouray and Silverton.* Ouray, Colo.: Ruth Rathmell, 1976.

Reichard, Gladys A. *Social Life of the Navajo Indians.* New York: Columbia University Press, 1928.

Rickard, T. A. *Across the San Juan Mountains.* New York: *Engineering & Mining Journal,* 1903.

Rico News. "Lone Cone Mining District." Rico, Colo.: *Rico News*, special edition, 1892.

———. "The Mining Industry, History, Production, and Future Prospects of the Rich Mines of Rico." Rico, Colo.: *Rico News*, special edition, 1892.

Rockwell, Wilson. "Gentleman of Fortune." *Roundup*, May 1966.

San Juan County. Combined Courts dockets and records.

———. Property Records and Transactions.

San Juan! A History. Author and publisher unknown, 1880s or 1890s.

San Miguel County. District and County Court dockets and records.

———. Marriage Records.

————. Property Records and Transactions.

————. Tax Records.

Sanborn Map and Publishing Company. Insurance Maps. Sanborn Map and Publishing Company, 1883–1910.

Scher, Zeke. "That Stormy Period When Telluride was in Rebellion." *The Denver Post*, Empire Magazine, August 9, 1981.

Schroeder, Albert H. "A Brief History of the Southern Utes." *Southwestern Lore*, 1965.

Sherman, Kandee Degraw. "You Could Have Guessed that Telluride is Haunted. It Is." *The Telluride Watch*, January 1, 1999.

Sloan, Robert, and Carl Skowronski. *The Rainbow Route*. Denver: Sundance Publications, Ltd., 1984.

Smiley, Jerome C. *Semi-Centennial History of the State of Colorado*. Chicago: Lewis Publishing Co., 1913.

Smith, Duane A. *Rocky Mountain Boom Town: A History of Durango*. Albuquerque: University of New Mexico Press, 1980.

————. *Silverton*. Ouray, Colo.: Western Reflections, 1997.

————. *Song of the Hammer and Drill*. Golden: Colorado School of Mines Press, 1982.

Smuggler-Union Mines and Mills. Telluride: *Telluride Journal* special edition, 1899.

Sons of Colorado, various issues.

Southwestern Cowbelles. *Big Bend and Dolores*. Southwestern Cowbelles Picture Roundup, 1982.

Spencer, Katherine. *Mythology and Values, an Analysis of Navaho Chantway Myths*. Philiadelphia: American Folklore Society, 1957.

Stewart, Omer C. "Escalante and the Ute." *Southwestern Lore*, 1952.

Stone, Wilbur. *History of Colorado*. Chicago: S. J. Clarke Publishing Co., 1919.

Suggs, George G., Jr. *Colorado's War on Militant Unionism*. Norman and London: University of Oklahoma Press, 1990.

Swadesh, Frances L. *Los Primeros Pobladores*. Notre Dame: University of Notre Dame Press, 1974.

————. *Hispanic Americans of the Ute Frontier*. Doctoral thesis. Boulder: University of Colorado, 1966.

Tallman, Marjorie. *Dictionary of American Folklore*. New York: Philosophical Library, 1959.

Teller, Joanne. *The Navajo Skinwalker, Witchcraft and Related Spiritual Phenomena*. Chinle, Ariz.: Infinity Horn Publishing, 1997.

Telluride Board of Trade. *Resources and Mineral Wealth of San Miguel County, Colorado, Past, Present and Future*. Denver: Publishers' Press Room Co., 1894.

Thayer, William Makepeace. *Marvels of the New West*. Norwich, Conn.: Henry Bill Publishing Co., 1887.

Trail, magazine, various issues prior to 1922.

Ubbelohde, Carl. *A Colorado History*. Boulder, Colo.: Pruett Publishing, 1965.

U.S. Government. Census records for 1880, 1890, and 1900.

————. Homestead records.

————. Mine Patent records.

Van Wagenen, Theodore Francis. *Notes on Colorado*. Personal journal. Denver Public Library, Western History Department.

Vigil, Angel. *La Mujer del Maiz: The Corn Woman, Stories and Legends of the Hispanic Southwest*. Englewood, Colo.: Libraries Unlimited, Inc., 1994.

Waters, Frank. *Midas of the Rockies*. Denver: Sage Books, 1949.

Weld County Vital Records. Marriage Certificate.

Wellman, Walter. *Indictment of Moyer, Haywood, and the Western Federation of Miners*. Published by Walter Wellman, c. 1905.

Wenger, Martin G. *Recollections of Telluride 1895–1920*. Booklet. Publisher and date unknown.

Whiting, Beatrice B. *Paiute Sorcery*. Publisher unknown, 1950.

Whitman, William. *Navaho Tales*. Boston: Houghton Mifflin Co., 1925.

Whitney, Ernest. *Legends of the Pike's Peak*, 1892. Publisher unknown.

Wilkins, Tivis E. *Colorado Railroads, Chronological Development*. Boulder, Colo.: Pruett Publishing, 1974.

Williams, Roger Neville. *The Great Telluride Strike*. Telluride, Colo.: R. N. Williams, 1977.

Wolle, Muriel Sibell. *Stampede to Timberline*. Chicago: Sage Books, 1969.

Wood, Frances. *I Hauled These Mountains in Here*. Caldwell, Idaho: Caxton Printers, Ltd., 1977.

Wright, Alice. "Ghosts Go Down in the Mines With Men." *The Daily Sentinel*, Mining Edition, 1976.

Wright, Carolyn and Clarence. *Tiny Hinsdale of the Silvery San Juan*. Big Mountain Press, 1964.

Wyman, Louis W. *Snowflakes and Quartz*. Silverton, Colo.: San Juan County Book Co., 1977.

Wyman, Mark. *Hard Rock Epic: Western Miners and the Industrial Revolution, 1860–1910*. University of California Press, 1989.

Newspapers

Alamosa Independent
Alamosa Independent Journal
Alamosa Journal
Animas Forks Pioneer

Aspen Daily Times
Aspen Democrat
Aspen Tribune
Boston Transcript
Boulder County Miner and Farmer
Boulder Daily Camera
Brooklyn Eagle (New York)
Burlington Hawkeye
Carbonate Chronicle (Leadville)
Central City Miners Register
Central City Register-Call
Chaffee County Democrat
Chaffee County Record (Salida)
Chicago Mining Review
Cochetopa Gold Belt (Iris)
Colorado Springs Gazette
Colorado Tribune (Denver)
Colorado Weekly Chieftain
Creede Candle
Crystal River Current News
Daily Democrat (Denver)
Daily Herald (Silverton)
Daily Muldoon (Ouray)
Daily Southwest (Durango)
Delta Chief and Independent
Denver Catholic Register
Denver Post
Denver Republican
Denver Times
Denver Tribune
Denver Weekly Times
Dolores News (Rico)
Durango Democrat
Durango Record
Durango Telegraph
Elk Mountain Bonanza
Elk Mountain Pilot
Evening Chronicle (Leadville)
Galveston News
Georgetown Courier

Glenwood Post
Globe-Democrat (St. Louis, Missouri)
Gothic Silver Record
Grand Junction News
Great Southwest (Durango)
Gunnison Daily News-Democrat
Gunnison Daily Review-Press
Gunnison Democrat
Gunnison Echo
Gunnison News
Gunnison News-Champion
Gunnison Republican
Harper's Weekly
Herald (Glasgow, Scotland)
Hinsdale Phonograph
The Journal (Hannibal, Missouri)
Kansas City Times
La Plata Miner (Silverton)
Lake City Mining Register
Lake City Phonograph
Lake City Sentinel
Lake City Silver World
Lake City Times
Lake City Tribune
London Illustrated News
Mining Exchange Journal (Denver)
Mining News (Telluride)
Montezuma Journal (Cortez)
Montezuma Millrun (Montezuma)
Montrose Daily Press
Montrose Enterprise
Montrose Press
Mountain Mail (Salida)
New York Evening Post
Ouray Herald
Ouray Times
Pagosa Springs News
Pitkin Mining News
Plaindealer (Ouray)
Public Ledger (Philadelphia)

Pueblo Chieftain
Red Mountain Pilot
Red Mountain Review
Revista Catholica
Rico Clipper
Rico Democrat
Rico News
Rico News-Sun
Rico Record
Rocky Mountain Herald
Rocky Mountain News
Rocky Mountain Sun (Aspen)
Saguache Chronicle
Saguache Crescent
Salida Herald
Salida Mail
Salida Record
San Juan Democrat (Silverton)
San Juan Herald (Silverton)
San Juan Prospector (Del Norte)
San Luis Valley Courier (Alamosa)
San Miguel County Journal (Telluride)
San Miguel Examiner (Telluride)
Seattle Post
Sentinel (Grand Junction)
Silverite Plaindealer (Ouray)
Silverton Democrat
Silverton Industry
Silverton Miner
Silverton Standard
Silverton Weekly Miner
Solid Muldoon (Durango)
Solid Muldoon (Ouray)
Southern Ute Drum
Telluride Daily Journal
Telluride Republican
Ute Mountain Ute Echo
Weenuche Smoke Signals
White Pine Cone (Gunnison)